LORDSHIP, KINGSHIP, AND EMPIRE

LORDSHIP, KINGSHIP, AND EMPIRE

The Idea of Monarchy,
1400–1525

THE CARLYLE LECTURES 1988

J. H. BURNS

CLARENDON PRESS OXFORD
1992

Oxford University Press, Walton Street, Oxford OX2 6DP
Oxford New York Toronto
Delhi Bombay Calcutta Madras Karachi
Petaling Jaya Singapore Hong Kong Tokyo
Nairobi Dar es Salaam Cape Town
Melbourne Auckland
and associated companies in
Berlin Ibadan

Oxford is a trade mark of Oxford University Press

Published in the United States
by Oxford University Press, New York

British Library Cataloguing in Publication Data
Data available

Library of Congress Cataloging in Publication Data
Burns, J. H. (James Henderson)
Lordship, kingship, and empire : the idea of monarchy, 1400–1525 /
J.H. Burns.
p. cm.—(The Carlyle lectures ; 1988)
Includes bibliographical references (p.   ) and index.
1. Monarchy—Europe—History. 2. Europe—Kings and rulers—
History. I. Title. II. Series
JC375.B87   1992   321.6'094—dc20   91–42781
ISBN 0–19–820206–7

Typeset by Cambridge Composing (UK) Ltd
Printed and bound in
Great Britain by Biddles Ltd,
Guildford and King's Lynn

For
Yvonne
. . . you shall be called My delight is in her
Isaiah 62: 4

PREFACE

The substance of this book was delivered as six Carlyle Lectures in Hilary Term 1988. A primary and agreeable obligation is thus for me to express my gratitude to the electors under the endowment in memory of A. J. Carlyle for the honour of the appointment and the opportunity it afforded me. I owe a special debt of thanks to Keith Thomas, as chairman of the electors, for his friendly and helpful welcome, and for his support throughout. Another such debt is due to the then Warden (Michael Brock) and the Fellows of Nuffield College for the hospitality I enjoyed during the term. If there was perhaps a certain irony in the fact that my first visit to that college was in connection with concerns no more recent than the sixteenth century, this did not make my sojourn there any less enjoyable and rewarding.

The material in the lectures has since been extensively revised and, in some directions (notably in Chaper 2), considerably expanded. Both in these modifications and in the original lectures I drew on work which was begun (or in some respects resumed) in 1982, during a period of leave from the Department of History, University College London. For this—as for much more over the past thirty years—I have to thank the College and my colleagues in the department. The invitation to deliver the lectures reached me shortly after my retirement and just before I went, for the spring semester of 1987, to the Department of History at the Johns Hopkins University as John Hinkley Visiting Professor. That appointment gave rise to a further debt which it is appropriate to acknowledge here, since it was during those rewarding months in Baltimore that I was able to focus my research upon the specific topic I had chosen as the subject of the 1988 lectures. Both on the Homewood Campus and in Washington at the Folger Institute Center for the History of British Political Thought, I met colleagues and students in whose company it was impossible to fall victim to any trace of sexagenarian inertia. John Pocock's Folger Institute seminar in which I had the privilege of participating was concerned with issues remote enough from those of fifteenth-century scholasticism; but that did not lessen the impact of my first personal encounter with his unflagging intellectual energy. If this book owes nothing directly to him, its author is deeply conscious of a debt which calls for acknowledgement here.

Several parts of the book have, in one form or another, been presented in various seminars and the like: in Oxford at two sessions following the completion of the lectures; at the Institute of Historical Research in London, under the rubrics both of the History of Political Thought and of Italian History; at the Eighth International Congress of Medieval Canon Law at San Diego in 1988; in the Johns Hopkins History Department (on an enjoyable return visit in 1990); and in the School of Law, University of California at Berkeley. In thanking the organizers of, and the participants in, these groups, I could wish that the final text had benefited from such discussions more than I fear it has; but I have done what I could.

It is never possible in such a context as this to acknowledge all those from whose conversation or correspondence over the years one's knowledge and understanding of a subject have profited. There are, however, two specific debts that I should mention. Angus MacKay, besides helping me in other ways in connection with the subject of Chapter 4, directed my attention to Nicholas Round's study of the fall of Alvaro de Luna. And Ralph Giesey in the course of correspondence about the work of Jean de Terrevermeille generously provided me with a copy of Jean Barbey's *La Fonction royale*, without which the first part of Chapter 3 could not have been written in the form it eventually took.

Like all scholars in fields of this kind I owe more than can easily be expressed to the great libraries where we have the privilege of working. In particular I have to thank the librarians and staffs of the British Library; the Bodleian Library; the Milton S. Eisenhower Library, Johns Hopkins University; and the Folger Shakespeare Library, Washington, DC. A particular word of thanks is due to the Librarian of the London Library, for allowing me to borrow the first volume of Melchior Goldast's *Monarchia* and to retain it for two separate periods, each of unconscionable duration.

In the process of turning the lectures into a book I have received every possible encouragement and assistance from the Oxford University Press; and I thank in particular Tony Morris and Anne Gelling of the Arts and Reference Division; Robert Ritter of the

Desk-Editing Department; and, for punctilious and helpful copy-editing, Lynn Childress.

It is not, I hope, out of place to add a word of appreciation to the anonymous readers who reported both on the project submitted to the Press and on the final text. Once again I have done what I could by way of response; but I am well aware of the fact that the book has not gained all that it might have done from advice which was always associated with reassurance and support.

It remains to add one final word of thanks. I have tried in the dedication of the book to acknowledge a more important debt in this quarter; but it is only right to add here my particular thanks to my wife for all the work she did as, in effect, an unpaid research assistant on both sides of the Atlantic. Much of what she did must have been inexpressibly tedious to any rational person; and I can only hope that there were some islands of enjoyment in the bibliographical Sargasso Sea.

J.H.B.

London
October 1991

CONTENTS

A CRISIS OF MONARCHY?

'THE fifteenth century opens in two of the principal countries with a revolution.' Thus, in 1885, Charles Plummer began his introduction to Sir John Fortescue's *Governance of England*.[1] After such a century as has passed since then, we might hesitate to apply the term 'revolution' to either of the episodes Plummer had in mind—the deposition of Richard II in England; and, in the Empire, the replacement of Wenzel IV of Bohemia by the Elector Palatine Rupprecht. Yet the implied suggestion that the fifteenth century was a 'time of troubles' for European monarchies was not misconceived. So much indeed is it confirmed by a broader review of the European scene that a much more recent historian devoted a chapter to 'The Fifteenth-Century Crisis of the Monarchies', having in mind the period down to and some way beyond the middle of the century.[2] The point merits consideration in a little more detail.

For France—to begin with the most powerful, the richest, and the most highly organized of all the monarchies—the moment of crisis came very early in the new century; and its impact was no doubt all the sharper because it followed so closely on what must have seemed the triumphant recovery from earlier troubles. The reign of Charles V (1364–80) had seen such achievements as may well appear to account for, if not to justify, the exalted claims made for kingship by the scholars and artists of his court. Yet less than a quarter of a century after the death of 'Charles the Wise', in 1404, the accession of John the Fearless to the duchy of Burgundy marked the beginning of a period of factional strife punctuated by assassination and aggravated by foreign invasion. All this took place, moreover, at a time when the French throne was occupied

---

[1] *The Governance of England: Otherwise called The Difference between an Absolute and a Limited Monarchy by Sir John Fortescue, Kt.*, ed. C. Plummer (Oxford, 1885), 1.

[2] G. Holmes, *Europe: Hierarchy and Revolt 1320–1450* (Fontana History of Europe; London, 1975), chap. 7.

by a king who, if he was neither old nor blind, was certainly mad and useless. Charles VI had indeed become a paradigm of the *rex inutilis*; and the beginning of his son's reign in the 1420s was to see the French crown at a low point from which its recovery—though in the end total and triumphant—was to be slow, difficult, and fitful. South of the Pyrenees, the Spanish kingdoms suffered many vicissitudes. A recent historian has written of 'the confusions of Castile' during the reigns of Juan II and Enrique IV, spanning the period from 1404 to 1474. And if 'the confusions of Catalonia' with which the same writer matches those of Castile–León arose specifically from a Catalan upheaval in the reign of Juan II of Aragon (1458–79), there had been ample confusion before that throughout the territories of the crown of Aragon. Already in 1396 Martí I had succeeded to the throne in an 'anarchic situation': his death in 1410 was followed by a disputed succession; and the change of dynasty, which in 1412 brought the house of Trastámara to the throne of Aragon as well as Castile, led to an exacerbation of conflict both in Catalonia and, at least during the reign of Alfonso V (1416–58), in Aragon itself.[3] Portugal alone among the Christian states of the Iberian peninsula enjoyed in this period a measure of peace and stability.

If we return northwards to Plummer's two revolutions, it hardly needs to be recalled that the accession of Henry IV in England raised dynastic issues which, in the third quarter of the century, were to result in civil war—a conflict not resolved till 1485 and even then not known with certainty to have been resolved by the Tudor accession. In the Empire the succession was again in dispute in 1410–11. It is true that the imperial reign of Sigismund (1410–37) saw some successes and some recovery in the prestige if not in the effective power of the emperor. At the same time, however, those years witnessed, in Bohemia (and thus outside the Empire as such, though subject to some kind of imperial suzerainty), a sharper challenge, perhaps, to the established authorities than anything previously experienced in medieval Europe. The Hussite challenge, with its religious dimension added to political animosities, frustrated Sigismund's claim to the Bohemian crown until very near the end of his life. At times, however, the challenge seemed to go

---

[3] J. N. Hillgarth, *The Spanish Kingdoms 1250–1516*, ii. *1410–1516: Castilian Hegemony* (2 vols.; Oxford, 1978), part 2, chaps. 3 and 4.

further than such issues and to threaten the very principle of authority itself. Had the fifteenth century known no conflict other than that with the Hussites, it would still be notable as a century of conflict and crisis.

In fact, elsewhere in central and eastern Europe the pattern of conflict recurs—in less dramatic terms than in Bohemia, but perhaps more menacingly, in the shadow of the greatest threat to fifteenth-century Christendom—the advance of Ottoman power. Here again there was occasional triumph as well as recurrent trauma. The kingdom of Hungary (also ruled by Sigismund until his death in 1437 and for long the subject of manœuvre and manipulation in the interests of dynastic diplomacy) threw up an indigenous hero in the person of John Hunyades. John's son Matthias Corvinus, king of Hungary from 1458 to 1490, sought to build on the foundations of military success an edifice of Renaissance kingship. ('Matthias', in Gibbon's words, 'aspired to the glory of a conqueror and a saint; but his purest merit is the encouragement of learning'.)[4] By then, however, Byzantium had fallen to the Turks, and no secure defence was to be erected against further Ottoman inroads. In the heart of Europe the Bohemian conflict remained unresolved. Here too an indigenous leader, George Poděbrady (governor from 1452; king 1458–71), achieved a good deal by way of recovery, but this was constantly at risk from both internal and external threats. The radical Bohemian Brethren (*Unitas Fratrum*) attracted support for their pacifist puritanism from town and countryside alike. The hostility of the post-conciliar papacy to even the moderate Hussite position adopted by George led in 1466 to his excommunication and deposition by Paul II. The Bohemian throne was claimed by Matthias Corvinus and the resulting conflict with Hungary was protracted into the reign of George's successor Ladislas II, son of Casimir IV of Poland. As for Poland itself, here perhaps we have an exception to prove the rule of monarchical crisis in the fifteenth century. The Jagiello dynasty, established in 1386, was to preside over territorial aggrandizement, economic prosperity, and cultural advance. Against this may no doubt be set Poland's withdrawal from a leading role in the defence

---

[4] E. Gibbon, *The History of the Decline and Fall of the Roman Empire*, ed. W. Smith (8 vols.; London, 1855), viii. 135. 'Italian fame', Gibbon adds in n. 34, 'was the object of his vanity.'

of Europe against the Turks, following Ladislas III's defeat at Varna
in 1444; and there was renewed and prolonged conflict under
Casimir IV with the Teutonic Knights (though it must be noted
that Poland emerged victorious and with substantial gains from the
conflict). Whatever potential for later problems there may have
been, the scale of Polish successes can hardly be questioned.

Yet the general impression of conflict and crisis remains and
could be further exemplified from realms of less preponderant
importance. In Scandinavia, for instance, though royal power—
specifically, Danish royal power—was consolidated, there was at
least one deposition (or at all events an enforced abdication by Eric
of Pomerania in 1439) and recurrent difficulties in holding together
by personal union territories of which each exerted its own
centrifugal force. In Scotland, whatever exaggeration there may be
in some historical accounts of the weakness of the crown, the
phenomena of royal minorities and factional strife were evident
enough for substantial parts of the century.

There is, however, one major monarchy yet to be considered—
still, arguably, the most important of all. The papacy had long been
the most impressive political organization in Europe. Here was a
formidable administrative structure, an elaborate legal system, and,
to back all this, a rigorous ideology of absolute monarchy. By 1400,
however, the papal schism had endured for over twenty years:
eighteen more were to elapse before a solution was found to that
stubborn problem. When the solution was found, moreover, at the
council of Constance (1414–18), it was based in part upon an
alternative ideology—a theory of the nature and structure of the
Church which had profound implications of a political kind. Those
implications were in some respects to be taken further and developed more radically by the conciliarists of Basle (1431–49). It is
true that what has been called the 'Little Schism', which followed
the council's deposition of Eugenius IV and election of Felix V in
1439, never challenged real comparison with the Great Schism of
1378–1418; and the rehabilitation of Eugenius's position had begun
before the council took its decisive steps against him. On the other
hand, the early years of his pontificate were spent in an enforced
exile from Rome which was arguably far more humiliating than the
more celebrated 'Babylonish Captivity' of his predecessors at
Avignon between 1305 and the beginning of the Schism. In one
way and another, indeed, the papal monarchy of the early fifteenth

century experienced disintegration and something like collapse. No temporal realm in medieval Europe had failed to resolve a disputed succession for as long as the forty years of the Schism. None perhaps had faced such a resolute and explicit attack on its principles no less than its practice as characterized the conciliarist literature of the late fourteenth and fifteenth centuries. The papal monarchy survived of course; and at no stage was its case allowed to go by default either in the political arena or in respect of doctrine. The world into which the papacy survived, however, was a world in which temporal rulers as well as popes had learnt some hard lessons. Those rulers were, moreover, prepared to assert and defend their claims in terms which might indeed have something in common with the claims of the papal monarchy: on both sides, after all, there was, or was believed to be, a 'democratic' challenge to be resisted. But the principles on which royal authority took its stand tended, in their practical applications, to erode papal authority as much as they undermined the position of those within the realm who might seek to challenge the 'absolutism' of the crown.

There is thus no difficulty in sustaining the view that 'a crisis of the monarchies' occurred in fifteenth-century Europe. The title of this chapter, however, and indeed the theme of the book as a whole, seem to postulate something more singular, so to speak: a crisis of monarchy as such. One obstacle to the acceptance of such a hypothesis is the fact that the European political scene in the period in question appears to have been dominated already by political societies that were not only territorial in their basis but characterized by variations which it is hard not to describe as, in some sense, 'national'.[5] Each of these societies may—indeed must—have had its own distinctive patterns of experience and its own way of envisaging that experience in image, symbol, myth, idea, and, ultimately, ideology. A significant pointer in that direction is the actual language of political discourse. One of the main works of Sir John Fortescue, for example, *The Governance of England*, is written, as are several of his minor works, in English. And even when Fortescue writes (as he does in his other major works) in Latin and endeavours (as he certainly does) to express his argument in terms of a general 'European' universe of discourse, his concerns

[5] Cf. B. Guenée, *States and Rulers in Later Medieval Europe*, trans. J. Vale (Oxford, 1985), chap. 3, 'State and Nation'.

are still concentrated overwhelmingly upon the institutions and the problems of the country in which he was native and active and which he sees as specifically different from other societies. In the Spanish kingdoms there was already a substantial political literature in both Castilian and Catalan. In Scotland—recognized by Fortescue as another instance of the *dominium politicum et regale* he saw above all in England—a theologian like John Ireland, thoroughly Parisianized though he was, could still write his *Meroure of Wyssdome* (1490) in the vernacular. In France a quarter of a century later—to add, of course, to much earlier instances—we have Claude de Seyssel's *Monarchie de France*.

Yet this was also the period of the great recovery and revitalization of classical Latin in one of the major achievements of Renaissance humanism. And at the same time the scholastic Latin of theologians, philosophers, and jurists retained much of its vitality and still more of its currency. Fortescue, as already noted, wrote substantially in Latin. Jean de Terrevermeille, a generation and more earlier, though writing, in the most direct and urgent sense, of and for a specifically French situation, did so in the Latin of the juristic literature in which he had been trained. The sources to be drawn upon in this book were, for the most part, written in the Latin of the schoolmen and based upon one version or another of the scholastic mode which had dominated the intellectual life of western Europe since the twelfth century. This makes it the more important not to forget or overlook the availability of the renascent classical alternative nor the fact that it was available to those whose intellectual centre of gravity, so to speak, might lie in scholasticism as well as to those who were committed humanists.

Much humanist political writing was no doubt expressive of a 'republican' ideal defined to a considerable extent by way of deliberate contrast with monarchy. The weight to be attached to 'classical republicanism' and 'civic humanism' is a matter that may be left for brief consideration at the end of this enquiry. Here, however, it is important to recall that there is a substantial humanist literature of princely government. Both the scholastic and the humanist mode contributed extensively to the daunting mass of 'mirrors of princes', with humanist production doubtless tending more and more to take the lead in that particular 'growth industry'. It may well be that insufficient attention is paid in what follows to the humanist share in the political writing of the fifteenth and early sixteenth centuries. The justification of the distribution of attention must be the argument that the most problematic issues in regard to monarchical government were still, in this period, discussed in the scholastic mode, utilizing a varying amalgam of languages originally devised for different purposes. The main elements in that amalgam were the scriptural and patristic language of the theologians; the essentially Aristotelian language of the philosophers; and the technical language of jurisprudence, whether civilian or canonistic.

In this sense it may be said that there was, in this period, a common language and methodology for the discussion of critical issues in regard to monarchy. This is not, of course, sufficient to establish that there was, in the sense suggested here, a single 'crisis of monarchy'. Nor does the existence of such a common language and mode of discourse entail the conclusion that a common purpose or concern united all those who used these means to articulate their ideas. As we shall see, highly specific issues were often at the heart of the concerns of particular writers, who, again, might react to the issues at stake in very different, even diametrically opposed, ways. The suggestion here, however, is that there was a certain underlying theme of crisis in much of what was written, a ground-bass in what is at times a counterpoint so intricate that it may be hard to catch and hold on to the notes that somehow sustain the whole. At this stage, in any case, all that is either necessary or appropriate is an essentially preliminary exploration of themes to be fully developed as the analysis in detail proceeds.

A somewhat indirect but useful approach may be made by considering some aspects of the historiography of political ideas in this period. The fifteenth century in particular has had, at least until quite recent years, rather a 'bad press'. The political thought of late scholasticism (using that term in the broad sense already suggested here) has received comparatively little attention and has been credited with little importance. The treatment accorded to those years in the Carlyles' great *History of Mediaeval Political Theory in the West* reflects this relative neglect and depreciation. In the remarkable sixth volume of that encyclopaedic work, carrying the story down as far as Mariana, Hooker, and Althusius—to the very end of the sixteenth century and even beyond—the fifteenth century is dealt with in some eighty-five pages. Not far short of three hundred are devoted to the century which followed—and which has conventionally been regarded as lying outside the medieval period altogether.[6] In a more recent and very different account of the subject, Walter Ullmann could spare perhaps half a dozen out of well over two hundred pages for the fifteenth century, including the Conciliar Movement.[7]

Now it cannot be maintained that proportions such as these were, in their respective contexts, mistaken or unreasonable. In comparison with the fundamental importance of earlier medieval developments, in the shadow of the great systems and syntheses of the thirteenth century and the radical questionings of the four-teenth, the late medieval period has little to offer that is strikingly new or creatively original. It is true that much of the sixteenth-century material brought together by A. J. Carlyle[8] under the rubric of 'medieval political theory' is at least as derivative as that which is to be found in the fifteenth century. Its significance, however, is inevitably heightened by the more intense scenes of conflict in which it was deployed. The fifteenth century may have been a time of troubles, of conflict and crisis for many monarchies; but (with the exception of the Hussites in Bohemia) it experienced nothing comparable with the religious revolution of the Reforma-tion and the ensuing 'wars of religion'. Yet it can still be argued that the political thinking of the pre-Reformation century needs and merits some degree of rehabilitation.

A process of that kind has been going on in recent scholarship in other fields of intellectual history. The rehabilitation of fifteenth-century philosophy may indeed appear to be a Sisyphean task; but even here—in logic, for instance, and in some aspects of natural philosophy—the record is less arid than may sometimes have been supposed in the past.[9] In regard to theology it is possible to go further and to say that the past two or three decades have seen a substantial positive revaluation of late medieval contributions. A

[6] Sir R. W. and A. J. Carlyle, *A History of Mediaeval Political Theory in the West*, vi. *Political Theory from 1300 to 1600* (6 vols.; Edinburgh, 1903–36), 133–218.

[7] W. Ullmann, *A History of Political Thought: The Middle Ages* (Harmonds-worth, 1965), 219 ff.

[8] Sir R. W. Carlyle died two years before the sixth volume of *Mediaeval Political Theory in the West* was completed.

[9] Cf. N. Kretzmann, A. Kenny, and J. Pinborg (eds.), *The Cambridge History of Later Medieval Philosophy* (Cambridge, 1982), chaps. 42 and 44. Important work on early 16th-cent. logic has been published by A. Broadie, *George Lokert: Late Scholastic Logician* (Edinburgh, 1983); *The Circle of John Mair* (Oxford, 1985). 'Perhaps', Broadie writes at the end of the second book (p. 266), 'after five centuries these writings will at last come into their own.'

theologian like Gabriel Biel—to cite the outstanding instance—will never rank with Aquinas or Duns Scotus or Ockham; but it is clear that he is far from being a negligible figure in European intellectual history.[10] There is thus a broader scholarly context in which to place a re-examination of what was happening to political thought in a period which has often seemed to be merely 'dead ground'.[11]

One element in this re-examination has been a revival of interest in conciliar ecclesiology—in the historical theology of councils as part of the life of the Church, including but not confined to what may be more narrowly identified as 'conciliarist' ideas. One part of this substantial body of work has particular importance for present purposes. In two important studies, published respectively in 1970 and 1979, Antony Black brought out the scope and significance of the more radical conciliarism which developed at the council of Basle in the 1430s and 1440s.[12] That phase of conciliarist theory had been—apart from the rather special case of Nicholas of Cusa—somewhat overshadowed in the history of political thought by the earlier 'classic conciliarism' of Pierre d'Ailly, Jean Gerson, and, to a lesser extent, Francesco Zabarella. In the first of the two books, however, Black put forward a thesis of even greater importance here: the view that the conciliarist ideology advocated especially by Juan de Segovia was regarded and represented by its papalist opponents as constituting a subversive, even revolutionary challenge to the very principle of monarchical authority—to that principle in the temporal as well as in the spiritual realm. It was further suggested that a papalist counter-ideology was promulgated and propagated, not only in the context of theoretical discussion, but also, and even more vigorously, in serious and energetic diplomatic efforts to establish a monarchical alliance with temporal rulers against the radical attack.[13]

[10] Cf. H. A. Oberman, *The Harvest of Medieval Theology: Gabriel Biel and Late Medieval Nominalism*, 2nd edn. rev. (Grand Rapids, Mich., 1967). The book was first published in 1963.

[11] Cf. J. H. Burns, 'Scholasticism: Survival and Revival', in id. and M. Goldie (eds.), *The Cambridge History of Political Thought 1450–1700* (Cambridge, 1991), 132–55.

[12] A. J. Black, *Monarchy and Community: Political Ideas in the Later Conciliar Controversy 1430–1450* (Cambridge Studies in Medieval Life and Thought, 3rd Series, 2; Cambridge, 1970); id., *Council and Commune: The Conciliar Movement of the Council of Basle* (London, 1979).

[13] See esp. Black, *Monarchy and Community*, chap. 3, 'Doctrine and Diplomacy'.

Such a hypothesis has the effect, if not of transforming the historical significance of the debate between papalism and conciliarism, at least of adding a new dimension to it. Since the work of Figgis, and perhaps indeed since that of Acton, it has been possible to argue that conciliarism was important for the history of political ideas because the attempt to embody 'constitutionalist' principles in the government of the Church gave rise to patterns of argument that were to be seminally important in the era of the Reformation and, above all, in the seventeenth century.[14] That view has lost neither its importance nor its plausibility. It has indeed been more recently developed with greater subtlety by Brian Tierney; and the transmission of conciliarist ideas to the seventeenth century by way of their early sixteenth-century exponents has been studied in detail by several scholars.[15] But just as Tierney's earlier work[16] and that of other historians radically changed the perspective in which medieval conciliar ecclesiology must itself be viewed, so Black's work has changed our understanding of the political significance of fifteenth-century conciliarism in and for its own time. If Tierney showed that conciliarism did not make its appearance either as an

---

[14] J. N. Figgis, *Political Thought from Gerson to Grotius 1414–1625: Seven Studies* (New York, 1960; first published Cambridge, 1907; 2nd edn. Cambridge, 1916), chap. 2, 'The Conciliar Movement and the Papalist Reaction'. Acton's position shifted somewhat. In 1859, in 'Political Thoughts on the Church', he seems unimpressed by Gerson's 'attempt to apply the principles of secular policy to the Church' (*The History of Freedom and Other Essays*, ed. J. N. Figgis and R. V. Laurence (London, 1907), 191–2). Eight years later, in 'Nicholas of Cusa', he saw the 15th-cent. reform movement as 'reviving and creating such institutions as might serve as bulwark against arbitrary despotism' (*Essays on Church and State*, ed. D. Woodruff (London, 1952), 246). Lecturing in Cambridge in the 1890s, he referred to the 16th-cent. 'Scots, who had heard the last of our schoolmen, Major of St Andrews, renew the speculations of the time of achism, which decomposed and dissected the Church and rebuilt it on a model very propitious to political revolution' (*Lectures on the French Revolution*, ed. J. N. Figgis and R. V. Laurence (London, 1910), 17).

[15] B. Tierney, *Religion, Law, and the Growth of Constitutional Thought 1150–1650* (Cambridge, 1982), esp. chaps. 4 and 5; F. Oakley, *The Political Thought of Pierre d'Ailly: The Voluntarist Tradition* (New Haven, Conn., 1964), 211–32; id., *Natural Law, Conciliarism and Consent in the Late Middle Ages* (London 1984); R. Bäumer, *Nachwirkungen des konsiliaren Gedankens in der Theologie und Kanonistik des frühen 16. Jahrhunderts* (Münster, 1971); H.-J. Becker, *Die Appellation vom Papst an ein allgemeines Konzil: Historische Entwicklung und kanonistische Diskussion im späten Mittelalter und in der frühen Neuzeit* (Cologne, 1988), chaps. B. 8–9, C. 5, D. 1–2.

[16] B. Tierney, *Foundations of the Conciliar Theory: The Contribution of the Medieval Canonists from Gratian to the Great Schism* (Cambridge, 1955).

unheralded *deus ex machina* to resolve the crisis of the papal schism or as a convenient by-product of secular 'constitutionalism' to serve the same purpose, Black for his part has shown that the argument about the structure of authority in the Church did not have to wait, so to speak, for a posthumous role in political debate. It was already in its own day part of a real and urgent political controversy.

Such an interpretation has a wider significance. It brings to our attention the point that, in this period as in any other, much of the importance of what we call 'political ideas' lies precisely in their being *political*—operative and effective to the extent that they are deployed in actual situations, in the relationships that are characteristic and constitutive of concrete political systems. No doubt this is only one element in the importance of such ideas. At a certain level of analytical penetration, or when a certain degree of systematic originality has been achieved, the contemporary significance of political ideas is subsumed in a broader relevance which (to a greater or lesser extent) transcends the limits imposed by a particular time and place. In the period examined in this book there may indeed be few works for which this kind of claim could be made. The *De concordantia catholica* of Nicholas of Cusa is perhaps the only plausible candidate for such an accolade. Its author, as it happens, provides an apt illustration of the other kind of importance political ideas can have—an importance which, in the exploration of the supposed 'crisis of monarchy' reflected in the political thought of the fifteenth and early sixteenth centuries, may be greater than that of radical originality or incisive analysis. It is a familiar fact that Nicholas of Cusa 'changed sides' in the conflict at the council of Basle between papalism and conciliarism. Ater he had gone over to the papal side, there was a notable confrontation between Cusa and the leading exponent of a resolutely conciliarist position, Juan de Segovia. Their debate gives us a more vivid sense of what was at issue in the ideological controversy over monarchical authority than we can derive from the more visionary pages of *De concordantia catholica*.[17]

Vitality may thus be found in what might otherwise appear to be

---

[17] Cf. the proceedings at the diet of Mainz, 1441, as recorded in *Deutsche Reichstagsakten*, xv; and see Black, *Monarchy and Community*, 108 ff.; id., *Council and Commune*, 122–3. On the movement of Cusa's thought, see P. E. Sigmund, *Nicholas of Cusa and Medieval Political Thought* (Cambridge, Mass., 1963), chaps. 9 ('From Council to Pope') and 11 ('*Explicatio Petri*').

inert and derivative arguments, if they are seen in political terms, as weapons of controversy wielded in particular conflicts. Seen in that light, moreover, such arguments may be revealed in what Burke called their 'distinguishing colour and discriminating effect'.[18] It follows that it will be necessary to say of many authors to be considered in these pages what Walter Ullmann said of one of them—Antonio de' Roselli: that he was 'above all a publicist'.[19] In saying this, however, it will be important to bear in mind that a publicist in the situations which constituted the hypothetical 'crisis of monarchy' was likely to be a man of substantial learning, whether in law, in theology, or in philosophy. He might even, indeed, combine (as Nicholas of Cusa, for instance, did) competence in all three basic scholastic disciplines. Again, he might well be (as Piero da Monte for one was) skilled in the rhetoric of classical humanism as well as in one or more of the scholastic modes of discourse.[20] This point about the intellectual equipment and, in some cases at least, the 'considerable calibre'[21] of the authors is worth making because their writings are so often polemical or propagandist in character. That might, but should not be allowed to, devalue the intellectual currency they helped to coin and circulate. The ideas in question, even when deployed in controversy, were still, frequently, ideas of great subtlety and sophistication.

To appreciate the full force of these ideas it is, however, necessary to apprehend them—up to a point at least—not only in their immediate fifteenth-century or early sixteenth-century manifestations, but also genetically, in the perspective of their origins and development. This raises problems as to the scope and range of the investigation; but these may be left aside for brief consideration at the beginning of the next chapter, in the preamble to an exploration of one particularly important instance—the notion of *dominium* or

---

[18] *Reflections on the Revolution in France*, in *The Works of the Right Honourable Edmund Burke* (8 vols.; London, 1801), v. 86: 'Circumstances . . . give in reality to every political principle its distinguishing colour and discriminating effect.'

[19] W. Ullmann, *Law and Politics in the Middle Ages: An Introduction to the Sources of Medieval Political Ideas* (London/Cambridge, 1975), 302.

[20] For scholastic technique as an essential qualification, cf. J. Haller, *Piero da Monte: Ein Gelehrter und päpstlicher Beamter des 15. Jahrhunderts: Seine Brief-sammlung* (Rome, 1941), *17: 'Wer also damals . . . als Piero da Monte in Padua studierte, Jurist sein wollte, der musste Scholastiker sein.'

[21] Ullmann, *Law and Politics in the Middle Ages*, 302, referring as above to Antonio de' Roselli.

lordship. Here, in what remains of this opening chapter, it is more relevant to review and in some measure explain the sequence of topics to be discussed in the book as a whole.

The order of discussion is to some extent indicated in the order of the key words used in the title of the book. That order is neither casual nor lacking in inner logic. 'Lordship' is evidently the most general, the broadest of these three terms, extending as it does across the whole spectrum of medieval society, including (but not limited to) what, in that society, we may properly regard as 'political' power. On the other hand, political power was certainly one very important form in which lordship was held and exercised; and kingship or royal power was the principal mode in which this political lordship was embodied and experienced in medieval Europe. The relationship between kingship and empire is arguably more problematic. The most helpful approach to the problem seems to be to regard *imperium* as embodying a fullness or plenitude of royal power in the same way as, in the theology of sacramental order, the bishop enjoys the fullness of priestly authority. At the same time, to proceed from lordship by way of kingship to the concept of empire is to proceed from that which is quite widely diffused into a more concentrated form of power and thence to something which, in principle, belongs at any one time uniquely to one ruler, who for his part claims to wield that power on a universal scale.

So much for the basic sequence of topics indicated in the title. On that basis it is plainly right to begin the more detailed discussion with the concept of *dominium* itself. When the focus of attention shifts to kingship, however, there is no inherent logic to determine the order of discussion. For that matter, there is no such inherent reason for choosing certain realms rather than others for particular consideration. The survival of especially relevant and helpful documentary evidence is plainly a major factor in making such a choice; and the kingdoms under scrutiny in the third and fourth chapters— France, England, Castile, and Aragon (with some reference to Naples)—earn selection partly at least on this basis. A supporting case could no doubt be argued on the score of their standing in the scale of European importance during the period, though this would perhaps raise issues more debatable than the manifest 'ideological' importance of such writers as Terrevermeille, Fortescue, and Sánchez de Arévalo.

As for the order in which the realms in question are dealt with, there is again no intrinsic or inherent logic. Chronology has a part to play, in that both crisis and ideological response came earlier in France than in either England or Spain. On the other hand, to turn from Terrevermeille to Fortescue has less to do with chronological considerations than with the interesting parallels that can be drawn between the two kingdoms and the explicit comparison Fortescue makes between England and France, having regard precisely to the form of monarchy he believes to be characteristic of each.

After further consideration of the principles and problems of kingship as these manifested themselves in the Spanish realms, the discussion moves on to the theme of empire. Or rather—and the point is of central importance—it moves on, as the title of the fifth chapter makes clear, to a special sense in which the term 'monarchy' was used. This referred not so much to one constitutional form among others as to the universal authority claimed by emperor and pope alike. The central importance of the papal monarchy is inescapable here, if only because, whatever its vicissitudes—its own experience of crisis, indeed—the papacy alone retained anything like a substantive claim to that universality. The retention in the title of this chapter of the term 'empire' is not rendered perverse by that undeniable fact, nor by the fact that already as early as 1300 it seems legitimate to 'doubt that the terms "universal Empire" and "universal monarchy" carried any meaning'.[22] Not only is it necessary to bear in mind and to assess the significance of the fifteenth-century revival of the 'imperialist' ideology itself, it is also essential to take account of the extent to which the 'absolutism' of the position ascribed to the emperor in Roman law was the model for the canon lawyers' conception of papal authority. And beyond these considerations lies the fact that, paradoxically but crucially, 'empire', for all its universalist connotations, was precisely what kings, great and small, had either claimed for themselves already or were to claim increasingly as the fifteenth century gave way to the sixteenth.[23]

---

[22] Guenée, *States and Rulers*, 7.

[23] For the claim that *Rex in regno suo est imperator*, see W. Ullmann, '"This Realm of England is an Empire"', *Journal of Ecclesiastical History*, 30 (1979), 175–203; also id., *Law and Politics in the Middle Ages*, 102–3, 182, 222 n. 2, and the references given there. A striking instance of such a claim is the assertion by the Scottish parliament in 1469 that the king of Scots had 'ful Jurisdiction and fre impyre' in the realm: cf. J. Wormald, *Court, Kirk, and Community: Scotland 1470–1625* (The New History of Scotland, 4; London, 1981), 3.

The fact remains that much of the most important thinking in this period on the subject of monarchy still referred to the papacy—Hobbes's '*Ghost* of the deceased *Romane Empire*, sitting crowned upon the grave thereof'.[24] This is true, moreover, not only on the 'absolutist' but also on the 'constitutionalist' side of the debate. That is the justification for turning, in the sixth chapter, to some elements in the conciliarist view of ecclesiastical authority and especially in the later expressions of that view. This late conciliarist thinking is important, for one thing, because it is clearly one of the principal forms in which the concept of 'limited monarchy' survived at a time when so many monarchical systems were developing in the direction of 'absolute' kingship. The evidence provided by the last major pre-modern confrontation between conciliarism and papalism is also important because it encapsulates both the achievements and the limitations of medieval thinking on the subject of monarchy. In the present context two points may be made. First, this epitome of a long and complex controversy provides an apt cue for a final chapter in which the 'crisis' of monarchy is reviewed in the light of the hypothesis that it had, by the early decades of the sixteenth century, been largely—perhaps even triumphantly—overcome. Secondly, however, the ecclesiology of John Mair and Jacques Almain takes the discussion back to its starting-point. For them the problem of political authority was an aspect of the theory of lordship, of *dominium*; and it is to that theory and some of its intricacies that the next chapter is devoted.

---

[24] *Leviathan*, ed. R. Tuck (Cambridge Texts in the History of Political Thought; Cambridge, 1991), 480.

2

LORDSHIP: THE PROBLEM OF
DOMINIUM

IT is of course in its political connotation and applications that the concept of *dominium* belongs to the present discussion. Neither in its origins nor in its development, however, was it in any sense a political term. If it is possible to isolate and analyse a 'political theory of *dominium*', this can be usefully done only in the context of a more general account of the concept to which the term refers. This raises in an acute form the difficulties and the dangers of imposing chronological restrictions upon such an enquiry. To consider the use of concepts of lordship or *dominium* exclusively in the period between the beginning of the fifteenth century and the first quarter of the sixteenth would produce nothing but meaningless distortions. Yet to embark without restraint on the search for 'origins and development' would be to undertake a virtually endless task. Its completion (if it could be completed) would involve, for example, a close scrutiny of some fundamental elements in Roman law together with some aspects of Aristotle's social philosophy, to say nothing of a wide range of scriptural and patristic sources. A compromise, however unsatisfactory, has to be found; and it must be acknowledged at once that the solution adopted below imposes severely abridged consideration of the earlier parts of the story, but also a good deal more attention to material from the thirteenth and fourteenth centuries than might be expected, or may be thought appropriate, in a book concerned primarily with the fifteenth.

Even in such a foreshortened analysis as this, the complexities of the problem are as inescapable as they are formidable. A preliminary approach—which is doubtless over-simplified—suggests that two major strands can be distinguished in the medieval notion of *dominium* as it eventually entered political discourse. There is, on the one hand, the essentially juristic use of the term—above all in the law and legal theory of property relationships. On the other hand, equally evident on the face of the record, there is a theological sense in which the term is used above all with reference to the power of God, but used in such contexts as ensure its relevance at the same time to human situations and human societies. Neither of these ways of thinking about *dominium* was, so to speak, fully autonomous: neither operated exclusively with its own material and its own terms of art. Each had certain affinities with what may best be regarded as philosophical assumptions or postulates— especially those of Ciceronian Stoicism in the case of juristic thought, and certainly (from the late twelfth century onwards) those of Aristotelian philosophy as part of the matrix of the theology of the schools.

That these two basic ways of envisaging and analysing *dominium* would meet and become intertwined with one another was always probable. What made it quite inevitable, however, was the place of the Church and the religious orders in the structure and functioning of medieval society. The Church in some sense represented the power and authority of God—the *dominium* or lordship of *the* Lord. Churchmen were also, however, unavoidably and increasingly, involved in those property relationships which were the essential subject-matter of the legal theory of *dominium* and its application through enforceable legal rules. There is no doubt a supreme irony in the fact that the most intense controversy on the whole matter developed out of attempts—made above all by members of the Franciscan order—to detach the spiritual life and mission of the Church completely from property-holding and the power that went with it. Ironic or not, that controversy and others closely related to it ensured that the legal and theological senses of the terms *dominium* would be closely interwoven in much medieval thinking. On one view—to be examined more fully at a later stage—it was a matter not so much of interweaving as of confused entangling of clearly distinct juristic ideas.[1] The issue suggested by that view lies essentially between the jurists and the theologians, and it is time now to take a nearer view of the ways in which the concept of *dominium* was used by those influential groups in the intellectual life of medieval Europe.

---

[1] Tierney, *Religion, Law, and Constitutional Thought*, 29 ff.; and see pp. 19–25 below.

The case for beginning this examination with the jurists is at once chronological and etymological, or at least linguistic. Chronologically, it is true, the lawyers may not have had an overwhelming lead: yet it does seem clear that they were ahead of the theologians in developing anything like a systematic theory of *dominium*. In any case the linguistic point tells decisively in favour of this way of opening the investigation. The word *dominium* is primarily a legal term, corresponding to a fundamental concept in Roman law. In that system it refers essentially to an absolute and exclusive right of ownership and control. Property in this sense was, in Roman legal usage and practice, sharply distinguished from other modes in which land or some other object might be accessible to one individual or group rather than to another. Such individuals or groups might, for instance, have acquired and so might enjoy the 'usufruct' (*ususfructus*) of a piece of property; or they might be in possession or occupation (*possessio*) of it. No such situation, however, altered or modified the owner's exclusive *dominium* in, or over, the property.[2]

When, in the late eleventh and increasingly in the twelfth century, the study of Roman law revived and expanded in Latin Christendom, the concept of *dominium* became both crucial and problematic. In a feudal society, of which the leading characteristic was the holding of lands by lords (*domini*), lordship was an absolutely basic fact of social life: *dominium* was therefore an essential concept in the juristic articulation of the social order. The problem was that feudal relationships did not allow for any such absolute and exclusive right as Roman *dominium* implied. The vassal or subtenant was regarded as having something more than mere usufruct or bare possession. He too was in his way a *dominus*, and to allow for this it was necessary to devise ways in which *dominium* itself could be divided.[3] It was for this reason that the jurists of the twelfth century developed the notion of *dominium utile*, a form of lordship which still preserved in the hands of the overlord the ultimate *dominium directum* (the 'eminent domain' as it came to be called in some legal traditions) while assuring to his vassal a tenure that was

    [2] Cf. W. W. Buckland, *A Text-Book of Roman Law from Augustus to Justinian*, ed. P. Stein, 3rd edn. (Cambridge, 1975), 185 ff.
    [3] See esp. E. Meynial, 'Notes sur la formation du domaine divisé du XIIᵉ au XIVᵉ siècle dans les romanistes', *Mélanges Fitting*, ii (Montpellier, 1908), 409–61; and cf. Oakley, *Political Thought of d'Ailly*, 67–70.

a great deal more than precarious—dependent on the lord's will or pleasure.

Essential though all this is to an understanding of medieval *dominium*, it is no more than a preamble to what are the main issues here. If the 'feudalized' theory of *dominium* had been (as the original Roman theory had perhaps been) no more than a theory of property-holding, its political importance would have been much less than its social and economic significance; but this was not the case. The feudal relationship involved not only a mutual interdependence of service and protection: it also involved jurisdiction. It involved the settlement of disputes and the exaction of penalties on the basis of rules of law. It was thus a relationship in which a crucial part was played by what was at least a quasi-political authority exercised by each lord at his own level and within the limits appropriate to that level.[4] Here again, of course, a Roman-law concept was being adopted and adapted. *Jus dicere* meant 'to give a judicial decision': the derivative noun *jurisdictio* meant, basically, the administration of justice and thence the legal authority manifested in that administration. In the medieval context, this could amount in the end to something very like legislative power, thus bringing the matter even closer to what we should think of as essentially political relationships. To see all this as an aspect of the *dominium* or lordship enjoyed by the *domini* or lords who exercised such powers might seem a natural enough conclusion.[5]

Yet, in the view already mentioned, 'confusion' would be an apter term here than 'conclusion'. Brian Tierney has argued that 'around 1200 any competent Roman or canon lawyer could discriminate between ruling and owning'; but that, a century or so later, 'various political philosophers and theologians' muddied this clear water. In particular, 'Giles of Rome . . . thoroughly confused, in the one word "dominion", the concepts of jurisdiction and property.'[6] Now it is perfectly true and abundantly clear that from

---

[4] Cf. R. C. Van Caenegem, 'Government, Law and Society', in J. H. Burns (ed.), *The Cambridge History of Medieval Political Thought c.350–c.1450* (Cambridge, 1988), 195 ff.

[5] On *jus dicere* and *gubernatio*, see e.g. Ullmann, *History of Political Thought*, 17–18; and cf. id., *Principles of Government and Politics in the Middle Ages* (London, 1961), 51–2, 157–8, 177–8.

[6] Tierney, *Religion, Law, and Constitutional Thought*, 30, 32.

the turn of the thirteenth and fourteenth centuries onwards *dominium* was extensively and elaborately used to cover both those concepts—and, for that matter, much more besides. It is no doubt true also that it was philosophers and theologians—especially the latter—who, rather than jurists, were responsible for that choice of language. Reasons for the choice will have to be considered later. First, the question of 'confusion' must be examined.

If we follow Tierney, as we may properly do, in seeing Giles of Rome as at once crucial and typical in the development of later medieval *dominium* theory, we shall certainly find a body of thought that is in many ways problematic. For one thing, there is the complicating fact of an apparent discontinuity between a predominantly 'Aristotelian' phase in Giles's thinking, represented by his *De regimine principum*, and the predominantly 'Augustinian' view expressed twenty years or so later in *De ecclesiastica potestate*.[7] It is true that the latter work is, in the immediate context here, more important. For one thing, the actual term *dominium* is not in fact prominent in the *De regimine principum* (nor for that matter in Giles's *De renuntiatione papae*). Yet his ideas in the earlier phase of his development were too influential and are too important in the wider perspective of an enquiry into late medieval ideas of kingship to be left wholly out of the reckoning here. What is worth noting is that, in *De regimine principum*, Giles prefers in general to use, not *dominium*, but a term more obviously linked to the concept of rule or government—the term *regimen*. And when the word *dominium* does occur, there is some reason to think that it is used in such a way as to suggest that the author of *De regimine principum* fully appreciated the force of the distinction between ownership and jurisdiction.[8]

The same is true, however, of the author of *De ecclesiastica potestate*. There, for instance, Giles draws an explicit distinction between diligence and wisdom applied to governing men (*in gubernatione hominum*) and the same qualities manifested in the

---

[7] On this, see Carlyle, *Mediaeval Political Theory*, v. 402–3; Ullmann, *Law and Politics in the Middle Ages*, 274–5.

[8] It is at any rate the case that in *De regimine principum*, II. i. 14, Giles deliberately used *dominium* as a synonym for *regimen*. Elsewhere, it is true, he uses it in a way that may seem to refer more directly to the ruler's territorial possessions than to his authority. Cf. III. ii. 9: 'decet uerum regem per usurpationem et iniusticiam non dilatare suum dominium'.

control of material goods (*in dominio rerum*).[9] *Dominium* is indeed a key word in this work; and Giles does use it in both the contexts just referred to. Even when he does so, however, he is absolutely clear as to the necessary distinction. It is in this connection that he claims to be following an unimpeachably theological source, albeit one that has been described as 'a source of first rate importance' for 'governmental questions'.[10] That claim will be considered in a moment. First, it is necessary to set out the terms of Giles's own distinction. This is between what he calls *dominium utile* and *dominium potestativum*. The first of these, also characterized as *fructiferum*, has to do with property and with the use or enjoyment by a *dominus* of what he owns. *Dominium potestativum*, on the other hand, is a form of lordship essentially concerned with jurisdiction: it is *jurisdictionale, ad quod spectat judicium exercere*.[11] The terminology strongly suggests that Giles had become acquainted with the juristic thought in which, as Tierney points out, the essential distinction had been made a century or more earlier. The terms Giles uses do not occur as such in the source he cites; and it is therefore necessary to ask what he did find there and why he turned in that theological direction instead of invoking what might seem to be the more obvious juristic texts.

Hugh of St Victor does not, in this connection, use the term *dominium* at all. Yet he does quite clearly make the relevant distinction, using for the purpose the term *utilitas* (for Giles of Rome's *dominium utile/fructiferum*) and *potestas* (for Giles's *dominium potestativum*). The second of these he elucidates by calling it *potestas justitiae exercendae* and using the word *jurisdictio* in connection with it.[12] Here, then, we have a theologian of the early twelfth century who is guiltless of the 'confused' use of the term *dominium* imputed to his thirteenth- and fourteenth-century successors. They certainly thought it appropriate to use the word *dominium* for both the functions or relationships which they still, none the less, wished to distinguish. Is it possible to account for this choice of language, which was to be so permanent and pervasive in later medieval writing on these problems?

---

[9] *De ecclesiastica potestate*, II. x; ed. R. Scholz (Weimar, 1929; repr. Aalen, 1961), 90 (hereafter Scholz edn.).
[10] Ullmann, *Law and Politics in the Middle Ages*, 254.
[11] *De ecclesiastica potestate*, II. x (Scholz edn. 86).
[12] *De sacramentis*, II. ii. 7, in Migne, *Patrologia Latina*, clxxvi. 420.

In seeking an answer to this question, it is helpful to consider the way in which the problem of *dominium* arises and is handled in the work of a major theologian of the thirteenth century not involved in the kind of polemical situation which determined so much of the writing we have to use as evidence for 'political thought' in the Middle Ages. To do this is not to ascribe to the theologian in question—Thomas Aquinas—any sort of uniquely authoritative position, but simply to use the evidence of an unquestionably influential system of ideas to illuminate the specific problem under investigation here. That evidence suggests that there were indeed powerful motives for such a theologian to use *dominium* as a key concept and term. After all, his primary and fundamental source-material was the Bible; and the Vulgate text was permeated by the figure of the Lord (*Dominus*) and by his omnipotent lordship. At the same time, there was no simple monolithic answer to the question as to how the term *dominium* and cognate terms might be applied. One possible solution to the problem lay for Aquinas in the notion of participation or sharing. Just as he defined natural law as a participation by rational creatures in the eternal law of divine reason, so he could regard the lordship enjoyed by creatures (whether angelic or human) as a sharing in the supreme dominion of their creator. The concept of divine lordship figures at an early stage in the *Summa Theologiae*; but we need not concern ourselves with the fundamental theological problems posed for Aquinas by that concept. It is sufficient to note that God is, of course, seen as 'truly lord' (*realiter dominus*).[13] The essence of that lordship lies in God's relationship to his creatures; and the question that brings the matter closer to the human level is that of the kind of lordship those creatures—or some of them—may themselves enjoy. Here Aquinas's discussion of the angelic hierarchies expounded by the pseudo-Dionysius becomes crucial. In the Dionysian scheme, certain orders of angel were, with scriptural warrant, given names, and one of these was the term *Dominationes*. Yet, Aquinas now suggests, lordship (for which *Dominatio* is evidently a synonym) 'is proper to God alone'. This difficulty is met by the argument that, while lordship does indeed belong to God 'uniquely and *par excellence*' (*singulariter per quendam excessum*), it is attributed scripturally to certain superior elements in the hierarchy of creation

---

[13] *Summa Theologiae* (hereafter *ST*) Ia, 13, 7 *ad* 5: cf. IIa IIae, 66, 1, esp. *ad* 3.

'by participation'. At the same time it becomes clear that, for Aquinas, the notion of lordship is inseparably connected with the activity of ruling, with government.[14] He does use the term *dominium* to refer also to property relationships; but it seems fair to say that, in his view, to be a lord is above all to rule or direct others.

It is nevertheless true that, when we turn to examine these matters in their direct application to human affairs, we find that Aquinas's most notable explicit use of the notion of participation has to do primarily with property relations. This is because the context is a discussion of the difference between two kinds of service, *dulia* and *latria*, the former having a connotation which includes the notion of slavery. Aquinas's argument is that God's *dominium* and man's differ in such a way as to require different forms of service. God has 'the full and primary lordship over the whole creation, which is totally subject to his power'. Man, however, 'shares a certain likeness of divine lordship': this yields 'a particular power over some [other] man or over some [other] creature', and that is the basis for a servile *dulia* quite different from the worship that is due to God as lord of all.[15]

Now this was, up to a point, straightforward enough. It was, after all, quite clear from the scriptural account of creation that God had given man, made in his image, a share in his lordship: he had indeed enjoined him to 'have dominion over the fish of the sea and over the birds of the air and over every living thing that moves upon the earth' (Gen. 1: 28). What was much less clear on this basis was the legitimacy of man's dominion over other human beings. That, it might even be argued, could not have prevailed in human relationships, at least 'in the beginning'—in the order of creation God had originally intended. Only after the Fall, only as part of a natural order perverted and corrupted by sin, could one man be 'lord' over others. How far this is compatible with the argument, in the *dulia/latria* discussion, that lordship over slaves is itself a 'sharing' in divine dominion is a question we need not pursue here. The essential point is that Aquinas did not in fact regard the 'despotic' power of a master over his slaves as the only form of human lordship. The correlative of lordship is subjection; but that

---

[14] *ST* Ia, 108, 5 *ad* 2 and 3.
[15] *ST* IIa, IIae, 103, 3.

subjection need not be servile. Even in the lost condition of sinless perfection there could and would have been subjection—and therefore lordship—of quite another kind. In this relationship, Aquinas maintains, the lord is one 'who has the office of governing and directing free men': his power is used, not (like that of the slave-owner) for his own selfish advantage, but for the good of his subjects.[16]

Elsewhere, and more than once, Aquinas invokes, as an analogical argument, another way of expressing essentially the same distinction. He does this in the course of analysing such matters as the psychology of human action, adopting the analogy used by Aristotle early in the *Politics*. The point, for both Aristotle and Aquinas, is that we can make a distinction between the kind of control exercised by the mind over bodily action and the control exercised by the rational over the appetitive element in the human personality. The former is analogous to 'despotic' control over slaves, the latter to 'royal and/or constitutional control' over free men, who are able, and in some circumstances entitled, to resist their 'lord'.[17] It is true that in such passages Aquinas is inclined to use the term *principatus* rather than *dominium*; but this does not affect the relevance here of the argument itself. Two points need to be noted. First, the concept of lordship is being associated with government rather than with ownership; and secondly, governing authority of this kind is presented as being entirely compatible with a 'political' as opposed to a 'despotic' relationship. Moreover, what is referred to as 'political' is also described, interchangeably, as 'regal' or 'royal'. The implicit 'political theory of *dominium*' is, at least potentially, a theory of kingship. Aquinas does not, it may be worth remarking, make use in this connection of the term *jurisdictio*; and indeed he seems, in the *Summa Theologiae*, to have used that term mainly in his analysis of ecclesiastical as distinct from temporal authority.[18] On the other hand, his whole theory of law and of the ruler's position in regard to law means that what he calls *potestas judiciaria* necessarily belongs to the ruler. The most

---

[16] *ST* Ia, 96, 4. This article is the most crucial; but the whole *quaestio*, on the theme *de dominio quod homini in statu innocentiae competebat*, is important. On this subject, see the full discussion by R. A. Markus, *Saeculum: History and Society in the Theology of St Augustine* (Cambridge, 1988; first publ. 1970), Appendix C, 211–30, esp. 219–27.

[17] *ST* Ia, IIae, 56, 5; 58, 2.

[18] *ST* IIa, IIae, 39, 3.

interesting development of the point comes at a late stage in the *Summa*, when the subject under discussion is the power of the risen Christ. That power is seen as essentially 'judiciary'; and such a power to judge others 'seems to belong to a lord', to whom it is committed or entrusted by God with respect to those who are subject to that lord's jurisdiction (and here Aquinas does use the word).[19] More particularly, indeed, judicial authority is associated with *royal* power and status.[20] Once again the theme of lordship merges with that of kingship.

In Aquinas, then, we have a major and widely influential thinker for whom the term *dominium* is certainly associated both with ownership and with jurisdiction and government. Yet it is hardly the case that he, or those who followed his lead, confused the two concepts. In what is arguably the most frequently cited of the passages from the *Summa* referred to above—that in which Aquinas distinguishes 'despotic' from 'royal' or 'constitutional' lordship— his argument turns precisely upon the differentiation of ownership from jurisdiction.

It must none the less be acknowledged that the theological impulse which made it seem natural to derive *dominium* in all its forms from the ultimate sovereignty of God could have sharply controversial political implications. When Giles of Rome became involved in the conflict between Boniface VIII and Philip the Fair, he interpreted the theory of *dominium* which he could reasonably claim to have found in Aquinas in a strictly hierocratic and radically papalist sense. If all lordship belonged essentially to God, the possession of any part of that divine sovereignty by any individual, whether as ruler or as owner, must depend for its legitimacy upon the authority of God's representative on earth, the pope. This did not entail the sacrifice of the well-established distinction between jurisdiction and property. What it did was to subordinate both these forms of *dominium*, not simply to an inoffensive and unproblematic doctrinal rubric, but to a papal *plenitudo potestatis* which could have direct and, to many, unacceptable consequences in practice. It was against this that John of Paris, following in many respects the earlier lead of Godfrey of Fontaines, reacted by vigorously asserting the *dominium/jurisdictio* distinction; by developing an essentially individual-

---

[19] *ST* IIIa, 59, 1,1.　　[20] *ST* IIIa, 59, esp. 3, 3; 4 *ad* 1.

ist view of property; and by denying to the Church any kind of jurisdictional primacy in temporal matters. It was, a little later, against the same kind of papalism that Marsilius of Padua and William of Ockham—concerned also, of course, with the relationship between such concepts as *dominium* and the Franciscan doctrine of apostolic poverty—reacted in their attempts to undermine the claims of the papacy to 'the fullness of power'.[21]

The interlocking and overlapping controversies of the fourteenth century are, manifestly, beyond the scope of such an essentially exploratory discussion as this, intended as it is simply to provide part of the background to the later theories and arguments which constitute the main subject here. It is necessary, however, to consider some elements in that complex pattern; and there are particular reasons for selecting, first, the work of Richard FitzRalph in the middle of the century. By then the Franciscan controversy, which had raged more or less continuously since, virtually, the time of Francis himself, was drawing to a close. Yet the claims and status of the mendicant friars in general were still highly contentious; and when FitzRalph, by then archbishop of Armagh, denied absolutely the evangelical basis and binding force of the doctrine of apostolic poverty, he incurred charges of heresy, the issue of which was still unresolved when he died in 1360.[22] His own teaching, with its emphasis on the inseparable link between *dominium* and grace, was to be carried further by Wyclif. FitzRalph's fundamental postulate resembles the position adopted by Giles of Rome in *De ecclesiatica potestate* inasmuch as he sees all human lordship as derived from God. It is true that he neither followed Giles in drawing extreme papalist conclusions from this nor anticipated Wyclif's contention that only the king could be regarded as the divinely constituted medium through which God's power was communicated to men. For FitzRalph, human lordship in general came directly from God. At the same time he expressed serious doubts as to whether any human power or authority truly merits the name of 'lordship' at

---

[21] Cf. J. Coleman, '*Dominium* in Thirteenth and Fourteenth-Century Political Thought and its Seventeenth-Century Heirs: John of Paris and Locke', *Political Studies*, 33 (1985), 73–100; J. Quillet, *La Philosophie politique de Marsile de Padoue* (Paris, 1970), esp. chaps. 11, 16; A. S. McGrade, *The Political Thought of William of Ockham: Personal and Institutional Principles* (Cambridge, 1974).

[22] For a comprehensive study of FitzRalph, see K. Walsh, *A Fourteenth-Century Scholar and Primate: Richard FitzRalph in Oxford, Avignon and Armagh* (Oxford, 1981).

all, being rather a mere *commodacio* by God, the one true Lord—a loan, or conditional grant. And the essential condition is that the recipient be in a state of grace. Grace and lordship are absolutely inseparable: for FitzRalph, to fall into mortal sin is to forfeit authority, property, or whatever else by way of lordship God may have conferred or allowed.[23]

It must indeed be acknowledged that there is, in FitzRalph's intricate and repetitive discussion, a baffling instability in the use of a terminology manifestly much influenced by the language of the jurists. That there is indeed positive confusion would be hard to deny. Yet, once again, one may question whether, even here, the author has simply lost sight of the distinction between property and jurisdiction. It is in fact—though not in those precise terms— a distinction he maintains with a good deal of emphasis. In one sense, it is true, he acknowledges that rulers—be they kings, dukes, marquises, counts; be they, under whatever title, the superiors of lesser lords—possess *dominium*. They have a subspecies of what FitzRalph calls, at one point, *dominium adventicium sive politicum*; the other subspecies are domestic and 'civil' *dominium*, the latter being concerned with 'the goods of a city or community' of many 'immediate lords'. Significantly, however, the term FitzRalph chooses to set beside *dominium domesticum* and *dominium civile* turns out to be, not *dominium regale* (or *principativum,* as Pierre d'Ailly was to call it[24]), but simply *regnum*. And he adds the striking comment that 'to rule [*regere*] does not imply lordship'. This is elucidated when he points out that although the ruler may, and sometimes must, interfere with the subject's property—for instance, by taxing it—this leaves intact the owner's essential *dominium*. For this reason FitzRalph is inclined (though without achieving any consistency in the matter) to prefer some such term as *prelatia* or *presidencia* for the jurisdictional or governmental aspect of what he and many others still tended to call *dominium*.[25]

More stubbornly persistent than even the poverty controversy

[23] *Summa Domini Armacani in Questionibus Armeniorum* (Paris, 1512), x, 4, fo. 75ᵛ: 'michi videtur nullus existens in mortali peccato habet aliarum creaturarum verum dominium apud deum sed tyrannus aut fur siue raptor merito est vocandus'.
[24] Oakley, *Political Thought of d'Ailly*, 76 and n. 7.
[25] Cf. FitzRalph, *De pauperie Salvatoris*, I. i; II. xxiv, xxv; in *Johannis Wycliffe De Dominio Divino Libri Tres*, ed. R. L. Poole (London, 1890), 280–1; 368–70 (hereafter Poole edn.).

was the long-running argument about the respective spheres and mutual relationships of 'the two powers'. 'Throughout the four-teenth century', it has been said, 'assemblies of clergy and laity met to debate the relations between the two powers. . . . Dialogues proliferated between knights and clerics to define the rights and powers of the two jurisdictions and to coordinate them.'[26] One such dialogue, forming part of the rich political literature produced during the reign of Charles V of France, merits some attention here as we enter the last quarter of the fourteenth century. The *Somnium Viridarii* or *Songe du Vergier* takes up and elaborates at length many earlier themes, drawing on a great variety of sources (including, as it happens, the work of Richard FitzRalph).[27] The ideological purpose of the book—more particularly of the French version of 1378, which differs significantly from the Latin text written two years earlier—is doubtless to sustain the claims of temporal monarchy, and specific-ally of the French crown, against papal hegemony. In this sense it was described by Walter Ullmann as a tract 'which revels in demolishing "historical" precedents so dear to hierocratic ideology' while asserting strongly 'the ascending theme of government', in which 'the Ruler's power was located in the people who elected him, but who as the bearers of political power could also depose him'. Deposition was, in particular, the sanction whereby the community could enforce the essential inalienability of the crown.[28] More recently Jeannine Quillet (having in view primarily the French text, whereas Ullmann considered primarily the Latin) saw it as 'perhaps the only "political" encyclopaedia left to us by the waning Middle Ages', reflecting the rise of national states, the decline of the Empire, and the critical condition of the church.[29]

The dialogue form contributes to this 'encyclopaedic' (if hardly systematic) aspect of the text by ensuring that many contrasting and indeed conflicting views are rehearsed in the *Somnium*.[30] In the

---

[26] J. Coleman, 'Property and Poverty', in Burns (ed.), *Cambridge History of Medieval Political Thought*, 644.

[27] Cf. n. 32 below.

[28] Ullmann, *Law and Politics in the Middle Ages*, 291–2.

[29] J. Quillet, *La Philosophie politique du Songe du Vergier (1378): Sources doctrinales* (Paris, 1977), 35.

[30] The Latin text (to which citations below refer) is in M. Goldast (ed.), *Monarchia S. Romani Imperi*, i (Hanover, 1611), 58–229. This is reproduced in F. Châtillon and M. Schnerb-Lièvre (eds.), *Revue du Moyen Âge Latin*, 22 (1966). The French text has been definitively edited by Marion Schnerb-Lièvre (2 vols.; Paris, 1982).

present context this is interestingly exemplified in parts of the debate for which notions of *dominium* are either explicitly or implicitly pivotal. Thus, in elucidating his contention that 'every human creature is subject to the pope', Clericus acknowledges that this does not imply papal lordship over all temporal goods and concerns. *Dominium*, he argues, has two forms, one based on divine law (or right), the other on human law (or right). In the truest and strictest sense, indeed, only God as creator has lordship: 'That lordship is real lordship, simple and absolute, and God is sole lord of all creatures'. The other form, termed *dominium legale* by the 'legists', *dominium humanum* by the canonists, is said by some to be grounded on the *jus gentium*, its various forms being determined by laws made by rulers (*leges principum*). The speaker, however, evidently regarding this as too great a concession to purely temporal authority, prefers the postulate that God himself conferred this *dominium* on mankind. That is why, while not in the strictest sense *verum dominium* (which belongs to God alone), it may reasonably be called *dominium verum legale vel humanum*, provided that it is recognized as being based upon a divine grant or concession. Similarly, Clericus argues, 'supreme lay power' is held immediately from God, though he adds that this still allows for various modes in which the holder of such power may be designated or appointed. This may be done directly by God himself, as it was in the case of Moses and (in respect of supreme authority in the Church) in the case of Peter. Peter's successors in the papacy, however, exemplify another mode: they are designated by an elective process, and yet, once so elected, they hold power immediately from God, to whom alone they are answerable. Yet again a ruler may acquire his authority 'by way of grant or gift or resignation of some other person'—he may indeed, in some instances, receive it from the whole community; but once again the ruler so appointed disposes of a power held immediately from God. As to the scope of that power in the temporal sphere, opinions differ, some asserting, some denying that a ruler has, in the strict sense, 'property [*proprietatem*]' in what is subject to his authority.[31]

To all this Miles responds by admitting the postulate of *duplex dominium*, which he proceeds to elaborate in phrases taken directly

---

[31] Goldast (ed.), *Monarchia*, i. 122–3.

from FitzRalph's *De pauperie Salvatoris*.[32] He develops at considerable length the theme of man's fallen nature and the consequent
necessity for forms of *dominium* which sinless creatures would not
have required. However, the polemical conclusion he reaches is
quite at odds with the position taken by his interlocutor: 'the
ecclesiastical power, being spiritual, ought not to seek lordship in
temporal matters'. In particular, it is not for the Church—specifically, it is not for the pope—to interfere in such things as the
deposition of an emperor or king. If a ruler deserves to be deposed
for misgovernment, it is for the people to depose him.[33] Later,
Miles gives his own account of the various ways in which royal
power may be established; and significantly he refers first to 'the
will and ordinance of the people'. This procedure is open, *de jure
gentium*, to any community not already subject otherwise to a
ruler. Secondly, an emperor or king ruling over different peoples
may set up kings in provinces which have none of their own.
Thirdly, anyone who has acquired *plenum dominium* over a
territory—whether by purchase, by conquest in a just war, or in
any other way—may either himself assume the title and substance
of kingship or confer these on someone else.[34]

It is evidently common ground between the disputants that
monarchical government is in principle superior to other forms.
For Clericus, however, the monarchical principle implies consequences that Miles cannot accept. The Church—the whole Christian community—is, Clericus argues, a single people, a single
'mystical body'. As such it must have a single head, and that head
can only be the pope. Both spiritual and temporal supremacy,
therefore, belong to the papacy, albeit that the latter is the pope's
solum secundum primariam auctoritatem and not in respect of its
immediate executive operation.[35] This 'primary authority' extends,
he later insists (in reply to an objection by Miles), to taking the
goods of laymen, whether knights or burgesses, in order to found
monasteries or churches where the needs of the Christian commun-

---

[32] These brief but not insignificant borrowings do not seem to have been noticed
elsewhere. They occur at Goldast (ed.), *Monarchia* i., 124, in a passage dealing with
dominium aut ius plenum possidendi: to be compared with FitzRalph, *De pauperie
Salvatoris*, I. vii (Poole edn. 290); I. xxiv (315); II. ii (336); IV. iv (441).

[33] Goldast (ed.), *Monarchia*, i. 124: 'Papa non debet eum deponere, sed populus,
a quo suam recipit potestatem tacite vel expresse'.

[34] Ibid. 128.

[35] Ibid. 150.

ity require this. Such overriding power, Clericus says, does not belong to a king or emperor by virtue of his temporal lordship over other princes and over his subjects in general.[36]

This, Miles responds, is to say that 'kings and temporal lords', holding their authority not immediately from Christ but from the Roman pontiff, are merely the pope's *ballivi seu praepositi*; and this is plainly not the case, for the pope could not depose the king of France as he might deprive a churchman of his benefice.[37] Clericus insists in reply that the conclusion Miles rejects is the right and proper consequence of the fact that, in any community, all powers of jurisdiction depend on him who, in that community, holds 'the fullness of power', as the pope does in Christendom. Not so, comes the retort: the pope is not sovereign over all, for the Church as such is greater than he is. It is true that Clericus had earlier acknowledged that a pope may be deposed for heresy; but, in his view, what happens in such a case is not a genuine deposition, but rather a declaration of the fact that, since heresy *ipso facto* cuts the heretic off from the Church, a heretical pope, being thus cut off, can no longer be head of the mystical body of Christendom. Clericus will not admit that there is any admissible sense in which the Church is superior to its head.[38] Summing up his position in one of his most vigorous assertions, Clericus declares that the monarchy of the Church (*principatus ecclesiae*) is a monarchy over the whole world both in spiritual and in temporal matters. The monarchy of an emperor or king, on the other hand, is *administralis et deserviens* in relation to this supreme power, by which such temporal rulers may be removed and deposed. Interestingly, the point is driven home by developing the analogy with the case of a king or other supreme ruler in 'a city or realm', where various kinds of dependent ruling power over 'towns, castles, and corporate bodies' (*multiformes potestates regitivae villarum, castrorum et universitatum*) may be exercised by those to whom such powers are delegated. This, however, leaves intact the 'royal power' whereby the king governs 'the whole realm and all its members'.[39]

---

[36] Ibid. 152.   [37] Ibid. 174.

[38] Ibid. 174, 175. The argument that a heretical pope is *ipso facto* deposed was well established in canonistic discussion, having been developed, in particular, by Huguccio: see on this B. Tierney, *Origins of Papal Infallibility 1150–1350: A Study on the Concepts of Infallibility, Sovereignty and Tradition in the Middle Ages* (Leiden, 1972), 49–53.   [39] Goldast (ed.), *Monarchia*, i. 190, 192.

What is striking here is that we have a model of monarchical
power which was, in itself, perfectly acceptable to both sides in the
debate. What divided them was not the question of the nature and
content of royal power; nor was it—though there were seeds of
disagreement here—the location of that power in the spiritual
government of Christendom. The contentious issue was whether
temporal rulers could claim to wield this kind of authority independently, each in his own right, or ruled only as 'bailiffs or
procurators' of the pope, who alone held the full power of
monarchy. The future lay, of course, with the former answer to
this question; but the issue was certainly not yet resolved as the
fourteenth century drew to a close.

The year which saw the completion of the French version of the
Somnium Viridarii also marked the beginning of the gravest crisis
of the medieval Church in the West. The Great Schism, when for
forty years there was no agreement as to who had the right to
exercise the monarchical powers of the papacy, precipitated among
other things a debate which, while ecclesiological in form, was to a
considerable extent political in substance. The literature of the
Conciliar Movement, which developed in response to the stubborn
scandal of a divided Christendom, is thus a major source for our
understanding of political ideas in the later Middle Ages. Here it is
neither necessary nor possible to summarize all that scholarship has
achieved—over many decades, but perhaps especially in the past
thirty or forty years—by way of exploration and analysis of that
literature. It so happens, however, that two key figures in the early
development of the conciliarism of this critical period made significant use in their work of the concept of *dominium*. For this reason,
the present chapter will be brought to an end with a brief
examination of some aspects of the thought of Pierre d'Ailly and
Jean Gerson.[40]

That there is real continuity between this part of the discussion
and what has gone before is a point neatly illustrated by the works
which mark the beginning of d'Ailly's protracted and in many ways

---

[40] On d'Ailly, see Oakley, *Political Thought of d'Ailly*; on Gerson, J. B. Morrall,
Gerson and the Great Schism (Manchester, 1960), and L. B. Pascoe, *Jean Gerson:
Principles of Church Reform* (Leiden, 1973).

convoluted engagement with the problem of *dominium*.[41] These works were written in the early 1380s, when the author, in his early 30s, was completing his formal theological training in the university of Paris. One of his main concerns was with the doctrine he found in Richard FitzRalph—the claim that *dominium* was legitimate only if the 'lord' who sought to exercise it was in a state of grace. As Francis Oakley has shown, d'Ailly wished both to modify the doctrine radically and yet to retain something of substance from it. Thus he rejected the view that one who, through mortal sin, lost justifying grace (*gratia gratum faciens*) also lost any claim to legitimate lordship, whether as owner or as ruler. This, we may say, differentiates d'Ailly's position from the various kinds of radicalism on this issue to be found in FitzRalph himself and in Wyclif. Yet d'Ailly was as concerned as FitzRalph (and, for that matter, Giles of Rome) had been to maintain that human *dominium* of any and every kind subsisted by the will of God, the one true Lord of all. And that was as much as to say that *dominium* did—must—depend upon and derive from the grace of God. If the grace in question was not *gratia gratum faciens*, it must, in d'Ailly's view, be a form of *gratia gratis data*, conferred by God not for the justification of the recipient but for the good of others through his agency. A priest or king could thus exercise God-given power for the benefit of his people even though he himself might lack the saving grace which heals the wounds of mortal sin. This is not, to be sure, the end of the argument or of the difficulty in understanding just what d'Ailly has in mind. The most straightforward part of his doctrine is the notion that 'the uncreated gift of divine approval' is 'principally' the ground of legitimate *dominium*.[42] Difficulties arise because this is not the *only* basis for the lordship we must regard as divinely ordained; approbation is not the exclusive mode in which God's 'effectual will' is expressed. Even unjust *dominium* may be permitted or indeed imposed by God for his providential purposes. Again, d'Ailly is satisfied that God is disposed to confer his approval upon varying structures and systems of authority in human society. So much is this the case that there is, as Oakley argues, a risk that this part of d'Ailly's doctrine may be left as no

---

[41] On which, see Oakley, *Political Thought of d'Ailly*, esp. 88–92. In what follows I am greatly indebted to Oakley's analysis.

[42] Ibid. 83–4 and n. 29, citing d'Ailly's *De legitimo dominio*: 'donum increatum divinae approbationis principaliter constituit aliquem justum Dominum.'

more than an empty endorsement of the Pauline principle that 'the powers that be are ordained of God'; for it is hard to see what variation in the forms and terms of *dominium* could not be represented as coming withing the seemingly flexible confines of the divine will as here conceived. Yet the real point, as Oakley goes on to argue, is a different one—or perhaps it is a way of expressing what has just been said so differently as to transform the significance of the point itself. God's will, for a thinker like d'Ailly, is no mere flag of convenience under which different political craft may legitimately sail. It is, in truth, the creative and governing power on which everything depends for its original and continuing existence. It is evidently the case (d'Ailly holds) that, as a matter of contingent fact (*de facto*), we find God lending his approval to the varying forms of authority and property. Since, however, all *dominium* is derived from divine will which disposes of a genuinely absolute power, we must acknowledge that God could at any time sweep away any or all of those structures and replace them by something entirely different: 'God can, without reference to any such created titles, by his totally free will, make anyone lord over anything that is susceptible of lordship, and overthrow any such titles.'[43] It is in this sense that we must understand and appraise d'Ailly's 'profound conviction of the importance of the divine role in the constitution of human authority'.[44]

Yet if this is the backdrop against which political disputes took place so far as theologians like d'Ailly and Gerson were concerned, such disputes dealt essentially with just those contingent structures which were endorsed rather than directly ordained by God. Obviously this presented special problems in the case of the polity of the Church. Here indeed was a jurisdictional structure permeated by the continuing presence of God, by whom it had been constituted at a particular moment in history. Besides, this structure enjoyed the constant assurance of God's favour: God did not in this instance, and would not, use his *potestas absoluta* to interfere with what he had established by his *potestas ordinata*. That establishment was—at least in the view adopted by d'Ailly, Gerson, and their conciliarist followers—something that could be understood in

[43] Cited from d'Ailly's *Utrum indoctus in jure divino* by Oakley, *Political Thought of d'Ailly*, 89 n. 41.
[44] Ibid. 88.

terms of its *political* character. The Church was a political society. Indeed, given its origins and its mission, it must be the perfect political society, the best of all possible polities. That 'best' might be variously interpreted. For some it was the classical *politia mixta*, combining the virtues of monarchy, aristocracy, and (though the term gave some pause and might be cautiously avoided) democracy.[45] For others—and this was perhaps in the end the prevailing view—it was a *politia regalis*; but this 'regal polity' had to be understood in such a way as to enshrine and safeguard the authority of the community as a whole.

Some of the later developments in this way of thinking about the Church, and therefore about monarchy as such, will be a major theme in a subsequent chapter.[46] Its earlier phases, in the 'classic' conciliarism of the late fourteenth and early fifteenth centuries, need not be examined here. It is, however, worth while to consider briefly, before turning to the general theme of *dominium* in more specific theories of monarchy in the fifteenth century, one other influential treatment of the theme. Few theologians of the late medieval period were more influential than Jean Gerson. In particular, his authority was paramount in the theology faculty of the university of Paris; and that university was one of the main centres of conciliarist ecclesiology. Now Gerson provided an account of *dominium* in its various forms and an analysis and classification of those forms which became standard for many later thinkers. A theory which, through various media (primarily, but by no means only, through the frequent printing and reprinting of Gerson's own works from the late fifteenth century onwards), was to circulate widely for 300 years must command some attention here.

Interestingly, the theory in question, though subsequently repeated in Gerson's more 'political' writings,[47] was first advanced in a work seemingly little concerned with such issues. This was the treatise *De vita spirituali animae* which Gerson wrote early in the fifteenth century and dedicated to Pierre d'Ailly. His subject involved him in a discussion of, among other things, the nature and

---

[45] See on this A. J. Black, 'The Conciliar Movement', in Burns (ed.), *Cambridge History of Medieval Political Thought*, 579; and cf. e.g. Gerson, *De potestate ecclesiastica*, in *Œuvres complètes*, vi, ed. P. Glorieux (Paris, 1965), 247–8. Typically, Gerson uses *timocratia* rather than *democratia*.

[46] Cf. Chap. 6, pp. 121–40 below.

[47] Cf. *De potestate ecclesiastica*, in *Œuvres complètes*, vi. 242–8.

authority of law; and in due course he also had to face the question
of lordship. He approached that problem by way of an analysis in
which the starting-point was his definition, much debated in recent
scholarship, of the term. *jus* or right.[48] This he takes to be 'an
immediate faculty or power pertaining to anyone according to right
reason'. In specific cases this *jus* may be divine or 'evangelical', it
may be natural, it may be human; but in every case it is to be
understood as a power pertaining immediately to its possessor,
being at the same time a power exercisable only in accordance with
'right reason'.[49] So understood, Gerson goes on to argue, 'right' is
the basis and origin of 'polities, various forms of jurisdiction, and
different lordships, kingdoms, and empires'. Under each of these
three headings—'polity', 'jurisdiction', and 'lordship'—there is a
divine, a natural, and a human form. The next stage is to recognize
that 'polities' in this broad sense are distinguished one from another
by reference to the laws which prevail in their government. Thus
the ecclesiastical polity (which is the commoner way of referring to
the *politia divina*) is regulated 'principally' by purely divine laws,
though there are of course 'certain decrees'—those of canon law in
effect—which govern some aspects of the life of the Church in so
far as this is a life lived here on earth rather than in the ultimate
blessedness of the Church triumphant.[50]

   To the term 'natural polity' Gerson attaches two meanings. On
the one hand, there may be said to be such a polity embracing all
created beings; but on the other hand, if we think in terms of
rational creatures living in the natural world—and that is the
context with which Gerson is primarily concerned—we must
conclude that 'a natural polity is a community principally governed
by purely natural laws'.[51] The analysis moves next to that ordinary
form of *politia humana* in which human law is the predominant

---

[48] See R. Tuck, *Natural Rights Theories: Their Origin and Development* (Cam-
bridge, 1979), 25–7. For a critically different view, see B. Tierney, 'Tuck on Rights:
Some Medieval Problems', *History of Political Thought*, 4 (1983), 429–41; also id.,
'Origins of Natural Rights Language: Texts and Contexts, 1150–1250', *History of
Political Thought*, 10 (1989), 615–48 (where the discussion ranges rather more
widely than the dates in the title might suggest).
[49] *De vita spirituali*, in *Œuvres complètes*, iii (Paris, 1962), 141. Tuck (*Natural
Rights Theories*, 25), in translating the defining phrase—*facultas seu potestas
propinqua*—renders *propinqua* as 'dispositional'; but it is not apparent that this is
either warranted by the Latin or apt to clarify the sense.
[50] *De vita spirituali*, in *Œuvres complètes*, iii. 143–4.
[51] Ibid. 144.

standard or rule. It is worth observing that Gerson does not present these categories as mutually exclusive in practice. His concern is, at a theoretical level, to analyse and distinguish factors which may be found empirically in varying conjunctions.

From polity the argument turns to jurisdiction; and it is important to note at once that Gerson here takes that term as connoting not simply the declaring of law but also, and mainly, the possession of power *over* law (*juris ditio* rather than *juris dictio*).[52] This power, again, can be taken in a more or less restricted sense; but if we take it in the sense adopted by those who deal with 'political' matters (*more loquendi politicorum*), we find that its essence is coercion. Once more we are told that the three categories—ecclesiastical, natural, and human—are rooted in the form of right or law from which each jurisdiction is derived. Specifically, jurisdiction in a purely human context—in civil or political society in fact—is a power conferred by human law.[53]

There follows an analogous account of *dominium*. Nor is it surprising to find that, since what we might call the 'constitutional' and 'governmental' dimensions have been dealt with already, Gerson can here use *dominium* to refer solely to the relation between persons and things. There is, moreover, a certain parallelism between his definition of *dominium* and his earlier more general definition of *jus*. Thus *dominium*, whether evangelical, natural, or human, is, in terms of the 'rules of right' appropriate to each case, a power to take something under one's control or for one's own use.[54] The further explanation of specifically human 'lordship' in this sense inevitably takes Gerson into the intricate debates of the previous century and more. He refers in this connection explicitly to FitzRalph and by implication to the Franciscan controversy. What is particularly relevant here is his insistence that, once we are dealing with the human situation as affected by the corruption of sin, we are obliged to recognize the indispensable need for coercive power to maintain a framework of law within which *dominium* in the form of property and all that goes with it may be peaceably enjoyed. This essential 'ruling and coercive power' may be acquired

---

[52] When he later resumed the topic in *De potestate ecclesiastica*, Gerson retained the former (highly dubious) etymology, but added the more usual derivation from *dictio* rather than *ditio* (*Œuvres complètes*, vi. 245).

[53] *De vita spirituali*, in *Œuvres complètes*, iii. 144.

[54] Ibid. 144–5.

in various ways, humanly speaking—by inheritance or election or the voluntary submission of subjects to a ruler; but in all its forms it is a gift of God. And that gift is *gratuitum gratis datum*: it is not forfeited or invalidated by the recipient's not being in a state of grace. On this basis Gerson restates his definition of *civile dominium seu politicum*: it is a form of lordship introduced because of sin, pertaining to the individual, by whom it may at will be retained, sold, given away, abandoned, or exchanged.[55] All this, however, is possible and valid only on the basis of human laws enforced by a duly constituted ruling power. This raises the question whether there is, in Gerson, some kind of 'political theory of *dominium*'.

It was suggested above that Gerson, in so far as he conducts an analysis on the basis of a distinction between *politia* and *jurisdictio*, and between each of these and *dominium*, might seem to have reserved the last of these three terms expressly and exclusively for property relationships. In the end, however, he did not maintain such a clear-cut position. The defining passages in this part of *De vita spirituali animae* are followed by a more elaborate investigation of the difference between *dominium civile* and *dominium evangelicum*. This need not be followed here in all its detail; but a crucial point emerges when Gerson discusses the various 'titles' by which 'civil dominion' may be held. The very first illustration he uses is that of the king of France, who 'holds his realm by virtue of hereditary succession based on the original consent of the citizens' (*titulo successionis haereditariae ex primario consensu civium*); and Gerson adds that 'there are certain public crimes for which the civil law would judge that this hereditary title was annulled by the withdrawal of the citizens' consent'.[56] Similarly, in an elective system such as the papal monarchy, there are rules of law determining the validity or invalidity of the elective process. This in turn opens up the whole subject of the polity of the Church, to which most of what remains of this part of Gerson's text is devoted. Even if much of the material in this tract had not been—as it was— deployed once again in Gerson's *De potestate ecclesiastica*, it should be clear enough that we have moved into the realm of political

---

[55] Ibid. 145 ff. The reference to FitzRalph comes at the outset of the discussion, on p. 145: 'nonnulli hanc materiam tractantes, nominatim dominus Armachanus. accipere videntur dominium divinum vel evangelicum et etiam naturale strictius quam sumpsimus'.

[56] Ibid. 151.

theory and stand on the threshold of Gerson's profoundly influential conciliarism.[57] It is also clear that the theory in question turns in some measure upon the concept of *dominium*; and the brief but significant reference, cited above, to the position of the crown in France supports the conclusion that this concept was to be crucial for thinking about temporal as well as spiritual authority in the new century, to which the next chapter will turn.

[57] See esp. ibid. 155, where Gerson considers the conditions in which 'concilium generale robur haberet ex Sede Apostolica et Christi approbatione'.

3

LORDSHIP AND KINGSHIP:
FRANCE AND ENGLAND

THE France in which Pierre d'Ailly and Jean Gerson spent most of their adult lives was the France of Charles VI—a realm which, within much less than a lifetime, passed from triumphant recovery under the rule of an outstanding king to something close to total collapse. The decline took place under a king who emerged from his nonage only to experience, almost at once, the recurrent trauma of mental breakdown. This happened in a country which, dominated (if hardly governed) by potentates with interests outside the realm, fell easily into the chaos of factional strife and foreign invasion. The invading power had itself experienced at the turn of the century a dramatic dynastic change brought about by the deposition of its king. And while the England of Henry V was to reach the apogee of success in the prolonged if intermittent conflict we know as the Hundred Years War, final defeat in that war came in the reign of Henry VI, under whom, at home, the Lancastrian claim to the throne was to be challenged and overborne in the Wars of the Roses. Theories of monarchy, ways of perceiving and understanding kingship, in fifteenth-century France and England were therefore, to a great extent, expounded in conditions of crisis; and two theories of this kind—each in its way a theory of *dominium*—form the subject of this chapter.

Jean de Terrevermeille (or Terre Rouge), the exponent of the first of these theories, was a younger contemporary of d'Ailly and Gerson. When he died in 1430—a month after the capture of Joan of Arc—the French recovery and reconquest had indeed begun; but Terrevermeille had been 'the exact contemporary of a half-century of exceptionally grave crisis for the monarchy'.[1] The

---

[1] J. Barbey, *La Fonction royale: Essence et légitimité d'après les TRACTATUS de Jean de Terrevermeille* (Paris, 1983), 63. Like all students of Terrevermeille I am greatly indebted to this, the first and so far the only comprehensive treatment of the subject.

perspectives in which Terrevermeille viewed that crisis were, in some important respects, different from those of d'Ailly and Gerson. The focal point of their careers was, initially and for many years, Paris, where they succeeded one another in the chancellorship of the university. Both in due course became involved in the high politics of the divided Church and played major parts in the decisive council of Constance. Terrevermeille on the other hand never achieved prominence or high office. Born at Nîmes in or about 1370, he was to live his life in Languedoc: active in the local affairs of his native city, he was appointed in 1418 royal advocate in the *sénéchaussée* of Beaucaire. He owed this appointment to the fact that by then the authority of the Dauphin Charles had been established in the region—an authority which, as we shall see, Terrevermeille strenuously upheld in his *Tractatus*, written at about this time. By 1418 civil war had raged for half a dozen years and more, and even before that Terrevermeille's part of France had become familiar with the evils of inadequate rule and positive misgovernment. In a deeply divided realm it may not always have been easy to determine who was rebelling against whom; but the passion with which Terrevermeille denounces rebellion undoubtedly reflects close firsthand experience of the evils of anarchy.

Terrevermeille's career was that of a layman and lawyer. His formation, accordingly, had not been by way of the arts-and-theology course of study that shaped men like Gerson and d'Ailly. The law school of Montpellier was his *alma mater* and his mind was nurtured on the juristic learning acquired through his training there. Montpellier had been established as a *studium generale* only in 1289, but it had been a centre of law teaching for a century and more before that.[2] By Terrevermeille's time it was admittedly in a state of decline, and it is not possible to say anything about the training he received there except what may be gleaned from his *Tractatus*. It is worth observing, however, that the one Montpellier jurist of note in the late fourteenth century, Jacques Rebuffe, was—in an established Montpellier tradition—a *maître praticien*. In his non-academic career, indeed, he was one of Terrevermeille's predecessors as *avocat du roi*.[3] Terrevermeille's own postgraduate career had no academic dimension; but he was evidently equipped

---

[2] See Ullman, *Law and Politics in the Middle Ages*, 97 and n. 1; cf. also 84 n. 2.
[3] Barbey, *Fonction royale*, 34–5.

for doctrinal exposition, or at least for the use in polemical discourse of the juristic concepts he applied in practical administration.

Only two works can be ascribed to Jean de Terrevermeille, and one of these—*De potestate papae*—has not survived, being known only from his own references to it in the three *Tractatus* known collectively under the title *Contra rebelles suorum regum*. This work (for it is indeed a single work divided into three 'tractates') owes its preservation to its sixteenth-century editor, Jacques Bonaud, and to the Lyons bookseller, Constantin Fradin, who urged Bonaud to undertake the editorial task. The resulting edition of 1526 is the sole basis for the text, no manuscripts being extant. Given the relative rarity of the book,[4] indeed, one may wonder whether its author's ideas would have commanded much attention had it not been for the fact that, sixty years later, François Hotman turned some of them to account in the polemical stress of the French wars of religion, reproducing part of Terrevermeille's text as an appendix to his own *Disputatio de controversia successionis regiae*.[5] It was evidently Hotman's truncated version of the *Contra rebelles* that was known to scholars like McIlwain and Kantorow-icz;[6] and it is certainly arguable (and the point must be considered more fully at a later stage) that the relative neglect of Terrever-meille's third *Tractatus*, constituting as it does fully half of his text, has yielded an impoverished and perhaps even a misconceived interpretation of his thought. For the moment, however, what matters is to place his ideas more firmly in the context of circumstances that led to their being expressed in this form.

The indignation which glows through what would otherwise be the somewhat opaque medium of juristic dialectic in the *Contra rebelles* was no doubt nursed through the years that saw the plight of France and of the French crown deteriorate from the desperate to the disastrous. The intermittent and ultimately total incapacity

---

[4] Barbey (ibid. 71–2 n. 37) lists nine copies, all but one (which is in Ghent) in French libraries. He does not record the Bodleian Library copy. The British Library does not have the book nor does the National Union Catalog record any American holding.

[5] Frankfurt, 1585; rev. edn. Geneva, 1586: for particulars, see Barbey, *Fonction royale*, 72–6 and nn. 45–9.

[6] C. H. McIlwain, *Constitutionalism Ancient and Modern*, 2nd edn. rev. (Ithaca, NY, 1947; first published 1940), 153–4, n. 10; E. H. Kantorowicz, *The King's Two Bodies: A Study in Medieval Political Theology* (Princeton, NJ, 1957).

of the king; the increasing intensity of factional strife; the outbreak and prolongation of civil war; the onset and progress of English aggression and conquest—all contributed to the situation Terrevermeille saw around him as he resolved to write 'against the rebels'. Specifically, however, it seems to have been events in the autumn and winter of 1418–19 that finally led him to demonstrate on paper his loyalties and his animosities. By then, in addition to France's other burdens, there were two rival governments, each claiming the legitimate authority of the crown. Already in 1417, the queen, Isabella of Bavaria, in alliance with the duke of Burgundy, John the Fearless, had attempted to set up a regency, at a time when the rival Armagnac party still held Paris, together with the person of the king and the support of the 14-year-old Dauphin. Another year saw those positions reversed, when Burgundy seized Paris and the king, while the Dauphin Charles with his Armagnac supporters retreated to Bourges. The final turning-point for Terrevermeille came, apparently, with the events of November and December 1418. For about a year before that the Dauphin had held his father's commission as lieutenant-general of the realm. On 13 November 1418 the king, now of course under the control of the Burgundian party, revoked this commission. The Armagnac riposte came in December, when, on the advice of his counsellors at Bourges, the Dauphin assumed the title of regent.[7] A major theme in the book Terrevermeille was now to write would be the defence of the Dauphin's absolute right to the regency in case of the king's incapacity.

A prerequisite for that defence was to establish the terms on which the French crown itself was held, and this is where, in the first *Tractatus*, Terrevermeille begins his argument.[8] It is here too that he makes most reference to, and use of, the concept of *dominium* or lordship. One common form of lordship, Terrevermeille acknowledges, is patrimonial: many things that are subject to human lordship are held 'as patrimony' (*patrimonialiter*). This is, essentially, the mode appropriate to private goods and possessions such as dwelling-houses. For obvious polemical reasons Terrevermeille is particularly interested in the mode of succession

---

[7] See Barbey, *Fonction royale*, 50–8 and the authorities cited there; and, for an outline account in English, Holmes, *Europe: Hierarchy and Revolt*, 243–7.

[8] Jean Barbey, it should be pointed out, begins his analysis with an exposition of the *corpus mysticum regni* as that concept is used in the third *Tractatus*.

associated with different kinds of *dominium*; and in the case of patrimonial possessions, he says, succession is by strictly hereditary right. There are, it is true, intricacies and complexities here, but these need not detain us.[9] The essential point for Terrevermeille's argument is that this mode of possession and succession is neither appropriate nor applicable to entities that are public rather than private. The examples he gives are such things as rivers, roads, and—especially—public offices. These are not, nor can they be, possessed as patrimony. Moreover, the succession to them is not and cannot legitimately be hereditary. The appropriate mode here is *successio simplex*. This takes place *per remotionem alterius*—when by death, resignation, or otherwise, the previous holder is no longer in possession. That holder, it is important to emphasize, has no say in the succession: his successor will be designated by whatever body or person has the right to do so. This is the arrangement which, *de jure communi*, applies to what we might call 'public utilities' and, more importantly for Terrevermeille's purposes, to all offices and honours of a public character.[10]

Now clearly the crown is, supremely, an office of the kind just referred to; and certainly Terrevermeille is committed to the view that royal authority is not to be held *patrimonialiter*, nor is the succession to it strictly hereditary. On the other hand, he does not regard it as an entity governed by *ius commune* and therefore subject to *successio simplex*. Besides that form of succession and the purely hereditary mode, there is a third possibility. This is what Terrevermeille calls 'quasi-hereditary' succession, and its foundation lies in custom. Such a custom may prevail in realms, duchies, and the like; and if and when it prevails in the form established in France it is a good, indeed an excellent custom—*est igitur optima consuetudo*.[11] The hereditary element here lies in the fact that, ordinarily, the first-born son, the *primogenitus*, succeeds his father. Yet the system is not strictly hereditary: it has in it an element of *successio simplex* in that the king who will in due course have a successor has no say in, or control over, the succession. In particular, he cannot dispose of the realm, as an ordinary individual can dispose of his private property, by will or bequest. Again, the

---

[9] See the discussion by Barbey, *Fonction royale*, 296 ff., 323 ff.

[10] *Contra rebelles suorum regum*, I. 1, concl. i–iii; (Lyons, 1526), fos. 9ᵛ–10ʳ (hereafter 1526 edn.).

[11] Ibid. concl. iv (1526 edn. fo. 10r).

eldest son, or anyone else who succeeds to the crown under this
system, is not and cannot properly be called *heir* to the king he
succeeds. It is at this point that the concept of *dominium* makes its
explicit appearance. Terrevermeille proceeds to examine the
rights—the kinds of lordship—enjoyed, respectively, by the heir
over his patrimony and by a king's successor over the realm. The
two forms of *dominium* are in fact specifically different from one
another. The private heir, having entered upon his inheritance, is
free to sell or otherwise alienate what he has inherited, and to
bequeath or devise it as he sees fit. None of these rights forms any
part of the king's *dominium* over the realm.[12]

All this is driven home in the fourteenth and fifteenth 'conclusions' of the first part of *Tractatus I*. The realm of France,
Terrevermeille declares, is possessed neither patrimonially nor
hereditarily: it is held solely *regia potestate et authoritate*. On the
other hand, this specifically *royal* power and authority is also
differentiated from the ordinary public *dominium* which is characteristic of those offices and honours which depend *de jure communi*.
Not only is its basis customary: the laudable custom of quasi-
hereditary succession is itself based on God's ordinance and express
approval.[13] Terrevermeille does not invoke the doctrine of *gratia
gratis data* as we have seen it in such theological writers as
FitzRalph and d'Ailly, but he is, none the less, insisting that the
king of France reigns by the grace of God and that quasi-hereditary
succession is in effect a divine right to succeed to the throne. Yet
the king's authority, divine as it is, can still, in certain extreme
circumstances, be forfeited. Obviously this does not mean that
there is, in Terrevermeille's view, anything like a 'right of resistance'
on the part of the subjects. We shall see later how vehemently he
rejects any such notion, and how deeply that rejection is ingrained
in the very substance of his conception of kingship. What he has in
mind here is a situation such as must have seemed imminent, or
indeed already present, in the France of 1418: the situation in which

[12] Ibid. concl. v–xiii (1526 edn. fos. 10ʳ–11ᵛ). Note esp. the following from concl.
x: 'reges Francae non poterant unquam neque posset rex modernus facere testamen-
tum de regno' (fo. 12ᵛ); and this from concl. xiii: 'successor in patrimonialibus
dominiis habet multo plenius ius quam rex in regno suo' (fo. 12ᵛ).
[13] Ibid. concl. xv (1526 edn. fo. 15ʳ): 'regnum Francie possidetur, & haberi &
possideri per reges consueuit, non patrimoniali aut hereditario modo, sed solum
regia potestate & authoritate, ex Dei tamen dispositione & expressa approbatione.'

the incapacity of a *rex inutilis* necessitates, if not in the full sense his removal from the throne, at all events the effective transfer of his authority to other hands. Terrevermeille's immediate concern is to insist that—in contrast to some situations which could arise in the private domain—the legitimate successor to such an incapacitated king (specifically the Dauphin in France) retains his rights, his *dominium*, absolutely intact. Leaving aside for the moment the question of the precise nature and scope of that *dominium*, we may now look more closely at the ways in which it is safeguarded against being challenged or undermined.[14]

In the first place, the successor to the crown does not owe his succession to any act performed or any law enacted by his father or, for that matter, by any other predecessor on the throne. His succession is assured solely, but completely, by the customary law of the realm, and that law is not subject to modification or interruption by any royal act, legislative or other. It was not by any such act that the customary law was constituted. Its establishing and its continuing authority are derived from and depend upon the consent of the community. This is the point at which we encounter for the first time Terrevermeille's use of the concept of the realm as a *corpus mysticum*, a 'mystical body'. His actual words in this crucial passage are as follows: 'quia consuetudo quae est iam in actu super hoc fuit et est introducta ex consensu trium statuum, et totius ciuilis siue mystici corporis regni.'[15] The tenses used here are perhaps somewhat problematic, but the intention is clearly to indicate a continuing as well as an originating role for the community conceived as a 'mystical body' articulated in the assembly of the estates. Terrevermeille goes on at once to argue that it is for the community to choose and appoint their king. He cites canon law in support of this position and invokes the biblical instances recorded in the second book of Kings.[16] Then, having expressly denied that the head of the body has any right to determine matters relating to the head*ship*, he adds that, just as ecclesiastical 'dignities' belong to

---

[14] Ibid. concl. xxiii (1525 edn. fo. 17ʳ⁻ᵛ).

[15] Ibid. concl. xxiv (1526 edn. fo. 17ᵛ): 'for the custom which is at present in force in regard to this matter was [or has been] introduced by the consent of the three estates and of the whole civil or mystical body of the realm.'

[16] Ibid. concl. xxiv (1526 edn. fo. 17ᵛ): 'iuxta gloss. c. Moses &c. si ergo &c. & text. xciii distinct. legimus: vbi dicitur, quod exercitus populi facit regem siue imperatorem: facit, quod habetur iiii. Reg. xi & xiiii. vbi patet quod populus sibi regem faciebat'. The biblical reference is to 2 Kgs. 11: 4–12; 14: 21.

the churches, so 'the dignities of the realm' (*dignitates regiae*) belong to the civil or mystical body. It follows that the head can do nothing in respect of those 'dignities' which would be prejudicial to the body politic or contrary to the will of those to whom they pertain. In this way Terrevermeille provides a theoretical framework for his insistence that the king cannot choose or nominate his own successor.[17]

An interlocking, overlapping set of terms is used in this part of Terrevermeille's analysis. In addition to the 'mystical (or civil) body', and the three estates in which that body finds its effective mode of action, there is the term *populus*. In the first of Terrevermeille's scriptural examples it was the army, the *exercitus populi*, that took the decisive action; in the second it was, simply, the *populus*. It is to the *populus*, then, in Terrevermeille's account of the matter, that the definitive ordering (*dispositio*) of these matters belongs. In a further development of his terminology, however, Terrevermeille construes this as meaning that the authority in question belongs to the *status regni et reipublicae*; and he adds that 'the king may not alter those things that are ordained for the public estate of the realm' (*ea, quae ad statum publicum regni sunt ordinata*). In this connection he explicitly invokes the parallel canon-law view of the pope's relationship to the *status ecclesiae*.[18]

It was this reference to the *status publicus regni* that caught the eye of C. H. McIlwain in his search for the medieval antecedents of 'constitutionalism'; and it is easy to understand why a writer like Jean Barbey sees here an essentially 'Anglo-Saxon' misrepresentation of Terrevermeille's doctrine. As already noted, McIlwain (and others) appear to have known the *Contra rebelles* only in the partial version preserved by Hotman—himself, after all, a 'monarchomach' with little reason to promulgate the teaching on faithful submission to royal authority, which we find at length in Terrevermeille's third 'tractate'. It is both proper and essential to emphasize,

---

[17] Ibid. concl. xxiv (1526 edn. fo. 17ᵛ): 'ad caput non spectat dispositio de capite eligendo ... dignitates regie sunt totius corporis ciuilis siue mystici regni: sicut dignitates ecclesiastice sunt ecclesiarum: igitur in preiudicium eorum (quorum sunt) aut preter eorum voluntatem caput nihil potest.'

[18] The passage quoted in n. 17 continues (fo. 18ʳ): 'Igitur in regno non est eius dispositio. Ceterum regum & principum dispositio ... pertinet ad populum: & ita in hoc pertinet ad statum regni & reipublice ... nam regi non licet immutare ea, que ad statum publicum regni sunt ordinata ... Et similiter notat. & dicit gloss. quod Papa non potest sibi facere successorem, quia hoc esset mutare statum ecclesie'.

as Barbey does, that it is indeed there, in *Tractatus III*, that Terrevermeille fully develops his understanding of the *corpus mysticum regni*; and the picture which emerges clearly from that development may well seem to have little if anything to do with 'constitutionalism'. Again, to suggest that Terrevermeille's theory as a whole should be seen as a structure built on the foundation laid in the passage just analysed would yield, both quantitatively and qualitatively, an oddly top-heavy edifice. It may well seem more reasonable to follow Barbey in taking the doctrine of the third 'tractate' as the framework into which the rest of the book must somehow fit. Yet the passage which culminates, as it were, in the concept of *status publicus regni* is surely too explicit and too fully developed to be treated dismissively. It may be that, in the end, some kind of 'third way' can be found through this problem; but for the moment the issue must be left open while the arguments of *Tractatus I* are further explored.[19]

The critical problem Terrevermeille faced in 1418 was not the general issue of the law of succession to the French crown. Had he been writing two years later, when the treaty of Troyes had purportedly upset the operation of that law in favour of Henry V, the situation would have been different. As it was, the crucial issue was the Dauphin's position during his father's lifetime. This led to a fuller development of the theory of *dominium*. In the world of patrimonial possession and strictly hereditary succession, Terrevermeille argued, a son naturally (*secundum naturam*) already has, together with his still living father, lordship over the father's goods. When the father dies, therefore, that event does not confer upon the heir any new *dominium*: what he then acquires is full administrative control (*plenam administrationem*) over what was already his as (to use a convenient term not, it seems, actually used in Terrevermeille's text) *condominus*.[20] In regard to *dominium* as distinct from *administratio*, he retains what he has no need to acquire. All this Terrevermeille applies equally to the *primogenitus* who, under the customary law of the realm, is the king's destined successor.[21] There may indeed be a sense in which it applies to that

---

[19] See Barbey, *Fonction royale*, 280–3; and cf. pp. 54–8 below.

[20] He does however use the terms *coadministratio* and *conregnare*: see Barbey, *Fonction royale*, 349 and n. 409.

[21] *Contra rebelles*, I. 2, concl. iii (1526 edn. fo. 18ᵛ): 'filius viuente patre est secundum naturam dominus cum patre rerum patris.' Applying the same doctrine

case with even greater force. It is, after all, arguable that, in the patrimonial mode, the heir, while his father lives, is only 'lord after a fashion' (*quodammodo dominus*). This appeared to be the Roman-law view of the matter; but, Terrevermeille insists, even if the qualification *quodammodo* may render the word *dominus* inappropriate for the private heir, this is not so in regard to the successor to a crown regulated as that of France is regulated. There are indeed, in the patrimonial case, factors arising from the father's right to alienate his property and so on which may erode or even destroy any *dominium* claimed by his heir. This is not the case in a realm where the king is expressly denied any right of alienation. The lordship enjoyed by the Dauphin is 'genuine and substantial' (*verum et reale*).[22]

Even so, the matter is not yet satisfactorily resolved. Terrevermeille cites Bartolus's definition of *dominium* as essentially an exclusive right to dispose of property as the *dominus* thinks fit; and even if this can be construed as applying differently to the patrimonial and to the public sphere, it is still the case that if there is to be *dominium* in any meaningful sense there must be some right of *administratio*. We know already that the patrimonial heir and the royal successor acquire, by the death of the father in each case, not the *dominium* they already in some sense have, but that *plenam* (or *plenam et liberam*) *administrationem* which was denied them before. This is not, according to Terrevermeille, to deny the existence of *any* right of *administratio* to heirs and successors *patre vivente*. The royal *primogenitus* in particular, with his *solidum dominium* safeguarded against all that makes the private heir's lordship precarious, does have some kind of right to 'administer'. Admittedly, since this must not be interpreted as a right to rule (*regere*), it is perhaps not too easy to see how it *is* to be understood. It is easier to see why the argument must, so to speak, be restrained at this point. Even though Terrevermeille may be happy to accept that the successor to the crown is not simply a lord but also a king,

---

to the royal case, Terrevermeille says (concl. vii; fo. 19ʳ): 'filius primogenitus est patre rege viuente simul cum eo dominus: ita quod obeunte patre filius non nouum dominium, sed solum plenam regni administrationem nanciscitur ... Et verius retinere dicitur quod habebat quam acquirere nouiter.'

[22] Ibid. concl. xi (1526 edn. fo. 20ʳ): 'illud dominium quod competit filio primogenito in regno & liberis in patrimonialibus viuente patre est eius verum & reale.'

this *rex iuvenis* must be placed firmly in a secondary position if the theory is to retain its emphatically monarchical thrust.[23]

If there are possible obstacles to accepting without reserve the logic of the argument, there is no difficulty in understanding why Terrevermeille argued as he did. The complex and perhaps ambiguous situation just considered prevails, and may well prevail without damaging consequences, in ordinary circumstances, with a competent ruler fully in control of the realm, while the 'young king' waits, as it were, in the wings. The crux comes—and had come as Terrevermeille wrote his book—when circumstances have become extraordinary to the point of creating a crisis of authority imperilling the very survival of the realm. With the titular king no longer in effective control and no longer able to reassert his position, the *solidum dominium* of his destined successor must take effect in 'full and free administration' of the affairs of the kingdom: he must, as of right, assume the *regimen regni*. This, however, both in general and in the specific circumstances of France in 1418, raised further issues. A problem arose, in particular, because the Dauphin, whose right to regency Terrevermeille sought to vindicate, was a minor. Could one who in law was not yet *sui juris* undertake the responsibilities of government? The answer to this question takes us back into other, more general considerations.

Once again Terrevermeille brings out a contrast between the private and the public sphere. A private owner exercising his *dominium* does so *jure proprio formato*—the right to do so is his own inherent right. Matters are different in the area of public administration. Here *rectores* or *administratores* (exercising *regimen* or *administratio*) do not act on the basis of any right belonging to them in their individual capacities. They act *jure commisso non proprio*: the right to act has been committed or entrusted to them. Moreover, whereas the private owner acts in respect of what is his own and no one else's, those in public authority act *in re aliena*— their actions necessarily affect matters that are the concern of other people. Now this, so far as it goes, might well seem to increase, not to reduce, the difficulty over the conduct of government by a regent (or a king) not yet of full age. That, however, is not Terrevermeille's view. The point he makes is that, precisely because of its 'other-regarding' character, public power cannot be legitim-

---

[23] Barbey, *Fonction royale*, 347–50.

ately exercised without counsel—without the advice of the leading men in the community. The language here—*cum consiliis, et arbitrio procerum, optimatum, et variorum sapientum*—might even be read so as to imply a requirement of 'advice and consent'. However that may be, the argument is associated explicitly with the authority wielded by kings, dukes, and other *sublimes potestates*. And however extensive or restricted the general implications may be, the point for Terrevermeille is that he has, he believes, removed any barrier to full acceptance of the Dauphin's irrefragable claim to rule as regent for the incapacitated Charles VI.[24]

For polemical purposes, then, this part of Terrevermeille's argument ends triumphantly with the emphatic assertion that, given the laudable custom of quasi-hereditary succession as established in the realm of France, the Dauphin's right to act as regent is absolute and paramount. No one has the right to appoint another coadjutor or vicegerent. The pope cannot do this, nor can the three estates as the civil or mystical body of the realm. On the other hand—and the point is an interesting one—Terrevermeille adds that, if circumstances were to render such an extraordinary appointment necessary, it *would* then be the responsibility of the estates to make it.[25]

The point just mentioned is, as it happens, taken up in the second *Tractatus*. In general, however, that part of Terrevermeille's text, with its fierce invective flaying the duke of Burgundy and his adherents for their treachery and rebellion, adds little to our understanding of the author's ideas. What may be regarded as the more theoretical dimensions of the book are resumed in *Tractatus III*. And it is indeed here, as Barbey argues, that we see fully and in depth Terrevermeille's understanding and use of the concept of the *corpus mysticum*. That body, we are now to be shown, is totally lifeless and incoherent without its head and without due recognition by subjects of their position as *membra mystica*. Both the thought and the language are strikingly vivid here and their impact is enhanced by the fact that the doctrine they express is addressed, not to subjects in general, as a group, but to each and every subject

---

[24] *Contra rebelles*, I. 3, concl. i, iii (1526 edn. fo. 25ᵛ).

[25] Ibid. I. 4, concl. v (1526 edn. fo. 30ʳ); II. 1, concl. vii (1526 edn. fo. 31ᵛ). In II. 1, concl. ix, Terrevermeille argues that cases in which the pope appears to have deposed a king or appointed an 'administrator' are always to be understood as referring to papal support or assistance to those who took the really effective action—the *maiores regni siue maiorem & saniorem partem* (1526 edn. fo. 32ʳ).

personally. One of the most dramatic metaphors Terrevermeille uses is that of the marriage bond. The subject is to cleave wholly to the king, otherwise he stands condemned as *infidelis et fornicator*.[26] Obviously the resonances here include that of St Paul's teaching on the relation between Christ and the Church.[27] What calls for closer scrutiny in an enquiry into Terrevermeille's contribution to fifteenth-century thinking about monarchy is a group of questions about the kind of unity he attributes to the realm and the kind of headship he ascribes to the king.

Taking first the question of unity, it is of course the case that the analogy between the body politic and a natural body is fundamental. It is arguable, however, that a still more crucial point is to be found in an essential difference between the two analogous entities. The physical organism is united, in Terrevermeille's phraseology, *unione compaginis*: there is a literal, structural joining together of its parts. This is to be contrasted, as well as compared, with the case of a *corpus mysticum*, which is united *solum unione voluntatis*—only by a unity of will. Nor is there, for Terrevermeille, any doubt as to where the necessary unity of will is to be found: 'in the mystical body of any kingdom and any other body of that kind the will is, and ought to be, only in the head'.[28] On the part of the subjects this is manifested in two ways: *in unione affectus*, in that the members of the body have the same goals or objectives (*idem volunt*) as the head; and *in unione effectus*, 'so that the members unanimously carry out the will of their head'.[29]

This is a far-reaching claim; and yet there may be a sense in which Terrevermeille carries the argument even farther. For him it is not simply the case that the 'mystical head', by ruling all the members *suo judicio*, is the life and salvation of the body. The head actually gives life to each of these members. It is here that Terrevermeille uses one of his most striking phrases: *caput mysti-*

---

[26] Ibid. III. 3, conc. viii (1526 edn. fo. 59ᵛ): 'sicut uxor . . . debet adherere viro suo . . . sic quodlibet membrum mysticum . . . suo supremo capiti mystico & soli domino in eis (que ad eum solum pertinent) adherere, et soli obedire . . . aliter autem est infidelis & fornicator.'

[27] Eph. 5: 23–5.

[28] *Contra rebelles*, III. 3, concl. iv (1526 edn. fo. 50ᵛ): 'in corpore mystico cuiuslibet regni, et alio quolibet, voluntas eius est, et esse debet, solum in capite eius.'

[29] Ibid. III. 2, concl. vii (1526 end. fo. 51ʳ).

cum influit esse in quodlibet suorum membrorum.[30] The concept and the language—the use of the verb *influere* in a transitive sense equivalent to the more classical *infundere*—are of theological provenance and inspiration.[31] By the fifteenth century, however, such language was being used in political or quasi-political context, as Terrevermeille uses it here. On closer examination, it is clear that the 'being' or life infused by the head of the body politic into each of its members cannot be either their natural or their supernatural being. The first of these belongs to the order of nature, the second to the order of grace. The 'mystical being' (*esse mysticum*) to be considered here is, as Terrevermeille also terms it, an *esse politicum*. It is the 'political being' of the subject that is infused by and from the head. The strength of such an assertion may be gauged by comparing it with some similar, and yet perhaps less emphatic views expressed towards the middle of the century. Piero da Monte, for instance, in a manuscript written about 1450, does regard the monarch as the source of all powers in the community; but the recipients of such powers are essentially those who would later be called the 'inferior magistrates'.[32] Similarly, and at much the same time, Juan de Torquemada claimed in his 1449 *Summa de Ecclesia* that all those who wield particular powers of political administration receive their jurisdictional authority from the supreme power.[33] Neither of these authors, however, maintained (as Terrevermeille did) that the 'political being' of *every member* of the mystical body of the realm is derived by 'infusion' from its head.

It is important to notice that Terrevermeille carefully distinguishes between the properly political relationship of head to members and, for example, the feudal relationship of lord and vassal. Once again we are dealing with different kinds of lordship or *dominium*; and we are told explicitly that a vassal does *not* receive from his feudal lord, as the 'mystical member' receives from the head of the body politic, the 'infusion' which constitutes and maintains his 'political being'. In one sense this is to reassert

---

[30] Ibid. III. 3, concl. ii (1526 edn. fo. 52ʳ).

[31] Cf. e.g. Aquinas, *ST*, IIIa, 8, 1, Art. 1: 'Caput enim influit sensum et motum in membra.' The question in which this phrase occurs is entitled *de gratia Christi secundum quod est caput Ecclesiae.*

[32] Black, *Monarchy and Community*, 62–3 and n. 1, citing Monte's *Contra impugnantes sedis apostolicae liber.*

[33] Ibid. 62: the passage from Torquemada (*Summa de Ecclesia*, II. 55) is printed by Black on p. 167.

Terrevermeille's initial distinction between the public and the private domain. It also involves, however, his insistence that the king is not merely the *caput mysticum*, he is the *caput mysticum supremum*. There are other, subordinate chiefs (*capita inferiora*), but only the sovereign can pour truly political life into the members of the mystical body.[34]

The exploration of the theme of unity in the *Contra rebelles* has thus taken us, no doubt inevitably, into the other set of questions mentioned above: those that concern the kind of headship Terrevermeille has in mind. Those questions are still, however, best approached by staying for the time being with the members of the body politic and asking what more can be said about the 'political life' they receive from their 'mystical head'. That life would, certainly, be one of faithful service, of implicit obedience, of love and loyalty expressed in active conformity to the ruler's will. Taking this together with the concept of the king as the sole source of 'political life' in all its forms may lead very naturally to the conclusion that what we are being offered is a theory of 'absolute monarchy'. If this is indeed the kind of headship Terrevermeille has in view, however, the question must at least be asked as to whether there is not some degree of tension, if not of outright conflict or contradiction, between this position and that which was advanced in *Tractatus I*. It is when this question is answered by suggesting that there is in fact a contrast between initial 'constitutionalism' and eventual 'absolutism' that Jean Barbey diagnoses an 'Anglo-Saxon' misunderstanding.[35] The problem here has to be faced and, if not solved, at least clarified in ways that may be relevant and helpful in later stages of the investigation of theories of monarchy in the period.

Baldly restated, the problem is this. In *Tractatus I*, the political community, envisaged explicitly as a *corpus mysticum* or *corpus civile*, appears to be treated as an entity subsisting, in some sense, independently of its head. The ruler, even if he has come to power by way of 'quasi-hereditary succession'—indeed, especially and explicitly in that case—holds his position on the basis of custom; but that custom is itself based on the consent of the community

---

[34] *Contra rebelles*, III. 9, concl. xiii (1526 edn. fo. 91 [misnumbered '95']): 'caput supremum mysticum magis influit esse conseruatiuum in membris quibuslibet suis quam capita illa inferiora.'
[35] *Fonction royale*, 290–1; cf. also 192–3 n. 188 and esp. 378.

expressed in and through the three estates. In *Tractatus III*, on the other hand, the ruler appears, not as the recipient, but as the source, the exclusive source, of authority. His subjects, deriving their very 'political being' from him, can claim no authority over him. They owe him the submission, the loyalty, and the love without which there can be no unity, and therefore no coherent life, in the body politic. The *corpus mysticum*, which had before appeared as the ultimate source of royal power, is now presented as being incapable of activity, perhaps even of existence, without the supreme authority which belongs exclusively to the king. The dilemma takes us to the heart of some of the most basic issues in the theory of monarchy in the fifteenth century (to say nothing of other periods), and it will inevitably recur in later parts of the discussion. For the moment it must suffice to explore possible ways of reconciling the seemingly discordant elements in Terrevermeille's thought.

Two possible modes of reconciliation suggest themselves. The first bears an essential similarity to a line of argument pursued by conciliarist thinkers in the context of political ecclesiology; and it is therefore only fair to point out that Barbey finds little trace in Terrevermeille of any sympathy with that point of view. Indeed, the milieu in which his thought was shaped was distinctly unfriendly towards conciliarism.[36] The fact remains that Terrevermeille's positions in his first and third 'tractates' might be squared with one another by way of the familiar distinction between taking the members of a group *ut universi* and taking them *ut singuli*. It has been pointed out already that Terrevermeille's concern in *Tractatus III* is essentially with the relationship between each individual subject and the head. Certainly he holds that a *corpus mysticum* is constituted by the totality of such relationships and that the life of that body flows essentially from its head. Yet precisely because this is so, because he emphasizes so strongly the constitutive importance of individual loyalty and service to the king, Terrevermeille excludes in this context the possibility of a corporate existence for subjects as a group. Things are quite different in *Tractatus I*. Here

---

[36] Ibid. 212: 'l'on connaît la tenace hostilité du Languedoc aux thèses conciliaristes'; and 283: 'A plusieurs reprises s'est manifesté le peu de goût du languedocien pour les théories conciliaires qui font résider le pouvoir dans l'*universitas*.' In this connection Barbey cites J. L. Gazzaniga, *L'Eglise du Midi à la fin du règne de Charles VII d'après la jurisprudence du Parlement de Toulouse (1441–1461)* (Paris, 1976), 32–42, 123–32. I have not been able to consult this.

we find little or no reference to the individual subject. And if it is true to say that, as Barbey points out, the concept of the *corpus mysticum regni* is far less prominent than it was to be in *Tractatus III*, it is also true that when it does occur in the first 'tractate', together with references to the *populus* and the estates, the part it plays in Terrevermeille's argument is absolutely crucial. The 'reconciling' interpretation on this basis would be that Terrevermeille operates in these different contexts with concepts that are, respectively, appropriate to each case. This would amount to saying that, although he does not use the terminology, his concern in the first 'tractate' is with *omnes ut universi*, while in the third he concentrates on *omnes ut singuli*.

That would not in itself be a self-contradictory procedure; but there is still some difficulty in accepting such a distinction as a satisfactory way of saving the coherence of Terrevermeille's position. Arguing on this basis was commonly associated (as we shall see in later instances[37]) with the view that the *universitas* was in some sense the ultimately supreme element in the system, with a degree of control over the ruler once established as well as what may perhaps be termed an originating or constituent role in regard to the ruling authority. It is hard not to share Barbey's feeling that this kind of 'constitutionalism' is decidedly at odds with the general direction and emphasis of Terrevermeille's thought. It is, at the very least, worth considering an alternative framework.

This second option, like the first, involves themes that will demand more extensive consideration at a later stage, in primarily ecclesiological contexts. Yet, given Terrevermeille's own use of arguments and analogies drawn from canon law, it is certainly not inappropriate to use such sources in interpreting his theory.[38] The relevant considerations are briefly the following. Theologians naturally saw the Church as the supreme and archetypal instance of the concept of a 'mystical body'; and the notion that the life of such a body was 'infused' by the head was deeply rooted in ecclesiological thinking. When, for example, Gabriel Biel says that the head of the Church 'pours spiritual life into its members' and

---

[37] Below, chap. VI.
[38] Cf. e.g. the reference to the *dignitates ecclesiasticae* in the passage cited in n. 17 above. Barbey (*Fonction royale*, Appendix III, 409) records 486 references in Terrevermeille's text to the *Corpus Juris Canonici* and 108 to canonists.

thus gives them 'sense and motion',[39] he is echoing what many earlier theologians, including Aquinas, had said.[40] In its life on earth, of course, the Church had what was sometimes called a 'secondary head', in the person of the pope, acting as Christ's vicar; and writers like Piero da Monte and Juan de Torquemada had applied the notion of 'infusion', as Biel was also to apply it, to the operation of papal authority.[41] What was 'infused' by this second-ary head, however, was (according to Biel) not the essential spiritual life of the individual Christian, but rather a certain authority, the power to teach and rule the Church, whether as bishop or as simple priest. The former comes, and can come only, from Christ himself; the latter comes, whether directly or indirectly, from the pope.

There is plainly a tempting parallel here. Just as Christ pours spiritual life into each believing Christian, it may seem, the king pours 'political being' or political life into each of his faithful subjects. The quasi-divine position this would ascribe to the king need not have been an obstacle to the acceptance of such a view. Giles of Rome for one—an authority Terrevermeille himself invokes—had, in his *De regimine principum*, referred to the prince or king as a demi-god (*semideus*); and writers at the court of Charles V of France had, in Terrevermeille's own lifetime, used even more extravagant language in their exaltation of royal power.[42] The parallel would in important ways accord very well with the image of the king as presented in Terrevermeille's third 'tractate', where it does seem as though the very life of the body politic flows exclusively from the ruler. Yet there are problems in such an interpretation. The power of Christ, in the theology of orthodox Catholicism, is not simply analogous to divine power, nor is it even simply derived from that source: it *is* divine power itself, belonging to the Son who is co-equal with the Father and with the Holy Spirit. It is a power that exists, so to speak, in its own right; it exists from all eternity; and if we suppose *per impossibile* that there had never been a Church for Christ to rule as its head, his power would

---

[39] Biel, *Canonis Missae Expositio*, ed. H. A. Oberman and W. J. Courtenay (5 vols.; Wiesbaden, 1963–8), i. 200 (hereafter Oberman and Courtenay edn.).

[40] Cf. n. 31 above.

[41] Cf. nn. 32 and 33 above.

[42] Giles of Rome, *De regimine principum*, III. ii. 15. On Charles V's court writers, see R. H. Gill, 'Political Theory at the Court of Charles V of France, 1364–80', Ph.D. thesis (London, 1988).

be unaffected and unabated. Such attributes cannot, obviously, be predicated of royal power in an earthly kingdom. That power belongs to the king only as head of a 'mystical body' apart from which he has, as king, no existence. 'No head, no body' may indeed be a valid maxim—though its validity is not entirely beyond question even in Terrevermeille's theory; but the maxim 'No body, no head' is not merely valid, it is self-evident. Again, the king's power is not in the last analysis an independent power subsisting in its own right. Specifically, Terrevermeille himself argues that it is based on custom grounded in the consent of the *corpus mysticum regni*. However true it may be that there can be no effective ongoing life for that body without its head, and however absolute that head's claim on the obedience and fidelity of his subjects, it seems to be the case that *some* kind, *some* degree of life inheres in the body politic independently of its ruler.

Yet to say this is not necessarily to say that there is, in such a theory as that which is deployed by Jean de Terrevermeille for his essentially polemical purposes, an uneasy combination or imperfect amalgam of 'absolutism' and 'constitutionalism'. It might be better to suggest something which will recur more than once in later chapters here: that late medieval and early modern thinking about monarchy allowed for, or even required, a structure which we (though not, of course, writers at the time) might want to call a 'constitutional' structure. Within it both the king's sovereign power and the corporate life of the *populus* had a place. This would imply that McIlwain was not mistaken in seizing upon Terrevermeille's reference to the *status publicus regni* as a point of real importance; but that importance may have less to do with 'constitutional*ism*' than McIlwain seems to have supposed.[43]

When we turn from Terrevermeille to Sir John Fortescue, from France in the first quarter of the fifteenth century to England in the third, we encounter both similarities and, of course, major differences. Once again, to start with, we are dealing with ideas expressed by a lawyer engaged in political controversy. On the other hand, Fortescue's training in Lincoln's Inn was a process very different from the education in civil and canon law received by Terrevermeille at Montpellier. The contrast need not, it is true, be overem-

---

[43] Cf. n. 6 above.

phasized. Both these writers belonged, after all, to a broadly similar cultural milieu: each could and did draw on a common store of scholastic learning to sustain arguments derived from their professional expertise. Fortescue may have a claim, as Terrevermeille assuredly does not, to be regarded as at least a forerunner of a less exclusively scholastic way of thinking.[44] And the fact that much of his writing was in English, not Latin, reflects the emergence and the needs of an educated public now less overwhelmingly clerical in its membership.[45] Yet there are still grounds for suggesting that we have not, with Fortescue, moved into a world Terrevermeille would have found alien or incomprehensible.

In regard also to the problems that precipitated the writings of these two lawyer-propagandists, there are resemblances as well as divergences. The basic theme of monarchy in crisis is common to both. It is true, and important, that for Fortescue, the crisis was at least as much a matter of 'governance' as of authority and succession. Indeed, if it is correct to conclude, as recent scholarship indicates, that the work we know as *The Governance of England* dates, at least in its original form, from the 1440s, and was thus written well before the major challenge to the house of Lancaster which issued in the Wars of the Roses, it would follow that Fortescue's earliest political concern was for the reform of government rather than with the basis of the authority to govern.[46] To that concern, moreover, he brought a different kind of political experience from that available to Terrevermeille. Even if we need not attach too much importance to the parliamentary experience which began in his 20s, the fact remains that Fortescue (King's

---

[44] On this, see J. G. A. Pocock, *The Machiavellian Moment: Florentine Political Thought and the Atlantic Republican Tradition* (Princeton, NJ, 1975), 9–12, 17–22; A. B. Ferguson, 'Fortescue and the Renaissance: A Study of Transition', *Studies in the Renaissance*, 6 (1959), 175–94; and id., *The Articulate Citizen and the English Renaissance* (Durham, NC, 1965), 111–29. For an earlier view, cf. H. D. Hazeltine, 'General Preface' in S. B. Chrimes (ed.), *Sir John Fortescue: De laudibus legum Anglie* (Cambridge, 1949; 1st edn. 1942), p. liii (hereafter Chrimes edn.): 'Fortescue's ascription of supreme authority to *ius divinum* and *ius naturale* represents the medievalism in his thought: the rationalism and the realism of his thought . . . represent the spirit of the early Renaissance.'

[45] On this, see P. E. Gill, 'Politics and Propaganda in Fifteenth-Century England: The Polemical Writings of Sir John Fortescue', *Speculum*, 46 (1971), 333–47.

[46] See D. Starkey, 'Which Age of Reform?', in D. Starkey and C. H. D. Coleman (eds.), *Revolution Reassessed: Revisions in the History of Tudor Government and Administration* (Oxford, 1986), 14–16.

Serjeant in 1441, Chief Justice of the King's Bench for two decades from 1442) moved much nearer the centre of political affairs than Terrevermeille ever did. His writings constantly reflect the attitudes and the anxieties of one who has seen at close quarters a system of government at work—or rather, more significantly, perhaps, failing to work.

Yet it is also the case that Fortescue's longest work, the *De natura legis nature*, like several of his minor pamphlets, was the product of concern as to the legitimacy, rather than the efficacy, of Lancastrian rule. And even when, as in his better known works, *The Governance of England* and *De laudibus legum Anglie*, he is mainly concerned with problems of administration and legal procedure, he is also careful to set out his position as to the nature and basis of monarchy in its different forms. It does no violence to Fortescue's own thought, therefore, to concentrate attention on issues of that kind—issues which, as in the case of Terrevermeille, belong firmly to 'the political theory of *dominium*'.[47]

It was certainly to the concept and theory of *dominium*, of lordship, that Fortescue turned when, in the early 1460s, the Yorkist challenge drove him to a searching scrutiny of the foundations of royal authority. Like Terrevermeille before him, he saw *regnum* as a public office; but since its function was to bear rule (*ad dominandum*), this office was a kind of *dominium*. Nor perhaps is it surprising, given the centrality of the law of property in the legal system in which Fortescue spent his professional life, that he should insist on the point that royal lordship is *dominium reale* in the strict sense of the term. His theory is, it has been aptly said, 'imbued with the real-property idea of kingship'.[48] Again, whereas Terrevermeille found it necessary to expound and justify a concept of 'quasi-hereditary succession' to the crown, Fortescue was quite satisfied with the view that the realm is hereditary in an entirely straightforward sense (*descendibile preregnantis heredi*). The king's son—for example, the prince who takes part in the dialogue *De laudibus legum Anglie*—is, quite simply, his father's heir. Indeed,

---

[47] J. H. Burns, 'Fortescue and the Political Theory of *Dominium*', *Historical Journal*, 28 (1985), 777–97.

[48] S. B. Chrimes, *English Constitutional Ideas in the Fifteenth Century* (Cambridge, 1936), 9; and cf. Hazeltine, 'General Preface', in Chrimes (ed.), *De laudibus legum Anglie*, p. xiv: 'the kingdom is regarded by Fortescue as real property of a public character, capable of descending to the heir of the preceding king.'

this strictly hereditary mode and right of possessing the realm is, for Fortescue, one of the crucial distinguishing features—and advantages—of that kind of *dominium* which is *regale* and not (or not only) *politicum*.[49]

The terminology just used alerts us to the comparative element in Fortescue's theory of *dominium* and provides the framework for a central part of his argument. In France and many other realms, he maintained, we find *dominium regale*. Elsewhere—in the city-states of the ancient world and, no doubt, in the Italian city-republics of Fortescue's own day—the prevalent form of government was *dominium politicum*. The critical point for Fortescue, however, was the claim that a third form, combining features from both these simple modes, subsisted—above all, though not only—in England. This *dominium politicum et regale* became the pivotal concept in Fortescue's theory. It has been so much discussed as to seem threadbare, but it is still an unavoidable topic for analysis here.[50]

Arguably the most important point to emphasize at the outset, especially in view of the order in which the two elements are usually presented (with *politicum* coming first), is that the 'regal' element carries the full implications of that term as Fortescue understood it. The king, that is to say, is a strictly hereditary ruler, and whatever authority he has is his alone. No *dominium regale*, even if it is also *politicum*, can admit any plurality in the exercise of those powers. A republic (as we would call it) must, like any other political system, make provision for *regimen*, for rule or government; and, while it may do this by entrusting the necessary powers to a single magistrate or *rector*, it may just as well do so by designating a number of *rectores*. The *regimen* under such a system, however, does not contain anything that Fortescue would have been prepared to call *dominium regale*: this is a case of pure *dominium politicum*.[51]

Yet, 'regal' though the authority of the king of England is (and we

---

[49] *De natura legis nature*, II. i; in *The Works of Sir John Fortescue*, ed. Thomas [Fortescue], Lord Clermont, and Chichester Fortescue (2 vols.; London, 1869), i. 167–8 (hereafter *Works*).

[50] Other perspectives on Fortescue's thought are usefully provided by J. L. Gillespie, 'Sir John Fortescue's Concept of Royal Will', *Birmingham Medieval Studies*, 23 (1979), 47–65; N. Doe, 'Fifteenth-Century Concepts of Law: Fortescue and Pecock', *History of Political Thought*, 10 (1989), 257–80.

[51] Cf. e.g. *De natura legis nature*, II. iv (*Works*, i. 118): '*politicum* solum dominium est quod plures recipit rectores, sed regale nunquam.'

do no violence to Fortescue's intentions by presenting the argument essentially in the English setting where his interest overwhelmingly lay), it is not, of course, exercised as pure *dominium regale*. It is part of the composite system of *dominium politicum et regale*; and Fortescue is quite clear that, whenever we can properly use the term *politicum* in such a connection, plurality of some kind *is* involved. He uses some fairly implausible etymology to underpin his position. What matters here, however, is not Fortescue's linguistic learning, but an important point he makes in the course of deploying it. He indicates that the involvement of a plurality of persons in the process he has in mind consists in what he calls *dispensatio*. That is not the easiest of terms to translate, and simply to Anglicize it as 'dispensation' does not help very much. 'Administration'—the term used by Chichester Fortescue in his translation[52]—is better, but carries the risk of reading the word too broadly and thus suggesting a power that would extend into those areas of 'government' which Fortescue seems to reserve for the king. A more cautious and perhaps more helpful interpretation may be sought by recalling the fact that *dispensatio* meant, among other things, 'stewardship'.[53] Now Fortescue also used, to elucidate one element in his suggested derivation of the word *politia* (whence of course *politicum*) the term *administratio*, with its general connotation of management and perhaps also having in mind its more specific legal sense in regard to the administration of an estate. To this it may also be relevant to add the point that, in Terrevermeille, the notion of 'administration' seemed to involve some share in the management of a domain still effectively possessed and ruled by a king.[54]

All this would suggest that Fortescue may have considered such terms as *dispensatio* and *administratio* relevant in the explication of the *politicum* element in his composite system because that element

[52] *Works*, i. 205. Chrimes, *English Constitutional Ideas*, 310, uses 'dispensation'.

[53] This was of course an extremely common medieval usage; and its scriptural associations are worth noting: see e.g. I Cor. 9: 17 (for *dispensatio*), and, for *dispensator* (='steward'), perhaps esp. Luke 12: 4—'quis putas est fidelis dispensator et prudens'.

[54] *De natura legis nature*, I. xxiii (*Works*, i. 85): '*policia* nanque a polos dicitur quod est *pluralitas*, et ycon *administratio*, quasi *regimen plurium consilio ministratum*.' The equation of 'ycon' with *administratio* (which is not made in the parallel passage in *The Governance of England* (ed. C. Plummer (Oxford, 1885), 112; hereafter Plummer edn.) is interesting in connection with the interpretation of *administratio*, which is thus given an 'economic' connotation, referring to household management. For Terrevermeille on *administratio*, see text at nn. 20–3 above.

was in some special sense concerned with the management of the public domain. There are two ways in which this argument might be developed. In the first place, one of the most familiar points in Fortescue's theory is his insistence that, under *dominium politicum et regale*, the king cannot levy texes without parliamentary consent.[55] Public needs, we might say, are in this context to be weighed against the legitimate rights of individual subjects; and this can be done only by means of a process in which the three estates of the realm take part. It is worth remarking, without reopening the intricate debate over Fortescue's claim to be following in his theory of *dominium* the lead of Aquinas and of Giles of Rome, that there is a significant echo of St Thomas here. In a context noted in an earlier chapter, a distinction is made in the *Summa Theologiae* between *despoticus principatus*, under which subjects 'have nothing of their own' (*nihil sui habent*) and *principatus politicus et regalis*, where the subjects, because they *have* 'something of their own' (*aliquid proprium*) are able, as free men, to resist the ruler if necessary.[56] It may be the case that, for Fortescue as compared with Terrevermeille, property rights had a different kind and degree of importance.[57] It does seem to be true that Fortescue was readier than Terrevermeille to assimilate public and private *dominium* to one another. Yet he does not, of course, abandon the distinction between the two. Nor is the status of private property merely, in Fortescue's thought, a touchstone for making that distinction: it is one of the bases for another, equally crucial distinction, between two modes in which political authority may be exercised. And it is no accident that the line of distinction in this case runs along the English Channel.[58]

There is, however, a second way in which one might develop the suggestion that the 'politic' element in Fortescue's composite system has a particular connection with the management of the public domain. If we are indeed to see political reform as one of Fortescue's primary concerns, having regard especially to the original purpose for which he wrote *The Governance of England*,

---

[55] *De laudibus legum Anglie*, c. 36 (Chrimes edn. 86, ll. 20–4).

[56] *ST*, Ia, 81, 3, *ad* 2.

[57] It must however be borne in mind that Terrevermeille wrote with much more limited purposes than those which directed Fortescue's works.

[58] The contrast between England and France is particularly prominent and pervasive in *The Governance of England*; but cf. also the discussion of torture in *De laudibus*, c. 22 (Chrimes edn. 46 ff.).

we are bound to notice his preoccupation with two issues that are relevant in the present context. One is the question of 'the fferme endowynge off the crowne'[59]—the essential importance of restoring and preserving a substantial measure of financial independence for royal government. This, in Fortescue's judgement, necessitated, *inter alia*, 'a generall resumpcion, made be auctorite off parlement' of royal gifts, together with a strict provision that the domain should not in future be alienated without express parliamentary assent.[60] The parliamentary factor here, as in regard to taxation, is clearly important. Yet it may be that Fortescue's other major concern as a reformer is even more important, as it is certainly more pervasive. It is a concern widely shared by fifteenth-century writers on monarchy: the king's indispensable need for counsel.[61] In Fortescue's case this concern is, so to speak, institutionalized; for he devotes considerable attention to the actual organization of the royal council.[62] It is also noteworthy that the council he has in mind has an essential part to play in the functioning of the parliamentary assembly.[63] This may not modify in any fundamental way the essential defining characteristics of the 'politic' element in *dominium politicum et regale*; and it is important to bear in mind the fact that the 'conciliar' concept of government would, in Fortescue's eyes, be equally desirable in the case of a pure *dominium regale*.[64] The fact remains that the council must surely be seen as an important aspect of the pluralistic *dispensatio* which is always essential to 'politic' rule.

Even now, however, we have not accounted fully for Fortescue's emphatic distinction between *dominium politicum et regale* and that which is *tantum regale*. When, in his *De natura legis nature*, he first defined the fundamental categories of *dominium regale* and

[59] *Governance*, chap. 19 (Plummer edn. 154 ff.); and cf. chap. 10 (131 ff.).
[60] Ibid. 143, 154–5.
[61] See J. Dunbabin, 'Government', in Burns (ed.), *Cambridge History of Medieval Political Thought*, 501–4; Quillet, 'Community, Counsel, and Representation,' in ibid. 545–54. Both authors emphasize the views of Gerson on the theme of counsel.
[62] See esp. *Governance*, chap. 15 (Plummer edn. 145–9).
[63] Ibid. 148, where Fortescue argues that the council should consider 'How also the lawes may be amendet in suche thynges as they neden reformacion in; where through the parlementes shall mowe do moe gode in a moneth . . . then thai shall mowe do in a yere, yff the amendynge theroff be not debatyd and be such counsel ryped to thair handes.'
[64] See esp. *De natura legis nature*, I. xxiii (*Works*, i. 85); and cf. Burns, 'Fortescue and the Political Theory of *Dominium*', 782–3 at n. 19.

dominium politicum, he did so in terms of law, in terms of the source and authority of the laws by which political society was to live. Political life, for Fortescue, was inseparably associated with two things: one was *regimen* or *principatus*—the rule or government without which human beings, even if they had remained free from sin, could not have lived happily and harmoniously together as God and nature intended.[65] The second necesssary condition for political life is the law in accordance with which legitimate government, in all its forms, must always be carried on. All rulers, all governments worthy of the name, are regarded by Fortescue as functioning within a legal framework. Under *dominium regale*, the ruler governs 'according to laws that he himself has laid down' (*secundum leges quas ipsemet statuit*). This means government by the will—at the nod—of the ruler: Fortescue refers explicitly to the king *qui ad nutum suum omnia dirigit in regno*, and likens such royal authority to that of God, whose will is law (*cujus velle est lex*).[66] Yet this kind of *jus regale* (as Fortescue calls it in his *Governance of England*) is not merely the exercise of arbitrary power. Under 'gode princes', laws so made may be 'right gode'. The maxim *Quod principi placuit legis habet vigorem* had been adopted by 'mony cristen princes'; and realms so ruled may well be 'most resembled to the kingdome of God'.[67] It may be, as we shall see, that there are, so to speak, degrees of divinity in different forms of government; but it is in any case important to note here that Fortescue's evaluation of *dominium regale* is by no means simply negative and hostile.[68]

Under *dominium politicum*, in direct contrast, the ruler or rulers (*rector, rectores*) govern 'by laws laid down by the citizens' (*secundum leges quas cives statuerunt*).[69] This 'republican' system is of course something with which Fortescue had little direct concern. It is, however, analytically essential to his argument; for

---

[65] *De natura legis nature*, II. xviii (*Works*, i. 131): 'homo, qui animal politicum est et sociale, non potest bene in societate viuere sine aliquo praesidente et regente.'

[66] Ibid. I. xvi (*Works*, i. 77); I. xxii (i. 84).

[67] *Governance*, chap. 2 (Plummer edn. 112).

[68] Plummer (p. 100) says that, for Fortescue, France is 'the type of a despotism'; but, though the point remains somewhat obscure, it seems that Fortescue would have drawn a distinction between 'despotic' and 'royal' monarchy. The term *dominium despoticum* seems to occur only twice in Fortescue's writings: cf. Burns, 'Fortescue and the Political Theory of *Dominium*', 786–7 and n. 32.

[69] *De natura legis nature*, I. xvi (*Works*, i. 77).

the whole theory of *dominium politicum et regale* turns upon establishing the nature and function of both elements. Nor does Fortescue leave his readers in any uncertainty as to the dignity and worth he ascribes to the 'politic' element in human society and government. If regal authority in its pure form is to be compared with that of God, we are also told that *dominium politicum* is the system that would have been appropriate for the whole human race if its original state of innocence had been preserved. Indeed, at one (slightly puzzling) point, Fortescue even suggests that God himself had governed the people of Israel 'politikely and roialy' until they had perversely insisted on having 'a kynge, a verray man that wolde reigne vpon hem only roialy'.[70] It is not possible to pursue here all the complex issues that arise at this stage. What is worth emphasizing is the fact that, in characterizing *dominium politicum*, Fortescue deliberately uses the word *cives*—citizens—to refer to the members of political society. It is also interesting to note that he sometimes uses the term *dominium civile* for what is essentially an association of people who are in some sense partners together: the composite term *sociale vel civile* points in the same direction.[71]

It is true that when we come to *dominium politicum et regale* the 'citizens' have become 'subjects' (*subditi*); that government is in some emphatic sense a matter for the king, wielding in certain important respects *potestas absoluta*; and that the members of the body politic do not and cannot make laws for themselves. Yet, if the king's authority and will are indispensable for the making of valid law, so too is the consent of his subjects expressed in the estates.[72] Underlying this view there is a conception of the nature and basis of political society as a *corpus mysticum*; and this calls for further scrutiny.

Political society, then, is, for Fortescue as for Terrevermeille, a

---

[70] Ibid. I. xvi (*Works*, i. 84); II. xlv (i. 163). It is to be observed, however, that, in the second of these passages, Fortescue seems to mean by *dominium politicum* a form of non-coercive authority rather than a non-monarchical form of government. The reference to the government of the Israelites is in *Governance*, chap. 1 (Plummer edn. 110).

[71] *De natura legis nature*, II. xlvi (*Works*, i. 163–4); and cf. Burns, 'Fortescue and the Political Theory of *Dominium*', 791.

[72] *De natura legis nature*, I. xvi (*Works*, i. 77). On 'absolute power' see ibid. I. xxiv (*Works*, i. 85–7). On lawmaking in general in Fortescue, see the articles by Gillespie and Doe cited above (n. 50).

'mystical body'.[73] Such an entity, as Fortescue understands it, is the result of a process of incorporation—that word is explicitly used in *The Governance of England*.[74] This does not mean, however, that the act or process in question creates a society with no previous collective existence whatsoever. In a fashion wholly characteristic of the thinking of the fifteenth and early sixteenth centuries, Fortescue assumes the pre-existing fact of a community—a *coetus hominum*. Following the view taken by Augustine from Cicero, he treats this basic social group as being bound together by common interest (*utilitatis communio*) and by shared moral principles (*iuris consensio*). These bonds, however, do not in themselves constitute a body politic—or indeed a body in any sense. This is because such a group lacks a head: it is *acephalus*. 'In political terms,' says Fortescue, 'a community without a head has no corporate capacity whatever.'[75] How is the corporate character which is essential to a genuinely political society acquired? To this question Fortescue offers two alternative answers. The process of incorporation may be the work, on the one hand, of a single person: the will of a conqueror or other strong man may simply impose political order and unity upon those who thus become incorporated as his subjects. Logically enough, Fortescue sees this process as the basis for *dominium regale*: at times he seems ready to allow an equation between 'regal' and 'despotic' lordship.[76] This would have some tendency to undermine the position he adopts elsewhere, accepting the legitimacy of *dominium regale*; but this is offset by the argument that the subjects' consent to, or at least their acquiescence in, a regime which, whatever its defects, is at any rate preferable to anarchic insecurity does confer royal legitimacy upon what would otherwise be mere usurpation of power.[77]

[73] Fortescue does not favour the term *corpus mysticum* to anything like the extent of its use by Terrevermeille; but he does use it twice in a key passage of *De laudibus legum Anglie*, c. 13 (Chrimes edn. 30).

[74] Chap. 2 (Plummer edn. 112).

[75] *De laudibus* (Chrimes edn. 30): 'in politicis sine capite communitas nullatenus corporatur.' Chrimes's translation (p. 31) renders *in politicis* as 'in bodies politic'. This seems illogical, since Fortescue's point is, precisely, that in this case we are *not* dealing with such a body. It seems better to take the phrase, like *in naturalibus* earlier in the sentence, as referring to a general field of enquiry or form of discourse.   [76] See n. 68 above.

[77] For the somewhat different accounts of this point in *De laudibus* and *Governance* respectively, see Burns, 'Fortescue and the Political Theory of *Dominium*', 786–7. Both versions are to be compared with *De natura legis nature*, I. vi–vii (*Works*, i. 68–71).

Incorporation in the case of *dominium politicum et regale* is quite a different process. It could indeed be called self-incorporation, though it is important to note that the process is one in which the king, or king-to-be, is involved as well as the people who are about to become his subjects. The point is perhaps made most clearly in Fortescue's interpretation of the 'Brutus' legend in *The Governance of England*. Referring to 'the fellowshippe that came into this lande with Brute', he suggests that, Brutus having been chosen as king, 'thai and he upon this incorporacion, instituting and onynge [i.e. uniting] of hem self into a reaume, ordenys the same reaume to be ruled and justified by suche lawes as thai alle wolde assent vnto'.[78]

In one or other of these two ways, then, a body politic is supposed to have been brought into existence; and such a body must have a head in the person of its king.[79] Fortescue does, as we have noted, refer to this political entity as a *corpus mysticum*, though he uses the term less frequently and develops the concept less elaborately than Terrevermeille. Moreover, in so far as he does develop the idea, he does so in a significantly different way from what we find in the *Contra rebelles*. Important though the head of the body politic is for Fortescue, concerned as he is to develop a theory and a programme for monarchical government, it is not from the head that the body derives its life. There is no question here of the king's 'infusing' political being into his subjects. In a natural body, Fortescue argues (citing Aristotle in support), it is the heart that is the *primum vivens*, from which blood—life-blood, we might well say—is transmitted to every limb or member.[80] What corresponds to this in the body politic is not the authority of the ruler as head: it is the will or purpose of the people (*intencio populi*) that constitutes the *primum vivens* in this case. And it is

---

[78] *Governance* (Plummer edn. 112). Cf. the account of the *Bruti comitiva troianorum* in *De laudibus* (Chrimes edn. 32).

[79] It is not clear how Fortescue would envisage the headship of a body politic governed by *dominium politicum* only, with no 'regal' element. What seems clear from the *De natura legis nature*, I. xvi (*Works*, i. 77–8), is the assumed existence under that regime of some kind of monocratic system: Fortescue refers to *ille . . . [qui] dominio politico preest*. His account, in the same passage, of the Roman constitution after the expulsion of Tarquin suggests that he saw 'the Consuls and the Dictators' as charged with this function.

[80] *De laudibus* (Chrimes edn. 30): 'in naturali corpore, ut dicit philosophus, cor est primum vivens, habens in se sanguinem quem emittit in omnia eius membra'. The Aristotelian reference is to *De partibus animalium*, II. 1 and III. 4; and cf. Aquinas *ST*, Ia, 20, 1, *ad* 1.

here that Fortescue locates 'political forethought for the service of the people' (*provisionem politicam utilitatis populi*). It is from the people's striving for its own well-being that this 'political fore-thought' is communicated to head and members alike. Thus, and not by 'infusion' from above, the body politic 'is nourished and quickened'.[81]

Even this does not exhaust the content and implications of this densely packed passage in *De laudibus legum Anglie*. Fortescue goes on to demonstrate again how crucial the function of law is in his thinking about society and government. It is, he says, by means of law that a human group hitherto lacking corporate capacity, 'becomes a people' (*populus efficitur*). In developing this point he makes use of a term we have already encountered in Terrever-meille—*compago*.[82] The function of law in the body politic, Fortes-cue argues, is like that of the sinews (*nervos*) in the natural body.[83] Deriving *lex* from *ligare*, to bind, he represents law as binding the mystical body together and preserving the resulting unity. He adds a further point, crucial to his argument at this stage in the text. What he calls 'the limbs and bones' of the body politic, 'denoting the whole truth by which the community is sustained . . . retain their own rights by means of the law'.[84] It seems clear that Fortescue is referring here to the individuals of whom the community is made up; and we are reminded that in this passage, in the thirteenth chapter of *De laudibus legum Anglie*, he is applying a general theory to the specific question of the origins and basis of *dominium politicum et regale*. The point just considered leads on immediately to the contention that, under the composite system which prevailed in England, the king could no more change the laws by his own authority than the head in a natural body can change the muscular or nervous system so as to deprive the limbs of their proper

---

[81] *De laudibus* (Chrimes edn. 30): 'sic in corpore politico intencio populi primum vivens est, habens in se sanguinem, videlicet, prouisionem politicam utilitatis populi illius, quam in caput et in omnia membra eiusdem corporis ipsa transmittit, quo corpus illud alitur et vegitatur.'

[82] Cf. text at nn. 28–9 above. Fortescue does not, however, like Terrevermeille, make the distinction between *unio compaginis* and *unio voluntatis*.

[83] The rendering 'sinews' is perhaps preferable to Chrimes's 'nerves'.

[84] *De laudibus* (Chrimes edn. 32). This is a difficult passage, and the translation above differs somewhat from Chrimes's version. In particular, the phrase *veritatis . . . soliditatem* is rendered as 'the whole truth' rather than as 'the solid basis of truth'. What is clear in any case is Fortescue's strong emphasis on the rights of subjects as safeguarded by the law.

strength and blood-supply. Accordingly, in kingdoms of this kind (*regna politice regulata*), the king holds power to protect, and only to protect, together with his subjects, their persons and their goods.[85] And he holds that power *from* the people for whose benefit it is to be used. Strikingly, Fortescue at this point adopts the imagery of power 'flowing', which we have seen in Terrevermeille; but the direction of the flow is reversed—here power flows from the people to the king.[86]

Fortescue and Terrevermeille, it can perhaps be said, occupy significantly different positions within what is broadly the same universe of discourse. Yet it may be both true and important to say that, in the subsequent development of thinking about these problems, the differences were to be more important than the similarities. If one were to single out an area of divergence which may be especially significant for those later developments, it might well be the notion of 'incorporation'. In particular, Fortescue's claim that political relationships are 'instituted' rather than natural—or at least that the best political system is one that is based on such a process—may be crucial. In any case, it was not, as we shall see in the course of the next chapter, a view with which all his contemporaries would have agreed.

[85] Ibid. 30–2. Cf. Ullmann, *Law and Politics in the Middle Ages*, 300–1, on the importance in Fortescue of 'the tutorial function of the king'. See further, on the 'tutorial' theme, esp. ibid. 58–9; also id., *History of Political Thought*, 56–7.

[86] *De laudibus* (Chrimes edn. 32): 'ad hanc [*sc.* tutelam] potestatem a populo effluxam ipse [rex] habet, quo ei non licet potestate alia suo populo dominari.'

4

THE SHAPING OF ABSOLUTISM:
SPAIN

THE Spanish contribution to political thinking in the late medieval
and early modern period presents something of a paradox. In and
after the sixteenth century, the united kingdom of Spain—to the
extent that it was indeed united—may be regarded as one of the
paradigmatic instances of absolute monarchy. Yet the Iberian
realms of earlier centuries have seemed, at least to some historians,
to be almost as exemplary in their 'constitutionalism'. Thus R. B.
Merriman could, in the first volume of his *Rise of the Spanish
Empire*, highlight the fifteenth-century activity of the Castilian
Cortes and the role of the *Justicia* in Aragon and Catalonia; while,
in the second volume, he could argue that already by the end of the
century Ferdinand of Aragon, ruling as a Machiavellian prince, was
establishing 'strong central monarchical government', or even 'royal
despotism'.[1] The Carlyles, again, although the case of Castile was
in some respects problematic for them, were in the end satisfied
that the Spanish kingdoms illustrated, as effectively as they believed
the realms of northern Europe did, what they regarded as 'the legal
or constitutional forms of medieval political societies'; and those
forms, it was argued, embodied a concept of kingship under law in
a real and substantial, not simply an ideal or theoretical sense.[2]

It is in some ways tempting to develop this provisional paradox
by suggesting that the putative tension between an emergent
'absolutism' and a persistent tradition of 'constitutionalism' is

---

[1] R. B. Merriman, *The Rise of the Spanish Empire in the Old World and the New*
(2 vols.; New York, 1918): cf. i. 217–18 (on the Castilian Cortes), i. 463–71 (on the
Justicia in Aragon); and, for the references to Ferdinand, ii. 78, 79.

[2] See, for instance, *Mediaeval Political Theory*, vi. 3: 'We have seen that the most
important political conception of the Middle Ages was the conception of the
supremacy of law, the law which was the expression, not merely of the will of the
ruler, but of the life of the community'.

reflected in a degree of divergence between the two main elements in the political structure of early modern Spain. Ralph Giesey has drawn attention to the fact that when, in 1551, a new compilation of the *Fueros de Aragón* was drawn up, the Castilian maxim that 'Laws obey kings' was rebutted on the ground that, in Aragon, laws took precedence of kings.[3] The matter, however, is a good deal more complex than would be implied by a simple contrast between Castilian absolutism and Aragonese (with a strong element of Catalonian) constitutionalism. Neither in practice nor in theory or principle was either term in the antithesis as unqualified as this would imply. Yet it may still be the case that, in looking to Spain for a fifteenth-century process which may be called 'the shaping of absolutism', we do have to look in the first instance at Castilian developments and Castilian sources.

As in the case of the general theory of *dominium*, so here in the investigation of the emergence of Castilian absolutism it is necessary to begin the search in a period considerably earlier than that with which most of the present discussion is concerned. The language of absolute monarchy in Castile—and it is, as we shall see, very much a problem in the language of political discourse that we are concerned with—is already, and crucially, deployed in the thirteenth century, in the work of Alfonso X the Wise (1221–84). In particular, that language is unmistakably present in the *Siete Partidas*. This seminal text may indeed, in Alfonso's own lifetime, have been no more than what Jeremy Bentham was to call a *projet d'un corps complet de droit*, a programme of legislation rather than an enacted code. In the mid-fourteenth century, however, the text of the *Siete Partidas* was formally enacted by the Cortes at Alcalá, in connection with the *Ordenamiento* of 1348. By these legislative acts Alfonso XI (1312–50) sought to impose firmer royal control over law and judicature. To say that is to make it clear, of course, that this was in no sense an established absolutism registering principles that were already effective in practice. It was, however, a significant attempt to bring those principles into play in the business of government.

As to the principles themselves, their source and inspiration is not in doubt. Both in the original thirteenth-century manifestation

---

[3] R. E. Giesey, *If Not, Not: The Oath of the Aragonese and the Legendary Laws of Sobrarbe* (Princeton, NJ, 1968), 119–31.

and in the fourteenth-century promulgation, the spirit and the language of Roman law are unmistakable. The *Siete Partidas* has indeed been described as 'a summary of Roman and canon law'.[4] Alfonso X had been guided by jurists schooled in Bologna—his *sabidores de derecho*. Their doctrines found legislative (or would-be-legislative) expression through the medium of a king who had been disappointed in his ambition to become Emperor, but who surely saw himself as 'emperor in his own kingdom'. Alfonso claimed *plena potestas*—power (to quote a convenient summary) 'to issue laws, do justice, strike money, declare war or peace, establish taxes [and] fairs, appoint governors, delimit provinces'.[5] All the attributes of *imperium*, of what would become known as sovereignty, are there. That there were 'enormous difficulties' in the way of implementing such principles may be accepted without hesitation or surprise. What concerns us here is, first, the concept of kingship that is expressed or implied in language of this kind; and, secondly, the fact that, hard as the task no doubt was, this was the way in which Castilian rulers meant and hoped to rule.

Now from the point of view adopted by the Carlyles in their *History of Mediaeval Political Theory in the West* this apparent emergence of absolutism was 'a stumblingstone and rock of offence'. It appeared to run directly counter to the view they presented of the medieval relationships of ruler, law, and community. Recognizing what they referred to as 'some tendency, even in recent and accomplished historians, to speak as though the Spanish kings at least in Castile claimed and exercised a legislative authority of a kind different from that which . . . obtained in the other countries of Western Europe', they sought to refute that view. Their counter-argument turned chiefly upon the authority of custom and the indispensability of counsel in the exercise of royal power. Neither point, however, really disposes of the problem. No medieval account of law and lawmaking could or did ignore those factors; but they did not in themselves refute Alfonso X's assertion that 'No one can make laws except an emperor or king or some other by their mandate'.[6] This is not to deny, nor to underrate the

---

[4] Hillgarth, *Spanish Kingdoms*, i. 101.
[5] Ibid. 298.
[6] Cited, from *El Especulo o Espejo de Todos los Derechos*, i, 1, 3, by Carlyle, *Mediaeval Political Theory*, v. 58 n. 2: 'Ninguno non puede facer leyes si no emperador o rey o otro por su mandamiento dellos.'

importance of the fact, that both in Castile and in Aragon (where the principles of the *Siete Partidas* also had their attraction for rulers) there were traditions of political life strongly resistant to such 'absolutist' principles. What can hardly be gainsaid is the character and the importance of the principles themselves.

It may indeed be misleading to apply the concept of 'resistance' in the way just suggested. It might well be argued that it was rather the Roman-law principles of royal *imperium* that had to fight—and often fought a losing battle—against the stubborn realities of society, politics, and government in what were still in so many ways fragmented and particularist realms. If it is in the end appropriate to speak of 'the shaping of absolutism' in late medieval Spanish thinking and experience, it must be emphasized that the word 'shaping' means no more than it says. The process to which it refers may often and for much of the time have been a pretty rough-hewn business. Yet the lineaments of the intended sculpture are in the end sufficiently clear. Alfonso X with his jurists aimed, as did those who succeeded them, at a monarchy capable of acting as the effective head of a *corpus mysticum*, in which unity was sustained in such a way as to transcend the particular claims of feudal jurisdiction and local privilege. The king, as God's vicar in temporal matters, was seen as wielding a public power which might not be either alienated or shared with other persons or corporate bodies within the realm, and in which of course he recognized no temporal superior beyond its borders.[7]

These principles were, as has been said, firmly restated and given the form and intended force of enacted law by Alfonso XI in 1348. In the latter part of the fourteenth century, on the threshold of the period with which we are primarily concerned, it is easy to see how and in what respects the hoped-for absolutism was being challenged. The challenges, in so far as they were based on principle and were not the mere assertion of one power against another, seem never, it is true, to have found any effective and permanent institutional vehicle. The Cortes of Castile and León, unlike those of Aragon and Catalonia, remained essentially an administrative instrument to be wielded by the crown—whether the effective wielding was at any given time in the hands of the king or of those who were for the moment in a position to act in his name. There

---

[7] Cf. Carlyle, ibid. 148, 360–1, citing the *Siete Partidas*.

were certainly times—notably in the reign of Juan I (1379–90)—
when issues of importance were raised and at least temporarily
resolved in the Cortes. The Carlyles rightly drew attention to the
meetings at Burgos in 1379 and at Bribiesca in 1387, when Juan was
prevailed upon to give undertakings that royal charters would no
longer purport to override the established law by use of the *non
obstante* clause, and to lay it down that whatever had been enacted
in Cortes might not be undone except in Cortes.[8] Yet even if those
provisions had been more secure than they were they would hardly
support the weight of constitutional significance the Carlyles laid
upon them. And they were not secure; for they were in truth
concessions by a king under pressure to a body lacking real power
to enforce them. The Castilian Cortes have been described as
institutionally dead by the early fifteenth century.[9] This does not
mean that the claims made and the principles asserted during the
reign of Juan II (1406–54)[10] are devoid of interest. It is with that
reign that Castile comes fully into the context of discussion here;
and the claims and principles in question are certainly significant.
Their significance, however, has less to do with any kind of effective
institutional balance in which the Cortes weighed independently in
the scales than with the relative strength at various times of political
forces at work and political positions adopted in a complex struggle
for power.

Much of Juan II's reign was dominated by the figure of Alvaro
de Luna.[11] Luna has been seen as a key figure in the establishment
of the principles and the ideology of royal absolutism, even if the
effective exercise of absolute power was in the event to elude both
Juan and his son Enrique IV (1454–74). Certainly it can be shown
that the language and formulae of absolutism were widely current
in royal documents during the period of his rise to power and his
preponderance.[12] It is also clear, not only that 'absolutist' claim was

---

[8] Carlyle, *Mediaeval Political Theory*, vi. 4–5.

[9] A. MacKay, *Spain in the Middle Ages: From Frontier to Empire, 1000–1500*
(London, 1977), 154–5. For a similar view expressed in 1966 by J. Valdeón Baruque,
see Hillgarth, *Spanish Kingdoms*, ii. 306: 'The Cortes were, Valdeón concludes,
practically dead.'

[10] Cf. L. Suárez Fernándex, *Nobleza y Monarquía: Puntos de vista sobre la
historia castellana del siglo XV* (Valladolid, 1959).

[11] On whom, see N. Round, *The Greatest Man Uncrowned: A Study of the Fall
of Don Alvaro de Luna* (London, 1986).

[12] This is thoroughly examined by Round, *Greatest Man Uncrowned*, chap. 4, to
which the discussion below is heavily indebted.

met at times by 'constitutionalist' counter-claim, but also that the language of absolute royal power could be used by both sides in the power struggle as the effective control over royal pronouncements passed from one faction to another.[13] This accounts for the complex pattern of 'ideological' statements issuing from the Castilian Cortes in the 1440s.

On one view, the document promulgated on 10 September 1440 in the Cortes meeting at Valladolid amounted to 'a constitutional charter'.[14] The Carlyles read it as a reversal of what had apparently been done at the Cortes of Palencia in 1431, which in turn they saw as an attempt by Juan II to repudiate 'the constitutional principles of the Cortes of Bribiesca (1387)'. The issue at stake was indeed that of the power to override or nullify outside the Cortes laws which had been made in that assembly; and certainly the 1387 provision was borne in mind both in 1440 and also in 1442 when, again at Valladolid, the Cortes returned to the matter.[15] The statements in question, however, must be read in a context of political circumstances which the Carlyles' account overlooks. On the one hand, the Cortes in question were assemblies with very limited representative credentials.[16] And in any case the aim of the aristocratic faction which had won temporary dominance in the early 1440s was to undermine the power of Alvaro de Luna precisely by persuading the king to use the royal power to invalidate the procedures which the favourite had turned to his own political advantage.[17]

Yet the documents of 1440 and 1442 remain important for the present enquiry precisely because they serve to focus attention on the formulae which had become central in the developing notion of monarchical power in Castile. When, in 1445, Luna and his allies were on the verge of regaining control, they promulgated, in the Cortes of Olmedo immediately before the decisive battle there, a document which, so to speak, forced the Carlyles to recognize the strength of the absolutist current which seemed to them to run so strongly against what they saw as the main stream of medieval

---

[13] See esp. Round, *Greatest Man Uncrowned*, 96; and cf. 119.

[14] Suárez Fernández, *Nobleza y Monarquía*, 110.

[15] See Carlyle, *Mediaeval Political Theory*, vi. 133–4.

[16] Cf. MacKay, *Spain in the Middle Ages*, 154: 'From the reign of John II the Cortes ceased to be representative assemblies in any meaningful sense.'

[17] Cf. Round, *Greatest Man Uncrowned*, 99.

(including medieval Spanish) thinking on the subject.[18] One notable feature of the Olmedo document is its reliance on the authority of Alfonso X and the *Siete Partidas*. The twenty-fifth law of the second *Partida* was reasserted and ratified. The purpose of that law was to define royal power; and in the words of Suárez Fernández, the power thus defined 'is the expression, the symbol, and the form of the common unity of the realm'.[19] Now in the polemics of the mid-1440s, the point of this appeal to the authority of Alfonso the Wise was that the opposing faction—rebels from the standpoint of the Olmedo Cortes—had themselves invoked the *Siete Partidas*. Their argument on that basis had been that it was the duty of subjects to protect the king even against himself, should he be inclined towards dishonourable or harmful conduct. Against this it was now argued that natural and divine law alike enjoined absolute submission to the king as God's anointed vicar.[20] No ill is to be done, said, or even thought against him. The concept and language of the *corpus mysticum* are present here as vigorously as in Terrevermeille's *Contra rebelles*, even if they are less elaborately developed. The king 'is head and heart and soul of the people': his subjects 'are his members and to him they owe all loyalty and fidelity and subjection and obedience and reverence and service'. All laws, all rights depend upon his power, which comes from God alone and not from any human source. Anything contrary to these principles can and should be revoked by the king's 'cierta ciencia e proprio motu e poderio rreal absoluto'.[21]

In such ringing terms, then, 'the banner of monarchy was unfurled in the fresh winds of Castile'.[22] Those winds, needless to say, were destined to blow in different directions and to varying effect before anything like an effective absolutism was established in Castile and beyond Castile in the early modern kingdom of

---

[18] See Carlyle, *Mediaeval Political Theory*, vi. 186–8.

[19] Suárez Fernández, *Nobleza y Monarquía*, 118.

[20] Carlyle, *Mediaeval Political Theory*, vi. 186 n. 1, citing *Cortes of Castile and Leon* (Madrid, 1861), iii. 18: 'que ningun no sea osado de tocar en su rrey o principe, commo a quel que es ungido de Dios, nin aun de rretraer nin dezir del ningunt mal nin aun lo pensar en su espirtitu, mas que aquel sea tenido commo vicario de Dios'.

[21] Carlyle, *Mediaeval Political Theory*, vi. 187 n. 2, citing as above, p. 483: 'el rrey . . . es cabeça e coraçon e alma del pueblo . . . ellos son sus miembros, al cual ellos naturalmente deuen toda lealtat e fidelitat e sujecion e obediencia e rreuerencia e servicio . . .'; and 188 n. 1, citing p. 492.

[22] Suárez Fernández, *Nobleza y Monarquía*, 118.

Spain. Yet although, within a few years of the Olmedo proclamation in which (it has been said) the king 'virtually laid claim to the
power of revoking whatever laws infringed his supremacy',[23]
Alvaro de Luna's dominance came to an end, that event itself
tended to strengthen the absolutist tide. This was because, in the
proceedings against Luna, it was necessary to establish the king's
right to override much that had been done by Luna in Juan's
name, employing precisely the absolutist formulae which were
now to be turned against him. This led, it has been argued by
Nicholas Round, to a consolidation and intensification of the
ideology of absolute power which represented something decisively different from the 'Alfonsist' roots in the *Siete Partidas*
whence it grew. It is no doubt possible to carry this thesis too far;
but it is hard to dissent from the conclusion that these Castilian
developments can be seen as 'marking a significant stage in the
growth of royal absolutism'.[24]

Yet the attempt to establish a 'working ideology of absolute
kingship' was at the same time 'to appeal to principles which were
less than universally accepted'.[25] Things might perhaps have been
different had Juan II not died in the year following the fall of
Luna. As it was, the reign of his son Enrique IV was to see the
power and prestige of the crown decline disastrously—to the point,
indeed, of what purported to be the king's deposition in the so-
called 'Farce of Avila' on 5 June 1465.[26] Aristocratic hostility to
royal favourites was once more a major factor in Castilian politics,
and the crisis leading up to the 'Farce' followed a train of events set
in motion by the fall of Juan Pacheco, marquis of Villena, and the
rise of Beltrán de la Cueva. The rebel nobles aimed at traditional
targets—not just the granting of office to unworthy favourites, but
also excessive taxation and the debasement of the coinage. Claiming
'the reformation of the kingdom' as their goal, they deposed
Enrique in effigy at Avila (in what seems to have been a unique
piece of political 'theatre') and proclaimed his young half-brother
king as 'Alfonso XII'. It is the ideology of this rebellion and of the
king's defence against it that calls for examination here.

[23] Round, *Greatest Man Uncrowned*, 91.
[24] Ibid. 101.
[25] Ibid. 118.
[26] On this, see the important article by A. MacKay, 'Ritual and Propaganda in
Fifteenth-Century Castile', *Past and Present*, 107 (May 1985), 3–43.

Some of the evidence on which to base that examination is admittedly in some respects thin and tantalizingly inferential. It seems clear that there was what Angus MacKay has called 'a constitutional debate waged by theologians and men of letters'.[27] The proceedings at Avila were, predictably, justified by an appeal to historical precedent—in effect, to the 'ancient constitution' of the realm. Precedents for deposition certainly existed: Alfonso X himself had been deposed, at least ostensibly, towards the end of his reign; and much more recently—a long lifetime before the date of the 'Farce'—Pedro I had been driven from the throne by his half-brother Enrique II, the first of the Trastámara kings. The procedures adopted at Avila, again, reflected the constitutional principle that Castilian kings were elected by the nobility (*electio*) and then acclaimed by the people (*laudatio*).[28] It must also be remembered that the example of the neighbouring kingdom of Aragon, with its strongly developed 'constitutionalist' tradition (to be examined more closely below), can never have been far from the minds of disaffected Castilians. That example must have been especially cogent at a time when relations between the two king-doms, with the Trastámara dynasty reigning, however uneasily, in both, were particularly close. More specifically, the early 1460s had been marked by a Catalan revolt against Juan II of Aragon. Those rebels had refused to be ruled by what Juan termed 'a law of Castile which is called the law of Spain'.[29] The Castilian rebels who staged the Farce of Avila were appealing to a law of Castile which bore some resemblance to the *Fueros de Aragón*.

What is more problematic is the character of what might be called the more academic contribution to the defence of the proceedings at Avila. Two points can, however, be made in the present context. The first is to call attention to the fact that, in ecclesiology and ecclesiastical politics, there was a Castilian contri-bution—or at least a contribution by a Castilian—to the case against absolute monarchy. In the debate on the authority of the papal monarchy which preoccupied so much attention in the later stages of the Conciliar Movement, Juan de Segovia (d. 1458) had arguably been the most important spokesman of his generation for

---

[27] Ibid. 12–13.
[28] Ibid. 19–20.
[29] Cf. Hillgarth, *Spanish Kingdoms*, ii. 271.

the conciliarist opposition to papal absolutism.[30] Segovia, in Antony Black's view, advocated what amounted to a system of 'parliamentary monarchy' in the Church, modelled on that which prevailed in the Spanish kingdoms.[31] So far as Segovia's native Castile is concerned, such a view would no doubt reflect myth rather than reality; but the survival of the myth must have had its importance for the ideology of resistance to monarchical domination. It is true that Segovia played no part in Castilian politics, and there is no evidence to suggest that his writings may have contributed directly to the development of political ideas in the realm. With the second of the two points mentioned above things are perhaps rather different. Alfonso de Madrigal, known as el Tostado, bishop of Avila from 1449 till his death in 1455, was a prominent Castilian churchman, committed at once to ecclesiastical reform and to resisting the vehement papalism of his fellow-countryman Juan de Torquemada.[32] We need not, therefore, assume that, in so far as there was a theological contribution to political debate in the reign of Enrique IV, it would have been wholly on the side of royal absolutism.

Nevertheless there was, of course, ecclesiastical support for Enrique against the rebels; and indeed the most substantial surviving item from the immediate debate provoked by the crisis is a speech delivered by Pedro González de Mendoza, bishop of Calahorra.[33] Addressing the Mendoza 'clan' and their allies, the bishop did not attempt to deny the king's personal and political deficiencies. He did, however, insist on the nobility's paramount duty to preserve the unity of the realm and urged those who had sought to depose Enrique to desist from their 'schismatic' rebellion. He invoked here the argument that the king as head of the body politic may need the application of 'those medicines which reason suggests', but that 'nature forbids' the removal of the head. To this he adds a further consideration:

We should specially consider that reason and justice do not allow us to take away the title which we did not bestow, nor to remove the dignity

[30] See Black, *Monarchy and Community*, esp. 22–34 and, for textual extracts, 141–61; also id., *Council and Commune*, 118–93.
[31] Ibid. 191–2.
[32] See Black, *Monarchy and Community*, esp. 58–80 and, for textual extracts, 162–72.
[33] MacKay, 'Ritual and Propaganda', 39–41.

from him who reigns by direct succession; because if kings are anointed by God in their lands, it should not be believed that those who are appointed by the divine will are subject to human judgment.[34]

This is of particular interest in relation to the most substantial 'theoretical' work that can be regarded as a by-product of the Farce of Avila.

The author of this work was Rodrigo Sánchez de Arévalo (1404–70), whose ideas call for more extended consideration here. Arévalo was not himself involved in the crisis surrounding the 'Farce', nor even in his native Castile at the time. For the last ten years of his life he was permanently in Rome. He does not seem to have resided in any of the four Castilian dioceses of which he was bishop successively from 1457 onwards. On the other hand, it is misleading to say that, after his involvement in the council of Basle, he 'spent most of the rest of his life in Rome employed in the papal administration'.[35] Apart from the fact that one of his most important functions in Rome was to act as the king of Castile's representative at the papal court, Arévalo spent prolonged periods in Castile in the 1440s and 1450s, engaged in ecclesiastical duties as well as in the royal service. His views on royal authority may or may not have had 'little relation to the realities of Spanish politics and society'; but they were certainly not the views of an intellectual in exile, isolated from 'reality'.[36]

Arévalo had studied law—probably civil as well as canon law, though he was primarily a canonist—at Salamanca in the 1420s. He seems also to have acquired some knowledge of theology, and the not unimpressive list of his writings includes at least one on a theological theme.[37] By the early 1430s he was, it seems, in the service of the bishop of Burgos, Alonso de Cartagena. This was an important source of influence on Arévalo's ideas. Bishop Alonso, the son of a Jewish convert who had preceded him in the see of

[34] Ibid. 40.

[35] H. B. Nader, *The Mendoza Family and the Spanish Renaissance 1350 to 1550* (New Brunswick, NJ, 1979), 22.

[36] For Arévalo's life and writings, see the comprehensive account by R. H. Trame, *Rodrigo Sánchez de Arévalo 1404–1470: Spanish Diplomat and Champion of the Papacy* (Washington, DC, 1958). On the question of political 'reality', cf. Nader, *Mendoza Family*, 24.

[37] *Brevis tractatus an mysterium Trinitatis probari possit naturali et humana ratione?* (Cod. Vat. Lat. 4881, fos. 174 ff.). This was directed against the views of Ramon Lull, the 13th-cent. Catalan *doctor illuminatus*.

Burgos, was a key figure in Castilian intellectual history. Both he and Arévalo were members of the Castilian delegation to the council of Basle; and from at least the autumn of 1434 till October 1439 Arévalo was involved, sometimes quite prominently, in the council's business. With the final breakdown in relations between council and pope, he went home with the rest of the Castilian contingent. He was still, however, deeply involved in the ecclesiastical politics of the new schism. In 1440 and 1441 he went as Juan II's ambassador to the papal court in Florence, then to Vienna, to the French court, to Naples, to Milan. Throughout, he acted, spoke, and wrote as a powerful advocate of the claims of the papacy against the conciliar challenge, adopting a firm ideological stance in support of monarchical principles. From that position he never departed, and he was still, at the very end of his life, upholding papal authority against what was by then hardly more than a vestigial conciliarist threat.[38]

Important as these phases in Arévalo's career are, they should not be allowed to obscure the fact, already mentioned, that from the summer of 1441 till June 1445, and again from sometime in 1450 till the end of 1456, he was largely at home in Castile. A canon of Burgos in 1440, he became archdeacon of Trevino in the following year. He played a part in Alonso de Cartagena's reorganization of the diocese of Burgos, of which he became vicar-general in the late 1440s. This means that he was fully aware of, and in some measure involved in, that critical phase of the political struggles in Castile which reached a kind of climax with the defeat of the forces opposed to Juan II and Alvaro de Luna at Olmedo in 1445. The cathedral chapter of Burgos, including Arévalo, took a decisive stand on the king's side in that crisis. Again, though not directly involved, Arévalo was in Castile when royal authority was, as we have seen, invoked decisively at the time of Luna's final fall. When Arévalo turned to political discourse, whether in the reflective or in the combative mode, he wrote with firsthand experience of what politics was all about.

This does not of course alter the fact that Arévalo's political writing is the work of an intellectual. He wrote, moreover, in a

---

[38] On this, see H. Jedin, 'Sanchez de Arevalo und die Konzilsfrage unter Paul II', *Historisches Jahrbuch*, 73 (1954), 95–119. Arévalo's *De remediis afflictae ecclesiae* dates from 1469; and in the year of his death, 1470, he wrote *De septem questionibus circa convocationem et congregationem generalis synodi.*

particular style or tradition, the nature of which it is important to identify before considering the concepts and arguments he uses. Helen Nader, in the opening chapter of her book on *The Mendoza Family and the Spanish Renaissance*, argues that in fifteenth-century Castile there were two contrasting, even conflicting forms of political and historiographical discourse, which reflected the interests and outlook of the groups or classes with and through whom kings had to work in their government of the realm. There were, on the one hand, the *caballeros*—the 'military professionals', as Nader calls them; and, on the other hand, the *letrados*, whom she defines as 'university graduates with advanced degrees in canon or civil law'. *Caballero* power was essentially military and judicial (in the administration of criminal justice), while the *letrado* power base lay in the *Audiencia*, with its civil and administrative jurisdiction. From these backgrounds issued two divergent views of the Castilian monarchy: a *caballero* view, in which the realm was regarded as 'secular, aristocratic, and particularist'; and a *letrado* view 'that placed the king at the apex of a divinely ordained and immutable hierarchy of institutions'.[39] The first of these views is said to have found expression in an essentially humanist historiography. The second—which, Nader argues, was to predominate almost to the exclusion of the other in fifteenth- and sixteenth-century Spain—the *letrado* view was expressed through a characteristically scholastic discourse.

Certainly there can be no doubt as to the scholastic, Aristotelian nature of the discourse we find in Arévalo. Even a brief glance at the *Suma de la política* which he wrote in 1455 is enough to show this.[40] It is none the less interesting to note that the *Suma* was written, not in the Latin of the schools, but in the vernacular. Its political purpose—we cannot call it polemical, since it was not the product of any immediate conflict or crisis—could evidently best be served by rendering the conventional wisdom of scholastic teaching in the Castilian which had long been the language of law and administration in the realm. The doctrine is indeed conventional enough, even if significant emphases can be detected in its presentation. What the text offers is a firm defence of monarchical

[39] Nader, *Mendoza Family*, 19–20.
[40] There are two modern editions of the *Suma*: ed. J. B. Perez, (Madrid, 1944); and the edition cited here, ed. M. Penna, *Prosistas castellanos del siglo XV*, I (Biblioteca de Autores Españoles; Madrid, 1959), 247–341 (hereafter Penna edn.).

government, in which the king is portrayed as the heart of the body politic, communicating *movimiento e influencia* to all its members. He is the *primum mobile* of the political universe, and the community over which he rules—whether city or kingdom (*ciudad o reino*)—is a mystical body of which he is the head.[41] Comparisons with Terrevermeille and with Fortescue obviously suggest themselves here; but it is more immediately relevant to point out that language of this kind had been used in Castilian public documents—notably by the Cortes at Olmedo ten years before Arévalo wrote his *Suma*.[42]

Arévalo fills out the picture somewhat by giving an account of what he regards as the four essential parts of a well-ordered polity. These are, first, the 'royal and ruling' (*real y principante*) part; secondly, the counselling part (*parte consiliatoria*); thirdly, the judiciary (*parte judicatoria*); and fourthly, the populace (*la cuarta, que es popular*).[43] The entire hierarchical structure is envisaged as being governed by law. Laws, it is true, must be backed by the king's authority; but the king for his part must respect the established law and refrain from the over-hasty introduction of new legislation.[44] More generally, indeed, 'every good prince and statesman must consider that his power in some things is limited'. The limits are stated by Arévalo in the following terms. The king must not seek to judge those who do not come within his jurisdiction—identified by Arévalo as 'priests and ministers of the law' (*los sacerdotes y ministros de la ley*). Again, the prince must not judge where there has been no formal accusation (*sin acusador*)—a matter much debated, of course, among canon lawyers. He must not decide arbitrarily (*según su alvedrio*): instead, he must shape his will to the law, save where urgency or equity demands action formally (though not substantially) at variance with legality and legal justice. Finally, the ruler is not to relax the punishment annexed to a crime, even if asked to do so by the accuser; for this would be to do wrong both to the accuser and to the *común y república*. Above all, such an action would offend God, 'in whose place' the ruler 'holds the land' (*en cuyo lugar tiene la tierra*).[45]

That last phrase makes it clear that, despite the stated limitations,

---

[41] *Suma*, II, 1 (Penna edn. 282–3).   [42] Cf. nn. 20, 21, above.
[43] *Suma*, II, 7 (Penna edn. 292–4).   [44] Ibid. II, 10 (298).
[45] Ibid. II, 11 (300).

this is still the world of divinely ordained absolute kingship. The limits are important; but they may be described as procedural rather than constitutional limits. They are, as is so often the case in late medieval and early modern thinking, the defining conditions of a power that is, in constitutional terms, emphatically absolute. That is the concept of royal power to be found in Arévalo's later work, variously titled, but perhaps most helpfully known as *De origine ac differentia principatus imperialis ac regalis.*[46] This seems to have been written early in 1467 or perhaps towards the end of 1466. In any case the civil war precipitated in Castile by the proclamation of 'Alfonso XII' as king still continued, and the issues at stake in the conflict were being argued at the papal court in the hope of enlisting Paul II's support for one side or the other. Arévalo's brief was to defend Enrique against rebellion and usurpation; and this is plainly the context of the tract on royal and imperial monarchy. It was dedicated to Rodrigo Borja, then cardinal, later of course pope as Alexander VI—a dedication which merits at least a passing comment. Arévalo chose to address a fellow-Spaniard, albeit an Aragonese not a Castilian: an Aragonese, however, who may be supposed to have favoured the view of monarchy taken by Alfonso V, who, as king of Naples, had fostered the rise to power of the first Borgia pope, Rodrigo's uncle and patron, the nepotistic Calixtus III.[47]

Early in the *De origine* Arévalo takes up a theme which, among other things, reflects the *letrado* tradition to which he adhered: the antiquity and dignity of the Castilian monarchy. This had been defended elaborately and at length by his mentor Alonso de Cartagena at the council of Basle, when he sought to establish precedence for Castile over England among the conciliar delegations.[48] Now, over thirty years later, Arévalo resumed the theme

---

[46] References here are to the edition published in Rome in 1521 (hereafter *De origine*). The full title there is *Liber incipit de origine et differentia principatus imperialis et regalis et de antiquitate et iusticia utriusque et in quo alter alterum excedat et a quo et quibus causis reges corrigi et deponi possunt.* This edition was the work of Francisco de Fontecha, archdeacon of Arévalo, by whom it was dedicated to Cardinal Domenico Giacobazzi: there is also a prefatory letter to Fontecha from Leo X. The alternative title *De monarchia orbis* appears, with an abridged version of the *De origine* heading, in Cod. Vat. Lat. 4881, fos 1 ff.

[47] See D. Hay, *The Church in Italy in the Fifteenth Century* (Cambridge, 1977; repr. 1979), 35.

[48] For this speech, see Penna (ed.), *Prosistas castellanos* (n. 40 above), 205-33. Bishop Alonso was following a lead given by his father, bishop Pablo: cf. Nader, *Mendoza Family*, 21-2.

with objectives at once more extensive and more urgent. Its relevance in 1466–7 turned on an element in the Castilian case which was, in certain respects, widely accepted: the claim that Castile enjoyed absolute independence of the authority of the Empire. This meant that Arévalo could compare Castilian kingship—or at least the kind of monarchy which it exemplified—with the imperial monarchy on, so to speak, equal terms. The Empire was, of course, an elective and not a hereditary monarchy. Elected rulers, Arévalo argued, are 'given to their realms as *administratores ac rectores*'. For this reason they are not 'true lords' (*veri domini*); and accordingly 'such princedoms do not belong to their princes' (*tales principatus non sunt in bonis principum*). This situation is contrasted with cases in which 'kingdoms are conferred upon kings' (*regna conferuntur regibus*), and especially with cases where authority is conferred only upon members of a certain house and lineage (*de certo genere personarum et de certa stirpe*). In cases of this kind, Arévalo says, the realm is given to the king, not the king to the realm. Such an arrangement may have various origins or bases. It may be the outcome of a choice made by the subjects; but it may also have arisen because the leaders of what was to become the royal house were the first to occupy the land and have since defended it from enemies and have conferred other benefits upon its inhabitants. The relevance of this hypothesis to the Iberian experience of reconquest from the Moors needs no emphasis. What is particularly important in the present context is Arévalo's conclusion that kings of this sort are the 'natural lords' (*naturales domini*) of their realms: they are kings 'by natural right' (*de iure naturali*). In these circumstances the realm *is* in some sense the property of its king: *talia regna . . . certo modo sunt in bonis talium regum.* Such a king can 'transfer and transmit' his realm to his descendants. And in general, Arévalo argues, kings 'by natural right' in comparison with elected rulers have 'a fuller, more stable, firmer right' (*uberius et stabilius et firmius ius*) to the authority they exercise.[49]

Comparisons suggest themselves here between Arévalo's position and the defence by Jean de Terrevermeille, half a century earlier, of 'quasi-hereditary' monarchy. In this part of the argument at least, the Castilian canonist is at once more decisive and more vehement than the French jurist. Arévalo might well have accepted what

[49] *De origine*, fo. 13^{r-v}.

Terrevermeille had said about the authority of custom and the notion of a corporate framework for the realm articulated in the assembly of the estates; the evidence of the *Suma de la política* suggests that he would. We have seen in that context his acceptance of the principle that royal power has to operate within certain limits. What concerned him primarily, however, when he came, a dozen years later, to write his *De origine*, was the need to confront and refute what he took to be radically mistaken views about the *enforcement* of restrictions on the king, about sanctions alleged to be available if the king overstepped the limits of his legitimate authority. This is made clear in that part of the lengthy title of his tract which raises the question 'by whom and for what causes kings can be punished and deposed'.[50] In the Farce of Avila two positions had been adopted which Arévalo is concerned to reject. On the one hand, 'Alfonso XII' had been made king on the principle that royal authority in Castile was conferred by *electio* and *laudatio*; and this is met by the argument examined above, to the effect that Castilian kingship is *not* elective, it is 'natural' and hereditary. On the other hand, the *barones*[51] at Avila had dramatically asserted and exercised their supposed right, precisely, to 'depose and punish' Enrique IV. Arévalo's case against that claim now calls for examination.

That case turns on two essential points. The first is a development or corollary of the conclusion that the Castilian crown is held by 'natural right' not by election. From this it follows, Arévalo argues, that, as 'kings acquiring their realms by natural right', the rulers of Castile recognize 'no secular superior in temporal matters'. The word *secularem* here directs us towards the second basic point: Arévalo is clear from the outset that sovereign rulers of this kind 'cannot for their misdeeds be deposed or turned out of their realms *except by the Roman Pontiff*'.[52] His emphatic assertion of the authority of the pope in such temporal concerns reflects, of course, Arévalo's lifelong commitment to a strongly papalist position. Its immediate relevance in 1466–7, however, is equally clear. It was not, of course, that Arévalo either expected or wished Paul II to depose Enrique IV. He did, indeed, defend the pope's deposing power not simply in principle but also in practice, at much the

---

[50] Cf. n. 46 above.
[51] This term is regularly used by Arévalo in the *De origine*, both in association with, and in distinction from, *populus*: cf. e.g. the passage cited at n. 55 below.
[52] *De origine*, fo. 66^{r-v}.

same period: when Paul excommunicated and deposed the king of Bohemia, George Poděbrady, in December 1466, Arévalo set to work on an elaborate commentary on, and defence of, the bull of deposition.[53] In the Castilian case, however, other considerations applied. For one thing, Enrique had himself acknowledged papal authority in such matters, whereas the opposition at a certain stage in the controversy (perhaps despairing of papal support for their cause) seem to have denied its validity.[54] A more important consideration may have been that to uphold the pope's right to convict and to pass sentence in such a case must enhance the effect of the acquittal Arévalo hoped for.

At the same time it was important to make out the negative side of the case against the rebels, and Arévalo's case here is forthrightly stated: 'the barons and people of the realm cannot depose and punish such a king because they lack power, jurisdiction, and coercive authority over their prince.'[55] In defending this thesis Arévalo is very much the jurist, the advocate arguing almost as though he were in court. Preponderantly, the arguments are procedural and jurisdictional. Yet there is also what may be termed a philosophical or theoretical dimension. Arévalo invokes, for instance, the concept of the realm as a *corpus misticum et politicum*—as he had already done, of course, in the *Suma de la política*. His purpose in using that concept is not to establish any kind of corporate authority for the realm in contradistinction from the king. Rather, he argues that, just as, in the natural order, 'the body cannot in any way act upon the predominant soul' (*in animam praedominantem*), nor can matter act upon form, so, in the political order, the subjects cannot take action to depose a sovereign prince (*principem dominantem*). Customs or precedents seemingly at variance with these principles are of no validity because we are dealing here with matters of 'natural right'. Arévalo does not deny the community all rights and remedies in a case of alleged misrule; but such rights are restricted to denouncing the ruler's misdeeds—

---

[53] *Commentus et apparatus super bulla privationis et depositionis Georgii regis Bohemiae* (Venice, Biblioteca Marciana, Cod. Marc. Z–L CXCIV—B, fos. 1 ff.). Cf. Trame, *Sánchez de Arévalo*, 159–61.

[54] See ibid. 152–3.

[55] *De origine*, fo. 66ᵛ: 'Barones vero & populus regni talem regem deponere & punire non possunt ex defectu potestatis iurisdictionis & auctoritatis coactiue in suum principem.'

laying a complaint before a superior. And the superior in this context can only be the pope. Again, the representation of the community in, or by, the estates is recognized; but, Arévalo insists, that assembly has no power to alter the *regimen regni* or to make any change in its *status*.[56]

When the argument moves from general principles to matters of procedure, the immediate Castilian context becomes clearer than ever. Such proceedings as those which—we may infer—took place at Avila are hopelessly irregular and inadequate. Turning again to the notion of the realm as a body (*quoddam corpus*), Arévalo insists that such a body must be represented in an assembly (*per singulos in unum congregatos*) duly convened and properly constituted. And even if it were granted that such an assembly could claim the powers over the king which Arévalo denies to it, the proceedings would have to respect certain basic rules of equity which were manifestly violated in the case in point.[57] This line of argument warrants rather closer scrutiny.

The Cortes at Avila (which is plainly what Arévalo had in mind) were invalid because, even supposing that they had legitimate power to do what was claimed, the members had not been duly summoned for that purpose (*ad hoc specialiter*) and could not, therefore, act *collegialiter* on behalf of the realm as a whole. Yet what was supposedly reversed by the deposition of Enrique IV was in some sense the will of the entire community. And even if the leading men of the realm (*priores aut principales*) have discretionary power[58] to act in certain ways, this cannot extend to actions which modify or change what has been done and approved by the whole people (*id quod factum est et approbatum per totum populum*). The long-established authority of the king, accepted by the realm as a whole and, specifically, accepted by the very magnates who had now attempted to depose Enrique, might not be overturned in this way.[59]

Secondly, Arévalo maintains, if such grave steps were to be taken, it was essential to proceed 'with scrupulous deliberation' (*morose et cum magna deliberatione*). If a private individual was to be deprived of his rights, due judicial order was required: the person in question

---

[56] Ibid. fos. 66ᵛ, 67ᵛ.

[57] Ibid. fo. 86ʳ.

[58] This seems to be the sense of the Latin: 'etiam si habeant generalem potestatem aut liberum arbitrium'.

[59] Ibid. fo. 86ʳ⁻ᵛ.

must be properly summoned and fully heard. Yet in the far graver matter of punishing and deposing the king, Enrique had neither had proper notice nor been duly summoned. Moreover, those who were his accusers and those who bore witness against him were at the same time his judges. No one was heard in his defence before sentence was pronounced. Any one of these procedural defects, Arévalo claims, would have rendered the acts of the assembly at Avila null and void. And in addition to this, the case had been heard without allowing any adjournment, in a matter of days (*infra paucissimos dies*). Thus an issue surpassing all others in importance 'was, so to speak, determined before it had been opened' (*ante ut ita dixerim finita quam incepta est*). This again would of itself result in 'nullity and invalidity'.[60]

The procedural case against the 'Farce' is then summarily driven home:

> there was deficiency in the judge, in the summons, in the defence (all these being matters of natural right): there was likewise deficiency in proof, in trial, in examination—in fine, there was deficiency in all that pertains to the order and substance of any judicial act.[61]

Yet even if the proceedings at Avila had been all they should have been and were not, Arévalo could not accept that the deposition of Enrique would have been justified. Not only were the causes alleged for it inadequate. The disadvantages of thus subverting the established order almost always outweigh the promised benefits. 'Virtuous subjects' are reminded that changing the laws is profoundly harmful (*mutatio legum est valde damnosa reipublicae*) because, among other things, it interferes with the process whereby laws are strengthened by becoming customary and habitual. The same applies to changing the ruler (*mutatio principatus*). In that connection Arévalo suggests an interesting variation on a familiar theme, arguing that the king is himself the native or natural law (*lex nata*) of his realm. Even if the king's behaviour is positively scandalous—and scandal certainly warrants the expulsion from the community of those who cause it—he is to be tolerated, not made

---

[60] Ibid. fos. 86ᵛ–87ʳ.
[61] Ibid. fo. 87ʳ: 'Itaque vt paucis agamus, fuit defectus in iudice in vocatione in accusatione in defensione: quod est de iure naturali. Item in probatione in cognitione in examinatione & in omnibus que sunt de ordine & substantia cuiuslibet actus iudicialis.'

away with (*tollerandus non tollendus*). In his development of this argument Arévalo drew both on John of Salisbury and on the Bible. Since, he says, it is 'no trifling sacrilege' (*non paruum sacrilegium*) to speak or even to think ill of a ruler, it must be the most sacrilegious of crimes to take injurious action against him. Nor will Arévalo admit that such dutiful submission applies only in the case of the good, virtuous, innocent ruler and is not owed to one who is, or becomes, wicked and tyrannical. He allows that there are cases which demand the ruler's removal from office; but these are, essentially, cases of heresy, and their determination belongs, as such, not to the people or their representatives, but to the pope.[62] We are again reminded here that Arévalo's defence of absolute monarchy in the temporal realm is subsumed, as it were, under his broader commitment to the universal supremacy of the papacy.[63]

This combination of what may, for convenience, be called royalism and papalism makes Arévalo's work a particularly striking example of that monarchical ideology which has been identified as one of the principal features of political thought in the middle decades of the fifteenth century.[64] Yet, paradoxically, the arguments of the *De origine* embroiled Arévalo in controversy, not with a proponent of constitutionalism or conciliarism, or even with a defender of the lost cause of 'Alfonso XII', but with perhaps the strongest, certainly the most systematic exponent of papalist ecclesiology. The most direct response to Arévalo's tract came from his fellow-Castilian Juan de Torquemada. What aroused Torquemada's hostility—expressed in his *Opusculum, ad honorem Romani Imperii*—was primarily, as that title suggests, Arévalo's rigorous subordination of the imperial power to the papacy. These questions belong to the next chapter; and the point is mentioned here merely to underline what may not improperly be called the extremism of Arévalo's position at least in its papalist aspect.[65]

If the Trastámara dynasty had experienced troubled times since acceding to the throne of Castile, things can hardly be said to have

---

[62] Ibid. fos. 89ᵛ–91ᵛ.
[63] On Arévalo's papalism, see Black, *Monarchy and Community*, esp. 70, 103–4.
[64] Cf. ibid., esp. 80–4.
[65] Arévalo is described as 'one of the more rigorous pro-papal writers of the mid-fifteenth century' by J. A. F. Thomson, *Popes and Princes 1417–1517: Politics and Polity in the Late Medieval Church* (London, 1980), 10. For Torquemada's *opusculum*, see Trame, *Sánchez de Arévalo*, 156–9.

been easier for them in the lands which owed allegiance to the *Corona de Aragón*. Reference has been made already in passing to the Catalan revolt against Juan II of Aragon in 1461; and that in turn was to be followed by ten years of civil war. Such a protracted conflict obviously had many sources, nor is it the business of the present enquiry to analyse and evaluate these. What is relevant here is the point that the events of the 1460s were in part at least the product of divergent views as to the nature and authority of kingship. 'For at least a century,' it has been said, 'two concepts of monarchy had been at issue in Catalonia.'[66] On the one side, there were what the same historian calls 'absolutist ideas' upheld by the Trastámaras at least as vigorously as by their predecessors of the house of Barcelona. Over against these were ranged the deeply rooted concepts of *pactismo*, proclaimed by the dominant classes in Catalan society. It is this latter view that now calls for fuller examination here.

At the outset it is as well to emphasize the point that the tradition of *pactismo*, deeply ingrained in Catalonia, was also more or less strongly established in the other lands of the *Corona de Aragón*. In all its manifestations, what is strikingly characteristic of the tradition is the extent to which the principles of an essentially contractual view of royal power achieved institutional form. A few fundamental points may be worth recalling here to illustrate this. There was, first, the regularity and substantive character of meetings of the Cortes, whether in Aragon itself, in Valencia, or in Catalonia. Perhaps even more noteworthy was the establishment in all three territories of standing bodies which remained in being and in operation even when the estates themselves were not in session— the *Diputación* or *Generalitat*. There is, further, the significant role of the Aragonese *Justicia* as 'the guarantor of traditional liberties and privileges'.[67] These arrangements make it possible to speak of a 'new "parliamentary state"' in the 1370s, and to argue that, from the reign of the first Trastámara king onwards (Fernando I, 1412–16), 'there were two governments in Catalonia, that of the Crown and that of the *Diputació*'.[68] Whether a situation of 'dual power' is equivalent to 'constitutionalism' may be debatable; but

[66] Hillgarth, *Spanish Kingdoms*, ii. 278.
[67] MacKay, *Spain in the Middle Ages*, 114.
[68] Hillgarth, *Spanish Kingdoms*, ii. 240.

what is clear enough is that such a situation is incompatible, whether in practice or in principle, with absolute monarchy.

So far as the principles of the matter are concerned, it is to be noted that the doctrine (so to call it) of *pactismo* found expression in the work of an outstanding Catalan intellectual at the very threshold of the period with which the present enquiry is concerned. Francesc Eiximenis (d. 1408) has been paired with Pero López de Ayala (1332–1407) as a figure representative of the cultural life of the peninsula between the mid-fourteenth century and the end of the fifteenth.[69] He was a Franciscan and the view of society and government to be found in his writings clearly reflects the traditions of his order. Thus there are echoes of Duns Scotus in Eiximenis's rejection of any concept of natural political authority. Such power over men, equal as they are by nature, can be established only on the basis of consent and election.[70] Plainly this is a view that will serve readily to underpin *pactismo*. Eiximenis is entirely clear as to the contractual character of the arrangements that are made to set up and sustain the authority of government. It is indeed still possible—perhaps in some sense and in certain respects necessary—for that authority to be absolute. This 'absolutism', however must operate within a sphere delimited by 'pacts and conventions' functioning to the advantage of the community. What is precluded is such absolute power as is based on 'the ruler's own will', regardless of such limits.[71] It goes more or less without saying

[69] See ibid. ii. 206–12. The fullest account of Eiximenis's political ideas is by A. López-Amo y Marín, 'El pensamiento político de Eximeniç en su tratado de "Regiment de Princeps"', *Anuario de Historia del Derecho Español*, 17 (1946), 5–139. For extracts from the *Regiment* and other texts, see J. Webster (ed.), *La Societat catalana al siglo XIV* (Barcelona, 1967).

[70] For Scotus, cf. e.g. J. Quillet, 'Community, Counsel and Representation', in Burns (ed.), *Cambridge History of Medieval Political Thought*, 564: 'Duns Scotus had stressed the importance of *consensus* and *electio* in the delegation of political authority, as an agreement reached between strangers (by which he meant people belonging to different familes) can only perform its constitutive role if it expresses the mutual consent of everybody.' Eiximenis's essentially similar view is paraphrased by López-Amo y Marín as follows: 'Como los hombres son naturalmente libres, aunque hagan de vivir necesariamente en sociedad y bajo autoridad, esta la constituyen ellos libremente ... A la libertad natural sucede la libertad política' ('Pensamiento politico', 87). Cf. also 94: 'como per naturaleza todos los hombres son iguales, ningun tiene "per se" señoría sobre los demás. Y como por naturaleza todos los hombres son libres, no puede surgir el poder político con independencia de su consentimiento.'

[71] On the contractual relationship and the community's consequential right to depose a defaulting ruler, cf. e.g. *Regiment de Princeps*, c. 513, as cited by López-

that Eiximenis unreservedly condemns tyranny. What is more remarkable is the fact that his theory of government is by no means exclusively monarchical. He attached great importance to civic life and seems to have envisaged the possibility of a political world governed by communes rather than by kings. This was no doubt at least as visionary a prospect as the same writer's prophecy that the crown of Aragon would 'achieve monarchy over almost all the world'.[72] Yet the urban dimension of Eiximenis's thought remains both striking and important, for it reflects the balance of social forces which sustained Aragonese, and especially Catalan 'constitutionalism' in the later medieval period.

Both the present and the future lay, of course, with monarchy, and increasingly with absolute monarchy. Even in Aragon the outcome of the struggle in the 1460s favoured the king, though the other side was far from being a mere lost cause.[73] When one turns from *pactismo* to the 'absolutist' side of the argument in the *Corona de Aragón*, the most immediately striking point may be that the field of debate, so to speak, extends significantly beyond Spain and its adjacent islands. Alfonso V of Aragon (1416–58) has been described as a 'great renaissance monarch';[74] and the description is doubtless apt enough for the king who became known as *Alfonso il Magnanimo*. The language of that sobriquet, however, reveals the crucial point; it was as king of Naples, a realm which he made his own after a long and testing struggle, that Alfonso was able to claim and in some measure at least to wield absolute power. Nor is there any ambiguity as to the claims he made there for his royal authority. The documents of his reign in Naples bear the same marks of

---

Amo y Marín, 'Pensamiento politico', 112 n. 92: 'donchs la comunitat no contractant que aja prineps elegit, si lo princeps no es profitos a ca a que es elegit per la comunitat, reman en su plan poder de tolre al princeps la dita senyoria e l'us del regiment.' On absolute power, cf. *Regiment*, c. 408, cited by López-Amo y Marín (p. 116), referring to the ruler's 'imperi e . . . plena juredictio e senyoria'. Eiximenis's position may not be wholly unambiguous, but the fundamental *pactismo* cannot be doubted.

[72] See Hillgarth, *Spanish Kingdoms*, ii. 65, 200; and cf. Webster (ed.), *Societat catalana*, 47f.

[73] See Hillgarth, *Spanish Kingdoms*, ii. 296–7.

[74] Black, *Monarchy and Community*, 118. Alfonso's designation presents numerical problems: Alfonso IV as count-king of Catalonia-Aragon, he was to become Alfonso I as king of Naples. His specifically Aragonese title, Alfonso V, is perhaps to be preferred in the present context.

absolutist ideology as we have encountered in those of Trastámara Castile. The formulae favoured by Alfonso's Neapolitan chancery are at times even more striking than the exactly contemporary language used by or on behalf of Juan II of Castile. One example may suffice to illustrate the point. Here the king is said to be acting 'of our certain knowledge, by our free, unqualified, personal, gratuitous, and spontaneous will, and from the fullness of our royal, lordly, and absolute power'.[75] That authority was proclaimed as being of emphatically and unequivocally divine origin; and the king who wielded it 'represents the image of the supreme King'.[76] Renaissance prince Alfonso may indeed have been, and his policy of strengthening the royal administration in Naples may indeed have laid the foundations of what might have become 'a modern state'.[77] Yet in assessing the political doctrine he claimed to follow, we should perhaps do well to remember also that he recited the office and heard mass four times a day and was said to have read the entire text of the Bible fourteen times.

Judge it as we may, Alfonso's absolutism was certain to bring him into conflict with the *pactismo* of his Aragonese, and especially his Catalan subjects. In his Spanish domain, it is true, he was for much of his reign an absentee, with his wife acting as Lieutenant-General, an office to which the king's brother Juan of Navarre (later Juan II of Aragon) succeeded in 1454. The queen, Maria of Castile, was herself well respected; but the relationship between her husband and the *Corona de Aragón* was never easy. The Catalans in particular were hostile to a regime under which their traditional privileges were little regarded. When, in 1450, they sent envoys to Alfonso to complain of the tardy administration of justice, they were bluntly told that the fault lay precisely with their 'privileges and pretended customs and liberties'. How different from us! Alfonso said, in effect. In his Italian realm, won by conquest, his absolute power met with no such objections or

[75] E. Rogadeo (ed.), *Diplomatico Aragonese, Re Alfonso V (1435–1458)* (Codice diplomatico barese, 11; Bari, 1931), 111 (1443, no. 75).

[76] Cited by A. Ryder, *The Kingdom of Naples under Alfonso the Magnanimous: The Making of a Modern State* (Oxford, 1976), 32 at n. 21.

[77] In addition to Ryder, *Kingdom of Naples*, see id., 'The Evolution of Imperial Government in Naples under Alfonso V', in J. R. Hale, R. Highfield, and B. Smalley (eds.), *Europe in the Late Middle Ages* (London, 1965), 332–57; and cf. Hillgarth, *Spanish Kingdoms*, ii. 659–60.

allegations as would prevent justice being done.[78] At that mid-century point, it is tempting to say, two concepts of kingship confronted one another across the western Mediterranean. Yet it would be a mistake to leave the matter there, forgetting where this part of the discussion began. That starting-point was not between the Spanish and the Italian spheres of Aragonese influence: it was in Aragon itself and above all in the long-drawn-out conflict of the 1460s in Catalonia. When Juan II emerged victorious from that conflict, it was, no doubt, a seriously qualified victory that he had won. By the settlement at Pedralbes in October 1472, the privileges of the Catalans were confirmed even if the civil war had disastrously undermined the prosperity of Catalonia. Yet there was a victory; the monarchy was decisively strengthened; and the case for royal absolutism certainly did not go by default. The views of Francesc Eiximenis, at the outset of that hundred years' conflict referred to above between the rival concepts of kingship, may be compared and contrasted with those expressed at the end of the period by another Catalan scholar-bishop. Joan Margarit i Pau not only brought Gerona over to the side of Juan II at a critical point in the struggle: as a historian he also provided ideological support for royal authority, representing Juan II as the heir of the Goths, and approximating to what has been called the 'extreme monarchist' position of the Aragonese jurist Gonzalo Garcia de Santa Maria.[79] If it is the case, then, that by the 1470s and 1480s 'the Castilian exaltation of monarchy was penetrating one of the redoubts of *pactismo*',[80] that may serve to consolidate the thesis argued in this chapter. The Spanish realms had indeed contributed to 'the shaping of absolutism', even if the heritage transmitted there from the fifteenth to later centuries was not by any means a simple or monolithic structure.

[78] See Ryder, *Kingdom of Naples*, 31 at n. 17, also 160–1; and cf. Hillgarth, *Spanish Kingdoms*, ii. 263–4.

[79] See ibid. ii. 205; and cf. R. B. Tate, *Joan Margarit i Pau* (Manchester, 1955), of which an expanded version in Catalan was published as *Joan Margarit i Pau, Cardenal i Bisbe de Girona, la seva vida i les seves obres* (Barcelona, 1976).

[80] Hillgarth, *Spanish Kingdoms*, ii. 205.

5

MONARCHY: PAPACY AND EMPIRE

IN the title of this chapter the word 'monarchy' is plainly being used in a sense different from that which it bears in the subtitle of the book. In the latter context, 'the idea of monarchy' refers to something alleged or supposed to be exemplified in various forms of 'lordship, kingship, and empire'. Here it is used, evidently, of something that is specific to the papal and imperial systems. Now this is a sense of the word less immediately meaningful to us than it was to writers and readers in the fifteenth century. They were of course familiar with the term 'monarchy' in what may conveniently and aptly be called its Aristotelian sense, denoting one among a number of constitutions or forms of government to be found in different political societies. They were also, however, familiar, in ways and in a measure remote from our experience, with the idea of a single, universal monarchy. Dante's *Monarchia*, for instance, is not a treatise on monarchy as a form of government but a tract powerfully arguing the case for the emperor's universal authority over Christendom—indeed, over the whole world. The matter is not made any easier for us—and indeed more than a little local difficulty was created at the time—by the fact that this universal monarchy had two heads. It is with ideas of that kind of universal monarchy, claimed by pope and emperor alike, that this chapter will attempt to deal.

Some preliminary obstacles should be cleared away at this stage. It is manifest that, as a basis for any practicable or applicable political programme, the idea of universal monarchy, whether papal or imperial, was, by the period with which we are concerned, null and void. The Roman eagle, whether clad in pontifical or in German feathers, was a dead duck. To that proposition, however, two riders are essential. The first is that what appears in hindsight to be almost self-evident was not necessarily so easy to see—let alone to say— at the time. The second rider is that the ideological potency of the concept of universal monarchy—and therefore part at least of its

importance in the history of political ideas—was not extinguished
by its impracticality. Many things which it was desirable or even
necessary—necessary for practical purposes—to say about monarchical government were still most readily expressed in terms of
universal monarchy. Sometimes indeed they might be expressible
only in such terms. There may be paradox, but there is no
contradiction, in the fact that the language of *imperium* and of
plenitudo potestatis was seized upon and exploited most eagerly by,
precisely, the territorial and 'national' monarchies of which the rise
marked the final collapse of both empire and papacy in their
medieval forms.

It can in any case scarcely be a surprise to find that much was
still being written and said in defence and exaltation of papal
monarchy throughout this period. After all, circumscribed though
the political aims and ambitions of the papacy may have become
after its post-conciliar restoration in the middle of the fifteenth
century, the claim to universal spiritual supremacy was unimpaired.
No doubt the seamless garment had been torn. The Utraquist
settlement in Bohemia had to be accepted; and the patched-up
union with the Eastern Churches achieved in and after 1439 soon
lost whatever slender chance it had had of survival with the mid-
century advance of Ottoman power. That such strenuous and
elaborate assertions of the papal claims as those formulated by Juan
de Torquemada should have been made just at this time may be no
more than an illustration of the truth that the owl of Minerva takes
her flight only in the gathering dusk. Even so, the subsequent
history of the papacy, down at least to the middle of the present
century, may suggest that this particular owl did not prove to be
merely the owl in the attic. Papal authority was, and was to remain,
real and substantial. More to the point in the present context, the
absolutism of that power within its sphere was to become more,
not less effective. The ideology of papal absolutism, as it developed
in and after the age of the great conciliar challenge, may properly
be regarded as a factor of prime importance for our understanding
of the ways in which ideas about authority developed in the late
medieval and early modern period of European history.

To say the same of concepts of imperial authority might well
seem a good deal less plausible. Are we not indeed faced, in this
case, with the owl in the attic—a rather shabby piece of taxidermy,
a bird looking as though it had been stuffed for a period far longer

than its brief life and had then been put away in the attic for longer than anyone cared to remember? There is a strong temptation to agree with such a judgement. After all, exemption from imperial authority—whether that exemption was juridically recognized or not—had long been the status of all the major territorial realms of Christendom. When we find that in 1469 'fre impyre' was claimed for a candidate as improbable as James III of Scotland, when we note the imperial crown that still adorns the chapel of King's College in Aberdeen, built in the reign of his son James IV, we may well conclude that *liberum imperium* had indeed been fragmented and the language of imperialism devalued.[1] Yet *the* Empire was still there; and, for the jurists who shaped so much of the political discourse of the fifteenth century, that empire still provided the essential context for the deployment and discussion of ideas about political authority. There was doubtless a good deal of arid legalism in this, and little to be seen (at least since the middle of the fourteenth century) of the more visionary imperialism of Dante or Engelbert of Admont.[2] At the same time the idea of empire was not simply taken over and adapted to the purposes of a purely German 'national' monarchy—on such lines as Lupold of Bebenburg seems to have envisaged.[3] Development of that kind was barred, or at least obstructed, both by the forces of particularism within the notional empire and by the predominantly dynastic interests and goals of emperors and would-be emperors. Yet the imperial title retained a certain aura and a certain allure, while the imperial structure, such as it was, preserved sufficient vitality to make it seem to some observers a suitable case for treatment—for reform and revival.[4]

Again, the dangers to which Christendom was exposed during the first half of the fifteenth century—the external threat from the Turks, the internal menace of the Hussite conflict and of the recurrent tendency to schism in the Church—perhaps generated a

---

[1] Cf. Chap. 1, n. 23.

[2] Dante's *Monarchia* hardly calls for annotation here. On Engelbert, see G. B. Fowler, *The Intellectual Interests of Engelbert of Admont* (New York, 1947); and Ullmann, *Law and Politics in the Middle Ages*, 79–80.

[3] Lupold's *Tractatus de juribus regni et imperii* is in S. Schard (ed.), *De jurisdictione, auctoritate et praeeminentia imperiali ac potestate ecclesiastica* (Basle, 1566), 328–409. On him, see Ullmann, *Law and Politics in the Middle Ages*, 290.

[4] Cf. esp. the anonymous *Reformation Kaiser Sigmunds*, written about 1439: ed. H. Koller, *Monumenta Germaniae Historica: Staatsschriften des späteren Mittelalters*, 6 (Stuttgart, 1964).

nostalgic longing for unity through universal authority. There is, after all, no nostalgia so potent as that which hankers after a state of affairs that never existed. However this may be, it is beyond question that the fifteenth century witnessed a notable revival of universalist ideology. The idea of monarchy in the sense of a single monarchical system embracing the whole of Christendom is one of the strongest elements in the political thought of the period.[5]

The problem for such ideologies had, of course, always been that universality and unity must, and yet could not, be combined with the dualism that had prevailed in Latin Christendom since the time of Gelasius I. That familiar theme needs no rehearsing here.[6] What does need to be emphasized is the fact that in, roughly, the second quarter of the fifteenth century there was a tendency for papacy and empire to draw together, a sense in which they might make common cause against ideas and forces that threatened, or could be seen as threatening, monarchical authority as such. This may serve, up to a point at least, to explain the character of the most important single text to be examined in this chapter—the so-called *Monarchia* of Antonio de' Roselli.[7]

To use the epithet 'so-called' of this impressive (and, in the present context, alluring) title may be to overemphasize the fact that *Monarchia* was not used formally as the principal title of the work until it was included in the first volume of Melchior Goldast's collection of the same name in 1611.[8] That title had, after all, served

---

[5] The point is discussed by J. P. Canning, in Burns (ed.), *Cambridge History of Medieval Political Thought*, 363–4; and, with more direct reference to the period envisaged here, by Ullmann, *Law and Politics in the Middle Ages*, 302–3. The fullest analysis is still that by F. Ercole, 'Impero e papato nella tradizione giuridica bolognese e nel diritto pubblico italiano del rinascimento', *Atti e memorie della R. Diputazione di Storia Patria per le provincie di Romagna* (IV. ser., 1; Bologna, 1911), 1–223.

[6] For a recent discussion, see J. A. Watt, 'Spiritual and Temporal Powers', in Burns (ed.), *Cambridge History of Medieval Political Thought*, chap. 14.

[7] The most extended study of Roselli and his *Monarchia* is still that of K. Eckermann, *Studien zur Geschichte des monarchischen Gedankens im 15. Jahrhundert* (Berlin, 1933). See also, besides other references in subsequent notes, J. H. Burns, 'The "Monarchia" of Antonio de'Roselli (1380–1466): Text, Context and Controversy', *Proceedings of the Eighth International Congress of Medieval Canon Law* (Vatican City, 1991).

[8] M. Goldast (ed.), *Monarchia S. Romani Imperii . . .* (Hanover, 1611; repr. in 1612 as the first of what was to be a three-volume collection), 252–556 (hereafter Goldast edn.) This edition is cited below: its division into parts and chapters is used for convenience, though it was the work of the editor, not of the author, nor of those who prepared the first printed edition (Venice, 1487).

from the outset—in cross-references within the text, for example—
as a convenient way of referring briefly to the work. Yet its use is
apt to give the impression that what we have here is precisely what
we do *not* have: Roselli did not produce a single, systematic,
organized treatise on the subject of universal monarchy. What was
printed for the first time in 1487 and reprinted in whole or in part
(or indeed in parts) during the sixteenth century, reaching the
nearest it has had to a definitive edition in the Goldast volume, was
what Jeremy Bentham would have called a *pasticcio*. It was a
composite, made up of different, and disparate, pieces, written at
different times for different purposes. The pieces were put together,
moreover, late in the author's long life (Roselli died in 1466 in his
mid-80s), perhaps even after his death. Certainly the work as we
know it was assembled some considerable time after the date, in the
mid-1430s, when the first elements in the text were written. It is a
significant fact that not one of some half-score of manuscripts
embodies the whole of what was committed to print in the Venice
edition of 1487.[9]

Yet composite—patchwork even—though it may be, the text
was evidently in its time a work of some importance; and it held
that position in some measure until at least the early seventeenth
century, when Goldast saw fit to reprint it. Its significance in
Roselli's own century is reflected in its having been placed on the
Index and by the appearance, in 1499, of a brief but vehement
riposte by Heinrich Krämer, OP, then inquisitor for Germany.[10]
Now it is plain that this condemnation was based on the charge
that Roselli's claims for the imperial authority violated the prerogatives of the papacy.[11] And it is true that the first and in many ways

---

[9] For these and other Roselli MSS, see A. Belloni, *Professori giuristi a Padova nel
Secolo XV* (= *Ius Commune*: Veröffentlichunge des Max Planck Instituts für
Europäische Rechtsgeschichte. Sonderhefte: Studien zur Europäische Rechtsgeschichte, 28) (Frankfurt-am-Main, 1986), 145–9; but cf. Burns, 'The "Monarchia"',
at n. 12.
[10] Henricus Institoris, *Opusculum in errores Monarchie* (Venice, 1499). The
colophon gives the title as *Replica f. Henrici Institoris aduersus dogmata peruersa
Roselli*. The dedication to Antonio Pizzamano is dated 23 Aug. 1496; but since it
also refers to Alexander VI's seventh year as pope, this is evidently a misprint for
1499: the colophon is in any case dated 27 July 1499.
[11] This need not mean that Roselli's 'imperialism' was the only 'perverse dogma'
critics detected in his book. J. A. F. Thomson, 'Papalism and Conciliarism in
Antonio Roselli's *Monarchia*', *Medieval Studies*, 37 (1975), 445–58, suggests (pp.
456–7, citing Eckermann, *Studien*, 142–3, 158–60) that Roselli's use of 'popular-

most interesting part of the text had been written for presentation to the emperor Sigismund. Yet it is also true that Roselli wrote, in the mid-1430s, as an official of the papal curia, and, moreover, as one who took a vigorous part in pope Eugenius IV's propaganda against the claims of the council of Basle.[12] He has indeed been regarded as a papalist writer and described as 'one of the most significant' of the publicists who took that side in the long debate on the nature and location of supreme ecclesiastical authority.[13] Even in that context, nevertheless, elements of 'conciliarism' have been discerned in Roselli's work.[14] That work is evidently ambiguous in its import as well as complex in its structure; and even in a summary account of the matter further consideration of Roselli's career is necessary.

Whether or not we are to give credit to the view that Roselli left the papal curia in a mood of frustration and disappointment at having been denied advancement to the full reward of his career there, it is certainly the case that he did, in 1438, leave the papal court at Florence and return to academic teaching. For the next quarter of a century and more he was to teach civil and canon law at Padua.[15] This did not, of course, entail anything like total isolation from the world of public affairs in which Roselli had lived for most of the 1430s. It is in fact quite clear that he continued to respond to (and in a limited measure at least to contribute to) that world.[16] For present purposes, the most important point is that, throughout the first half-dozen years or so of his Paduan career, Roselli devoted part of his time to revising and developing the *Monarchia* text of the mid-1430s together with the tract on the Empire which had perhaps been written rather earlier (and which was eventually to form the final part of the composite text published

sovereignty' arguments at certain points may have contributed to the 1540 condemnations of the *Monarchia* in Antwerp and in Toledo. Thomson acknowledges, however, that Roselli's 'imperialist tendencies' carried greater weight (p. 157 n. 47); and there is no real uncertainty as to where the gravamen lies so far as Krämer is concerned.

[12] On this, see Burns, 'The "Monarchia"', at nn. 48–59.
[13] Thomson, *Popes and Princes*, 10.
[14] Thomson, 'Papalism and Conciliarism'.
[15] Belloni, *Professori giuristi*, 145–9.
[16] See esp. E. Meuthen, 'Antonio Rosellis Gutachten für Heinrich Schlick im Freisinger Bistumsstreit (1444)' in H. Mordek (ed.), *Aus Kirche und Reich: Studien zu Theologie, Politik und Recht im Mittelalter* (Sigmaringen, 1983), 461–72.

in 1487).[17] The circumstances in which he did so were, essentially, those of the 'Little Schism' which followed the final breach between Eugenius IV and the council of Basle, culminating in the election of 'Felix V' as anti-pope in 1439. One major factor in the diplomatic manœuvring of the early 1440s was the attempt, constantly renewed though eventually fruitless, by the new emperor, Frederick III, to achieve a solution through the summoning of a new council of the Church. Not only did Roselli at some stage rededicate his tract on the Empire to Frederick; more significantly, he extracted material from the *Monarchia* text and developed it into a treatise on councils. This was completed at the end of 1444 and dedicated to the Doge of Venice (within whose territories Padua now lay).[18] In this treatise (subsequently incorporated, with confusing results, in the composite *Monarchia* text) it was natural that Roselli should give a fuller and in some ways more favourable account of conciliar authority, even though he remains very far from anything like a radical conciliarist position.

It will be clear from what has now been said that it cannot be an easy or straightforward task to identify and expound Roselli's view of 'monarchy' and monarchical authority. A start may be made by saying something about the kind of writing we are dealing with, the form of discourse to which *Monarchia* belongs. It is, of course, above all the work of a jurist, even if the more 'technical' aspects of juristic learning are much more evident in some parts of the text than in others.[19] Though Roselli shared the literary talents of his family, we are not to expect much literary grace in his major work. Nor is it the product of much philosophical reflection. Such philosophy as we may find in it comes at second hand, notably from Dante, though it is hardly possible to accept the claim that it was Roselli who brought that earlier and more visionary *Monarchia* back into fifteenth-century awareness.[20] At the same time, the argument is certainly conducted in the style of scholastic discourse; and while Roselli's original intentions as to its presentation are by

---

[17] This is part V of Goldast's text: cf. Burns, 'The "Monarchia"', at nn. 24, 65–7.

[18] Cf. Burns, 'The "Monarchia"', at nn. 65–9.

[19] Such 'technicalities' are especially evident in Goldast's part IV.

[20] This claim is made by Eckermann, *Studien*, 77. Of greater importance is the evidence of Roselli's unacknowledged borrowings from Dante, which is examined by B. Nardi, 'Fortuna della "Monarchia" nei sec. XIV e XV', in id., *Nel mondo di Dante* (Rome, 1944), 161–205.

no means clear, there is some evidence for his having envisaged the characteristic scholastic schematism of 'articles', 'questions', and so forth.[21] As always, such a method creates difficulties for any attempt to identify the precise position the author himself adopts amid the welter of propositions, objections, and counter-propositions. In this case, as has been suggested, the ambiguous development of Roselli's thinking in response to changing circumstances compounds the difficulties. Some points at least, however, are clear enough.

The first such point is the rigour and vigour with which Roselli asserts an absolute dualism of spiritual and temporal authority. He does this even—perhaps indeed especially—in those parts of the *Monarchia* text which belong most probably to the mid-1430s— the high point, it may be said, of Roselli's curial career. In developing his analysis of papal and imperial power—the central theme of the original treatise—he had to consider the hierocratic view in which temporal authority, including that of the emperor, was derived, under God, from the papacy. Roselli sets out elaborately the arguments in favour of that position—but only to reject them and to assert vehemently that the power of the emperor no less than that of the pope comes directly from God. This view informs his lengthy discussion of the Donation of Constantine.[22] Roselli's view of the effect of that transaction—he does not question its authenticity or, properly understood, its validity— involves the concept of lordship: it was *dominium utile* only, in respect of the exercise of temporal jurisdiction in the States of the Church, that was acquired by the pope. *Dominium directum* remained with the emperor: the integrity of the Empire was unimpaired. As for the oath sworn to the pope by the emperor at his coronation—and Roselli mentions that he had himself been involved in drafting the terms of the oath sworn by Sigismund in 1433—it entailed spiritual, not temporal subordination.[23] Certainly the pope's spiritual supremacy could have temporal consequences: a heretical emperor, or even an emperor whose conduct indicated

---

[21] Cf. Burns, 'The "Monarchia"', at n. 28.

[22] See on this Burns, 'The "Monarchia"', at nn. 94–5. The *locus classicus* is of course D. Maffei, *La donazione di Costantino nei giuristi medievali* (Milan, 1969), where Roselli's views are fully considered.

[23] *Monarchia*, I. lxv (Goldast edn. 194); and cf. Burns, 'The "Monarchia"', at n. 51.

the possibility of heresy, could be deposed by the pope. It was also the case in Roselli's view, however, that in certain temporal respects the pope was subordinate to the emperor; and the emperor might also have a role (albeit essentially an enabling role) in the procedures to be adopted when the Church, acting through the instrumentality of a general council, had to deal with the problem posed by a heretical pope.[24]

Such areas of actual or apparent overlap between the two powers were inevitable, given the inescapable fact that both pope and emperor ruled over a single Christian community with one ulti-mately supreme goal or purpose—the eternal salvation of its members. It was still, for Roselli, the case that the two authorities were 'completely separate and distinct'.[25] This absolute dualism, however, is matched by a dual absolutism. Over half a century ago, in what is still the most extensive discussion of the *Monarchia*, Karla Eckermann said that Roselli 'grants to his Emperor all the attributes of an absolute ruler. He is not a delegate of the people nor is his imperial office an *officium publicum*. He is therefore *legibus solutus*, and bound only by divine and natural law.' As for the pope, he likewise, within his spiritual jurisdiction, 'is the theocratic, absolute sovereign, who rules his Church as the emperor rules the Empire'. And this leads to the summarizing, clinching assertion—'The pope is the Church as the emperor is the Empire'.[26] It is also entirely appropriate to note, as Eckermann did, that the same kind of absolutism was at the same period being claimed by other writers, sometimes for the pope, sometimes for the emperor, sometimes for both, and indeed sometimes for other rulers alto-gether. As we shall see, claims of that kind were to be made by Aeneas Sylvius Piccolomini, Piero da Monte, and Juan de Torque-mada. And we have seen something already of the developing ideology of absolute monarchy in the Spanish kingdoms, in Naples,

---

[24] See *Monarchia*, I. xxiv (Goldast edn. 368): 'potest Imperator ... supplere defectum vel impotentiam Papae si Cardinales essent negligentes'; and cf. v. xxx (556) on Sigismund's role at the time of the council of Constance.

[25] Ibid. I. xxxvi (Goldast edn. 277): 'immo penitus sunt operationes [Papae et Imperatoris] separatae atque distinctae. Et caesar in temporalibus, nisi a Deo, a nullo noscitur dependere.'

[26] Eckermann, *Studien*, 104–6, 108, 117. There is an echo here of a well-known phrase of Cyprian: cf. Ullmann, *Principles of Government and Politics*, 141–2, referring to 'the Cyprianic view that the bishop was in the Church and the Church in the bishop'.

and in France. Roselli's 'absolutism' locates him in a heavily cultivated area of fifteenth-century political thought.

Yet here as elsewhere a degree of caution is necessary in the interpretation of such ideas. Roselli does indeed say, for instance, that 'the church is in the pope' (*ecclesia est in Papa*); but he says at the same time that the pope is 'in the church' (*Papa* [*est*] *in ecclesia*).[27] It may be reasonable to refer to 'the personalization of power' in the monarchical ideology of this period.[28] Yet such a phrase could be misleading if it resulted in any tendency to overlook the fact that the whole of Roselli's argument is conducted in terms of a corporate conception of society—a conception in which neither head nor members can claim meaningful independence. It is true that Roselli uses the neoplatonic language of infusion to describe the relation between the ruler and the body politic: life is poured into the body from the head or the heart. We know already, however, from the case of Jean de Terrevermeille in particular, that the 'absolutist' implications of such language did not preclude the simultaneous holding of a view in which the *corpus mysticum* enjoyed, potentially and even actually, what we might call 'a life of its own'. Similarly, Roselli, steeped as he was in the lore of canon law, argued that the ruler could override the ordinary provisions of the law and supply its deficiencies by acting *de absoluta potestate vel de certa scientia*.[29] Once again, however, we can recognize that such formulae need not carry the totality of what is apt to be understood by our term 'absolutism'. In particular, *absoluta potestas* is to be taken as referring to an element which was regarded as an essential attribute of any viable political system, not as something which was a defining characteristic of 'absolute' rulers.

If we return to the account given by Karla Eckermann and consider more closely her reference to Roselli's ruler, whether emperor or pope, as being '*legibus solutus*, and bound only by divine and natural law', the inadequacy of such a statement will

---

[27] Cf. *Monarchia*, III. xxvi (Goldast edn. 441). The whole of the lengthy discussion of these matters in III. xxvi: (pp. 432 ff.) is important.

[28] Black, *Monarchy and Community*, 67–73. There are three references to Roselli in this context, the most important being at pp. 70–1.

[29] For 'infusion', see e.g. *Monarchia*, III. xxvi (Goldast edn. 440): 'quemadmodum omnia membra recipiunt influxum a capite sensus & motus secundum alios a corde, & non econtra: sic tota ecclesia.' For action *de absoluta potestate vel de certa scientia* see e.g. ibid. III. xx (417). The *certa scientia* concept is especially prominent in the account of papal powers to which Goldast's part IV is largely devoted.

become apparent. The laws of God and of nature were of course of great importance as fundamental norms for a jurist like Roselli; but they did not comprehend the whole of the framework within which he envisaged the operation of government. They were necessary but not sufficient conditions for the legitimate exercise of authority. The emperor, for example, certainly enjoys 'universal lordship' (*dominium universale*); and yet this does not imply or include *dominium rerum singularum*. Lordship of that kind—the ownership of particular things—is grounded in the *jus gentium*: it forms no part of 'the rights of empire' (*jura imperii*). Even those *jura imperii*, for that matter, are not simply the emperor's, to do with as he pleases. He cannot dispose of them as though they were his property. Were he, for instance, to seek to subject the empire to some alien authority, he would violate fundamental law and his action would be *ultra vires* and thus invalid.[30]

Underlying this part of Roselli's argument we can discern the notion that a monarchical power conferred directly by God can none the less be regarded as, in some sense, inhering in the community for whose benefit it exists and is to be used. What God confers is not in any sense a personal power specific to the individual upon whom it is conferred. It is certainly power *over* a community; but it exists *for* that community, and if it is used in ways damaging to the common good it may—Roselli seems to think—revert to the community. His theory then, 'absolutist' though it may be, is not a theory of non-resistance: he allows explicitly for the legitimacy of disobedience and resistance in certain extreme circumstances. There are, moreover, institutional means for dealing with situations of this kind: the community, even when the validity of its ruler's authority is in question, is not a formless mass but an organized body capable of collective action. This implies the existence and the legitimacy of representation through some kind of council. The question of Roselli's 'conciliarism' in the context of the Church—and that is in fact the context in which he mainly discusses the matter—belongs more properly to the next chapter. It is important to establish here, however, the point that

[30] For the ruler as *legibus solutus*, see ibid. 1. lxxi (298); for *dominium universale* and *dominium rerum singularum*, ibid. 1v. viii (462); for the argument against alienation of the *jura imperii*, ibid. 1. xlvii (277); and cf. ibid. 1. lxvi (291): 'bona enim principos non sunt sua, sed suae dignitatis . . . & ideo non videtur illa posse alienare irreuocabiliter'.

the essential elements in his thinking on the subject are of general import and application.

In an interesting phrase which Roselli seems to have added to the text when the separate 1444 treatise on councils was incorporated in the expanded *Monarchia*, he declares that 'general councils are of the very nature of monarchy'.[31] In the original text of the mid-1430s he had cited a well-known passage from Book III of Aristotle's *Politics*, which argued, in the medieval Latin version, that the *regimen civitatis* must be lodged either in the whole body of citizens or in its weightier part; and the citation was, naturally enough, retained when the passage was used in the 1444 treatise.[32] Taken together with the remark about the integral part played by 'general councils' in monarchical systems, this makes it clear that monarchy is indeed, for Roselli, to be understood properly only in what we may call its corporate matrix.

There are thus what we might call 'constitutional' means of dealing with the problem of misrule or with the interruption or suspension of the ordinary processes of government. That is not, however, the whole content of this part of Roselli's thinking. The means just referred to might well be available only if and when misgovernment had provoked positive resistance; and Roselli explicitly allows for this extremity. To this end he invoked a classic argument from Roman law; an unjust judge may be resisted by force, even to the point of killing him if that becomes necessary; and he supports the view that, analogously, a people may depose a tyrannical ruler.[33] At an earlier point in the text, and dealing explicitly with temporal authority, Roselli referred to Aquinas's commentary on the *Sentences* of Peter Lombard for the argument, which he accepts, that in the last resort the killing of a tyrant may be justified.[34] It is important, of course, not to overstate the case and to attribute to Roselli a 'radicalism' which he certainly did not profess or advocate. He makes it perfectly clear that drastic action of this kind would not be legitimate for anything other than extreme tyranny; and, on the basis of his interpretation of imperial authority, he argues that, where the defaulting ruler is subject to that universal power, it is for the emperor (and, accordingly, neither

[31] Ibid. III. I (379): 'ipsa generalia concilia de genere sunt monarchiae.'
[32] Ibid. II. xx (357), also III. ii (382); and cf. Burns, 'The "Monarchia"', n. 113.
[33] Cf. *Monarchia*, II. xxiii (Goldast edn. 366).
[34] Cf. ibid. I. lxix (294–5).

for the ruler's subjects nor for the pope) to take the necessary measures.[35] It is after all a jurist's theory we are considering; and what Roselli consistently looks for in the first instance is a tribunal with the appropriate jurisdiction to deal with the problem in question. If that problem arises from heresy in a pope, the relevant tribunal is a general council of the Church; if it is a problem caused by misgovernment in a realm or city subject to the Empire, then the emperor is himself the legitimate judge. Only if the tyrant is a ruler recognizing no superior—the emperor himself, in fact—and then (it seems) only if the matter cannot be adequately handled by the 'secular council' of the Empire is it either necessary or right to turn to the *ultima ratio* of rebellion or tyrannicide.[36]

Such measures, even in their more 'constitutional' forms, are by definition extraordinary. In all ordinary circumstances, Roselli would clearly uphold the monarch's right to absolute power and urge the duty of subjects to maintain implicit obedience. It is, therefore, entirely legitimate to regard him as a proponent of a monarchist ideology at a time when there were grounds for thinking that monarchy, together with the principle of authority which sustained it, was under threat of subversion.[37] That sense of danger, of the need to rally the forces of order against the many-headed menace, is even more strongly present, perhaps, in the case of Piero da Monte.[38] Born in Venice between 1400 and 1404, da Monte studied civil and canon law at Padua, where he graduated on 15 July 1433.[39] In that year he wrote a text which, like Roselli's much more voluminous work, came to be known as *Monarchia*. This is

[35] The passage just cited in n. 34 makes it clear that the right of 'popular' resistance prevails only where the king guilty of acting *contra salutem regni universalem* recognizes no superior. Later Roselli is careful to reject the view that the pope has power to depose rulers (other than those who are *temporally* subject to him) except for heresy; and to assert, rather, the authority of the emperor over defaulting kings. He illustrates the point by citing the emperor's part in the replacement of Eric of Pomerania by Christopher of Bavaria on the Danish throne (cf. ibid. iv. xxiv (509) and iv. xl (526)).

[36] Ibid. ii. xvi (413): 'concilium seculare non est iudex causae Caesaris, qui est dicti concilii caput . . . nisi ipse conueniretur vt tyrannus & scandalizans vniuersale bonum imperii secularis: quia tunc posset a suo concilio seculari iudicari'.

[37] See Black, *Monarchy and Community*, 80–4; and cf. 112–29.

[38] On whom, see esp. Haller, *Piero da Monte*; also Black, *Monarchy and Community*, 99–102, on Monte's diplomatic activity in England in the 1430s.

[39] Cf. Haller, *Piero da Monte*, 13–14. Monte's principal teacher was Prosdocimo Conti, whom Antonio de' Roselli was to succeed at Padua and who had himself been a pupil of Francesco Zabarella.

indeed more limited in scope as well as in length than Roselli's treatise: when it was printed, in part, for the first time in 1476/7, it was entitled *De potestate Romani Pontificis et Generalis Concilii*; and when it was reprinted in the 1549 Lyons collection of juristic texts, it was described as *Tractatus Conciliorum generalium*.⁴⁰ The implied concentration on the question of papal as against conciliar authority reflects the fact that Piero da Monte was immediately involved in the conflict between Eugenius IV and the council of Basle. He entered the papal curia, where he was thus a younger colleague of Roselli; and like the latter he was to play an active part in the papal diplomacy directed against the council in the 1430s. Yet the title *Monarchia*, used in the Lyons edition of 1512, was not altogether inapposite; for da Monte does in fact, both in this text and elsewhere, uphold 'monarchist' views of a more general kind.

In particular, writing at the very time when the rapprochement between pope and emperor was perhaps at its closest,⁴¹ Piero da Monte goes out of his way to uphold imperial power. In one passage, for instance, he uses a comparison we have encountered, apropos of royal power, in Jean de Terrevermeille: the authority of the emperor is like that of a husband. What he receives from the electors is *plenum jus*. With this, of course, comes corresponding responsibility: 'Just as the husband is the defender of his wife, so the emperor is the protector of the commonwealth and of its individual members and also indeed of the churches.'⁴² He insists

---

⁴⁰ The 1476/7 edn., published in Rome under the title *De potestate Romani Pontificis et Generalis Concilii*, comprises about one-third of the text printed in the 1512 Lyons edn. cited below, which uses the title *Monarchia* followed by a very lengthy indication of the subject-matter. Becker, *Die Appellation vom Papst*, 332–3, refers to an edn. published in Rome in 1537. The text was included in several later collections: in *Volumen II Tractatuum ex variis legum interpretibus collectorum* (Lyons, 1549), 71–80, as *Tractatulus Conciliorum generalium*; in *Tractatus Illustrium Iurisconsultorum*, xiii/1 (Venice, 1584), 144–53, as *Monarchia, sive De primatu papae et maiestate imperatoris*; in J. T. de Rocaberti, *Bibliotheca Maxima Pontificia*, xviii (Rome, 1698), 100–37, as *Tractatus Conciliorum generalium*. Black, *Monarchy and Community*, in his one reference (p. 86) to the *Monarchia*, cites the 1584 edn.: his other references for Monte's views are to the unprinted *Contra impugnantes sedis apostolicae auctoritatem liber* (Cod. Vat. Lat. 4145 and 4279): this was written about 1450.

⁴¹ The date is clearly indicated by Monte's references to Sigismund's imperial coronation (*Monarchia*, 1512, sig. g iiiiʳ), which took place on 31 May 1533, and to his own incorporation in the council of Basle in November of that year (ibid., sig. c [i]ʳ).

⁴² Ibid. sig. g iiiiʳ.

too that the emperor alone has the most important of all the powers in the imperial constitution—the power to make law.[43] That power is, it is true, exercised, like all political powers, on behalf of the people; and it is also true that the emperor's authority has an elective source.[44] This does not, however, alter the fundamental fact that, ultimately, the authority comes from God. And certainly (as we shall see) to recognize that in certain respects the community has a part to play in the constitutional process is as far as possible from implying any sympathy or respect on da Monte's part for 'the people' as a political entity.

Both da Monte's understanding of the divinely ordained, sacred character of political (and specifically of imperial) authority and his opposition to any kind of 'populism' may be more clearly understood by examining his account of the status and powers of the papal monarchy. That the government of the Church was and must be monarchical is made absolutely clear: time and again da Monte reiterates the standard view that monarchy is, by any and every criterion, the best form of government.[45] This was the basis on which the Church was established—and established, of course, by 'him by whom kings reign'.[46] Christ gave the power of the keys to Peter as head, to the other apostles only as members of a body whose unity depends absolutely on the 'plenitude of power' given to the 'one shepherd'. That shepherd—Peter or his successor— 'governs, orders and judges all matters at his own will and pleasure (*pro libito voluntatis*)'.[47] Whether that absolute power extends in its fullness to temporal as well as spiritual concerns is a point on which da Monte is perhaps not entirely unequivocal. There is, inevitably, a measure of dualism in his answer. Thus, in the *Repertorium Juris* which he seems to have compiled twenty years or so after the tract which became known as *Monarchia*, he says that 'the pope cannot exercise his plenitude of power in matters pertaining to temporal

---

[43] Ibid. sig. g iiiᵛ: 'illud quod est maximum in imperio, est legem condere generalem & hoc soli principi conuenit'.

[44] Ibid. sig. g iiiᵛ: '[imperator] ex sola electione plenum ius imperiale consequitur.' Cf. sig. b [i]ʳ: 'Certum est ... quod imperator representat populum christianum cum in eum translata est plena potestas'.

[45] Cf. e.g. ibid., sig. d viiʳ: 'optimum regimen multitudiniis est quod regitur per vnum qui omnibus presit'.

[46] Ibid.: 'regimen ecclesie ... dispositum fuit per eum per quem reges regnant & legum conditores'.

[47] Ibid. sig. a iiiiʳ.

jurisdiction; and again that 'the pope should not interfere in the emperor's jurisdiction nor the emperor in the pope's'.[48] Yet it may be that the dualism is less strenuously asserted here than in Roselli's treatise. When da Monte considers the pope's duty to 'supply the deficiencies of the emperor and correct his vices', he notes that Baldus had treated this as applying only in ecclesiastical matters, since in temporal concerns the emperor had no superior. This view da Monte rejects, holding instead that the pope is the emperor's superior even in temporal terms.[49] The coronation and anointing of a new emperor by the pope, to which da Monte is careful to refer in the *Repertorium*, may indeed bring out the sacred character of imperial authority;[50] yet the ceremony might also serve to emphasize imperial dependence on the papacy. It is therefore interesting to find that in 1433 da Monte did not uphold the view that papal coronation and unction were essential prerequisites for the wielding of imperial authority: election of itself conferred *plenum ius* upon the successful candidate.[51] And it was 'by divine will and permission' that emperors and kings alike held their power. Even if force had in fact been the original means of their obtaining it, God had authorized this for the sake of a common good to which monarchical government was the best means.[52]

Piero da Monte's resolute monarchism was associated with vehement opposition to 'populism'. The persistence of this element in his thinking appears in the *Repertorium*, where he both cites the canonistic maxim, *Populus docendus est non sequendus*, and observes that 'to yield to a people in tumult is not to their benefit

---

[48] *Repertorium Iuris* (Nuremberg, 1476), s.v. *Papa* (this edn. lacks pagination, folio numbers, and signature indicators). The date of composition of the *Repertorium* is indicated by a number of references in the text to events in the 1450s—in particular, to Frederick III's visit to Italy for his imperial coronation.

[49] *Repertorium*, s.v. *Papa*: 'Papa supplet defectus imperatoris et corrigit vicia eius ... quod dicit Bal[dus] non procedere in temporalibus quia in ilis imperator non habet superiorem ... contrarium est verum quod etiam papa est superior in temporalibus imperatori'.

[50] *Repertorium*, s.v. *Imperator*; and cf. *Monarchia*, 1512, sig. b [viii]ᵛ, where, however, Monte insists that anointing does not imply any kind of sacramental or quasi-priestly ordination: the anointed king or emperor remains a layman.

[51] This is clear from the passage cited from *Monarchia* in n. 44 above, where Monte confronts directly the question whether a duly elected emperor needs papal 'examination, anointing, confirmation, and coronation' before he is *verus imperator*, and answers firmly that this is *not* the case.

[52] *Monarchia*, 1512, sig. [f vii]ʳ.

but to their detriment'.[53] These views, restated in the relatively peaceful conditions of the 1450s, had been formed in the stressful 1430s. To start with, in 1433, da Monte already faced a situation in which the council of Basle had passed a 'suspended sentence' of deposition upon the pope.[54] The first concern of a papal apologist was therefore to refute the conciliar claim to exercise that kind of jurisdiction; and this da Monte undertakes vigorously. He cannot and does not deny the validity of such jurisdiction in all circumstances. It was well established that a council could act in the case of a pope who had fallen into heresy: yet even here da Monte's view is that the conciliar sentence of deposition is only declaratory of a previously existing *de facto* situation.[55] And no offence other than heresy, however incorrigible the offending pope, however great the scandal, can authorize deposition. The pope is in the most exalted sense 'the Lord's anointed' (*christus domini*), and as such he may not be 'touched' any more than Saul, despite his offences, was to be 'touched' by David.[56]

From a papalist point of view matters went from bad to worse in the middle and later years of the decade. Piero da Monte was active in the diplomatic service of the papacy in those years; and further striking evidence of his hatred and fear of 'the people' is to be found in documents originating in that activity. Thus, at the court of the young Henry VI of England in the early winter of 1437, da Monte denounced the *concilium populare* of Basle, 'where clamour prevails, not rational discourse'.[57] At much the same time, writing to Eugenius IV about the *Monitorium* issued by Basle on 19 October, he referred to the view taken by 'all who are possessed by zeal for the Lord's house'—the view that 'a sword has been put into the hands of madmen, to stab the prince of the Church, to shed innocent blood, and to destroy the entire ecclesiastical monarchy'. Those responsible for such enormities are 'mad dogs, no longer to be tolerated, but to be removed from the face of the earth,

---

[53] *Repertorium*, s.v. *Populus*. The *Populus docendus* . . . maxim is also cited in *Monarchia*, 1512, sig. b [vii]ᵛ.

[54] In July 1433 the council had decreed Eugenius IV's suspension if he did not within sixty days revoke his bulls (issued at the end of 1431) purporting to dissolve the assembly at Basle.

[55] *Monarchia*, 1512, sig. d iiiiʳ.

[56] Ibid. sig. d [viii]ʳ.

[57] Cf. Haller, *Piero da Monte*, 252: 'Item concilium populare est . . . ubi clamores praevalent et non rationes.'

blotted out of the book of life'.[58] The threat, moreover, was not to
the papacy only, or to the Church alone. Writing to Eugenius in
May 1438 about the reply given by Archbishop Chichele to an
embassy from Basle, da Monte reported with evident satisfaction
the archbishop's insistence that 'every kingdom, every province and
region, all cities and peoples—the whole world' was in danger of
being led astray and thrown into disorder by the scandal and error
emanating from Basle.[59] When the council, in the summer of 1439,
proceeded to the final extremity, deposed Eugenius, and elected
Felix V, da Monte wrote to Cardinal Beaufort not only to argue
that this was to set up 'a vicar of Antichrist' and to replace the
apostolicus by an apostate, the one 'prince of priests' by a schismatic, but also to point out the great evils all this implied for 'every
kingdom, province, and nation'.[60]

Piero da Monte perhaps illustrates most clearly—and doubtless
more clearly than the somewhat equivocal Roselli—the thesis that
an attempt was being made, in the 1430s and 1440s, to rally support
for a defence of monarchy as such against a subversive 'democratic'
challenge from the conciliarists of Basle.[61] Certainly monarchy in
its imperial form found notable defenders. Most notable of all,
perhaps, was Aeneas Sylvius Piccolomini. Historian of the council
of Basle, later pope as Pius II, Aeneas Sylvius was also a major
figure in the developing humanism of the mid-fifteenth century.
Whatever may be thought of the force and sincerity of his arguments in *De ortu et authoritate Romani Imperii*, they are presented
with an eloquence that puts the ponderous Roselli somewhat in the
shade.[62] 'Oratory', it has been shrewdly said, 'became the art form
of the new political ideas'[63]—even though one may question just
how new the ideas were.

[58] Cf. Haller, *Piero da Monte*, 41.

[59] Cited ibid. 66.

[60] Cited ibid. 106–7.

[61] On this, see Black, *Monarchy and Community*, 85–6 and *passim*; and on the
'democratic' tendencies of the council itself, cf. P. Ourliac, 'La Sociologie du Concile
de Bâle', *Revue d'Histoire ecclésiastique*, 56 (1961), 2–32.

[62] The text is most conveniently available (with German translation) in G. Kallen,
*Aeneas Silvius Piccolomini als Publizist in der 'Epistola de Ortu et Auctoritate
Imperii Romani'* (Cologne, 1939), 51–100 (hereafter Kallen edn.): the Latin text
used is taken from R. Wolkan (ed.), *Der Briefwechsel des Eneas Silvius Piccolomini*
(2 vols.; Vienna, 1909). See also B. Widmer, *Enea Silvio Piccolomini in der sittlichen
und politischen Entscheidung* (Basle, 1963), esp. 103–67.

[63] Black, *Monarchy and Community*, 125.

Piccolomini had, as it happens, studied law under Roselli at Siena.[64] He subsequently became secretary to Cardinal Niccolo Albergati, the pope's senior representative at Basle in the early years of the council. Later Piccolomini was himself an active participant in the council and, for a time, a committed conciliarist. Gradually, in the mid-1440s, he moved towards the full commitment to Eugenius which came in 1445. At this stage, however, Piccolomini was in the service of the emperor Frederick III, having become secretary to the imperial chancery as a protégé of the chancellor Kaspar Schlick in 1443. Just at that time, as Antony Black has pointed out, the emperor's authority had been challenged in Switzerland; and Piccolomini's correspondence shows that he chose to regard this, as da Monte and others had seen the claims of the Basle conciliarists, in terms of a radical threat to monarchy as such, perhaps to all consitituted authority. A couple of years later Piccolomini elaborated his position in Aristotelian terms, using the concepts of natural lordship and slavery to sustain a hierarchical view of society culminating in its royal or imperial head.[65]

With this background, then, Piccolomini turned, in 1446, to his most explicit exposition of the case for imperial authority. The immediate context of the *De ortu* was the situation within the Empire, where Frederick III's policies were being obstructed by 'disruptive princely politics';[66] and the work itself has been described as 'surely an attempt to promote Frederick's confidence in his authority vis-a-vis lesser princes in the Empire'.[67] Piccolomini pursued that objective, however, at the highest doctrinal or ideological level. If he adds little to the traditional stock of imperialist ideas, he expresses them with notable force and clarity, and with an 'absolutist' emphasis that is of particular interest in the present discussion.

The argument begins with an account, drawing particularly on Cicero and Horace, of the origins of *civilis vita* and the basis of *regia potestas*. It was Horace's *utilitas* that led to the establishment

---

[64] See as to this Burns, 'The "Monarchia"', n. 45.

[65] See J. B. Toews, 'The View of Empire in Aeneas Sylvius Piccolomini (Pope Pius II)', *Traditio*, 24 (1968), 471–87; and cf. Black, *Monarchy and Community*, 123. Black refers briefly, Toews at some length, to Piccolomini's *Pentalogus de rebus ecclesiae et imperii*, which is not directly considered in the discussion below.

[66] Toews, 'The View of Empire', 480.

[67] Stieber, *Pope Eugenius IV*, 286 n. 20.

of kingship; and while 'utility' was no doubt *iusti prope mater et aequi*, the laws which secured the order of justice were the product of 'the king's decisions'—and the phrase *arbitria regis* carries an important emphasis on the royal will as the source of law.[68] When Roman power becomes the focus of discussion, it is presented first in a historical perspective provided by Aristotle, Orosius, and Livy: Rome is seen as the last in a line of imperial powers stretching from the Assyrians to Alexander the Great and Carthage.[69] More specifically, it was Julius Caesar who established the principate; 'for by him the government of the state was transferred in perpetuity to the emperors'.[70] This was the imperial power, approved by Christ himself, which was to be one of the *duo luminaria* enlightening and ruling the whole world; and the rule in the case of the Empire was true lordship or dominion. The power had indeed belonged originally to the *populus Romanus*; but it had been totally and irrevocably transferred to the emperors by the *lex regia*. That law thus became the basis of a monarchical regime better fitted than any alternative to maintain peace in justice.[71] There can be no valid exemption from this universal authority: the emperor holds, as of right, *directum dominium* over every province.[72]

With these fundamental positions established, or at least asserted, it is possible to look rather more closely at the character of imperial power. It is, for one thing, a power exercised without any obligation to render an account of the reasons for what is being done. Whatever the emperor does is to be patiently borne and regarded as having been done with God's permissive authority; for 'the heart of the king is in the hand of God'.[73] As *legum dominus*, the emperor has full legislative authority and is himself not subject to the laws (in accordance with which, however, he ought to pass judgement).[74] His *suprema potestas* should not be used without the most serious reason (*sine magna et augusta causa*).[75] Yet when necessity demands its use, it is a formidable power indeed. Warning his readers that what he is going to say will perhaps strike some of them as harsh, Piccolomini insists that, when the needs of the state demand it, the emperor is entitled to take from any of his subjects, even from one who has 'deserved well of the commonwealth', his land, his house,

---

[68] *De ortu*, Kallen edn. 54–6. [69] Ibid. 58. [70] Ibid. 60.
[71] Ibid. 66. [72] Ibid. 74. [73] Ibid. 78–80.
[74] Ibid. 84–6. [75] Ibid. 86–8.

his other possessions, in order to apply them to the common good.[76] Against this, as against any imperial act of sovereign power, there is no appeal. In that connection Piccolomini uses an argument which we shall encounter in its application to the papacy by Juan de Torquemada. Caesar alone, he says, has as much power without the princes of the Empire as he has when acting together with them. He supports this claim by arguing that 'supreme power loves unity and flies spontaneously from the many to the one'.[77] Nothing useful, accordingly, can be achieved by bringing in the princes. Everything needful in respect of *summa potestas* ... *summaque authoritatis plenitudo* is the emperor's; and 'what is already full cannot be made any fuller'.[78]

However remote such language may have been from the political realities of Frederick III's situation in the 1440s, Aeneas Sylvius had certainly provided one of the most vigorous statements of imperial absolutism. Twelve years after writing the *De ortu*, he himself occupied, as Pius II, the other throne for which *plenitudo potestatis* was claimed. In the year of his election, 1458, another statement of the imperialist position was produced. The author was Peter von Andlau, who entitled his work *De Imperio Romano-Germanico*. The title is an interesting one, in view of the fact that we are now dealing with a German, not an Italian writer; and Walter Ullmann suggested indeed that Peter von Andlau was advocating—as Aeneas Sylvius manifestly was not—'a purely German empire'.[79] That may be something of an overstatement, though it is noteworthy that the nineteenth-century editor of von Andlau's work described it as 'the first systematic exposition of German constitutional law'.[80] Certainly it is significant that the text was first printed—and reprinted—in the early decades of the seventeenth century, when German jurists were deeply engaged in analysing and criticizing the constitutional structure of the Empire.[81] By then indeed such concerns were purely German. In

[76] Ibid. 80.   [77] Ibid. 88–90.   [78] Ibid. 92.
[79] Ullmann, *Law and Politics in the Middle Ages*, 302–3.
[80] J. Hürbin, *Zeitschrift der Savigny Stiftung für Rechtsgeschichte, Germanistische Abteilung*, 12 (1891), 34 ff.: cited by Ullmann, *Law and Politics in the Middle Ages*, 303 n. 1.
[81] See on these writers, J. H. Franklin, 'Sovereignty and the Mixed Constitution: Bodin and his Critics', in Burns and Goldie (eds.), *Cambridge History of Political Thought 1450–1700* (Cambridge, 1991), 309–28. Von Andlau's *De Imperio Romano-Germanico libri duo* was printed at Strasburg in 1612; and this text was followed in

the mid-fifteenth century the term Romano-Germanic might still have seemed appropriate.

However that may be, Peter von Andlau certainly states his case in a way that is of some theoretical interest. Although, like Aeneas Sylvius, he uses a historical perspective, the framework of his discussion is more analytical. He takes some trouble to consider the various forms of government, with particular emphasis on a distinction similar to that which Fortescue employed at much the same time—between societies that are ruled *regaliter* and those ruled *politice*.[82] Unsurprisingly, his preference is for the former, exemplified above all in the Empire. Yet he goes some distance out of his way to state the case *for* the 'politic' alternative. Thus 'the rulers of cities' (*rectores civitatum*) are bound by the 'municipal laws', whereas kings are free from any such coercive restraint. In such regimes (republican, as we should call them) there is a stronger impetus towards identifying private and public interest, and the benefits of this are illustrated, von Andlau says, by the power and prosperity of Venice. There, incidentally, the Doge has a power that is 'tempered and limited'. Where such limits are lacking, as they are in the case of regal (and presumably *par excellence* imperial) power, von Andlau acknowledges that tyranny frequently results.[83]

None the less, Peter von Andlau was persuaded that the arguments in favour of monarchical rule were far stronger. It cannot, admittedly, be claimed that he gives monarchy an absolute preeminence. This is because of his interesting insistence that, in such matters, circumstances alter cases: that, in accordance with Aristotle's teaching, political regimes should be organized in accordance with the 'disposition' of the people who are to be governed. Thus, von Andlau argues, some regions are 'servile by nature'; and these are fit for 'despotic and regal government'. Elsewhere, however, the people may be 'vigorous and bold, outstanding in genius and diligence': such people necessarily require a 'political' system of

---

the edn. cited below: *Repraesentatio Reipub. Germanicae sive tractatus varii de Sacri Romani-Germanici Imperii regimine* (Nuremberg, 1657), 1–115 (hereafter 1657 edn.).

[82] *De Imperio*, 1. viii (1657 edn. 27): the heading of the chapter is: 'An conveniat imperium & quodlibet regnum magis regaliter quam politice gubernari'.

[83] Ibid. 1. viii (27); and cf. 1. ix (32): 'Dux Venetorum temperatum limitatumque regimen habet, qui suam potestatem a Senatu Venetorum, veluti a Sole Luna, mutuare perhibetur.'

government. That form of *dominium* (the term is expressly used) 'flourishes', we are told, 'in Italy and in many other regions'.[84] It is reasonable to suppose that von Andlau had the German imperial cities in view here; and it is also worth bearing in mind that the Hanseatic towns were still near the height of their prosperity and power as he wrote. Yet monarchy retained its ultimate superiority in his eyes; and it will hardly do to suppose that he had in mind that 'despotic' form of monarchy which was suitable for peoples of slavish character. He did in fact distinguish—though he may not have maintained the distinction consistently—between *principatus despoticus* and *principatus regalis*. Neither form of rule, he says, would have been necessary had mankind preserved its original innocence: some kind of 'politic order' would then have sufficed.[85] The similarity to Fortescue is striking here, both writers drawing, of course, upon Thomist concepts. Peter von Andlau, however, does not develop the notion of a regime that is at once 'regal' and 'politic': he seems rather to think that, for most societies, regal government provides the best security against those factors which threaten the common good. In particular, he is of course concerned to argue the case for the supreme authority of the emperor, who is *dominus et princeps mundi*.[86] When this is combined with von Andlau's recognition of the need for a diversity of regimes appropriate to different societies, we may well conclude that his conception of the imperial role is not unlike that advocated by Dante: a role that consists not so much in any kind of universal direct rule as in an ultimate responsibility for peace and justice throughout the entire empire.

It is also the case that Peter von Andlau's view of the emperor's power is noticeably less 'absolutist' than the view taken by Aeneas Sylvius. The latter would, admittedly, have had no difficulty in endorsing the accepted principle that 'kings were established for the sake of their kingdoms, not kingdoms for the sake of their kings'.[87] Peter von Andlau, however, took this to imply limitations on royal, and specifically on imperial, power which are perhaps more stringent than some other imperialists would have found acceptable. It is true that when he argues, for instance, that the emperor cannot deprive his subjects of what is theirs by virtue of

---

[84] Ibid. i. ix (31).　　[85] Ibid. 1.i (6).
[86] Ibid. ii.viii (83).　　[87] Ibid. i. iii (11).

the *jus gentium*—cannot, in particular, deprive them of their property—he is careful to say that such things may not be done *sine causa*. This of course leaves open the path that leads to justifiably drastic action in case of necessity. Nor would any imperialist have had difficulty in agreeing with Peter von Andlau that the emperor cannot in any circumstances arbitrarily alienate any of the 'rights of the Empire' (*jura Imperii*). The issue is very much one of nuance and emphasis; and in that sense the impression made by *De Imperio Romano-Germanico* does seem significantly different from that left by reading Piccolomini's *De ortu et authoritate Romani Imperii*.[88]

There is also, however, a more striking difference between Peter von Andlau's account of the Empire and that given by Antonio de' Roselli. The latter's 'imperialism' was such as to incur ecclesiastical condemnation because of Roselli's insistence that the emperor derived his authority directly from God and not through the medium of the Church, as represented by the papacy. That is described by Peter von Andlau as 'not far short of heresy'.[89] His own view envisages a single hierocratic pyramid, in which the papal power established by Christ and conferred upon Peter and his successors is the source of the imperial authority; and the latter in turn is the source of all 'the other subordinate kingdoms, duchies, principalities, and lordships in the world'. Power flows down from the apex of the pyramid by a process of 'emanation'.[90] Peter von Andlau's view is thus in the end a monistic view; and if his imperialism seems to transcend the specifically Germanic context in which it has been said to find its place, it also stops short of the rigorous dualism of a Roselli.

It remains, by way of conclusion to this chapter, to say something more about the systematic and highly developed papalism which is

---

[88] Ibid. II. viii (83). The passage is perhaps worth quoting *in extenso*: 'Quanquam autem praedixi, quod Imperator sit dominus & princeps mundi, non tamen potest tollere ea quae sunt de iure gentium, sine causa: & sic non potest tollere alicui rem suam, sine causa. Quia Imperator licet habeat de jure jurisdictionem in universo, non tamen habet dominium rerum privatarum, quae olim fuerunt concessae occupantibus . . . Non potest etiam ad libitum alienare jura Imperii praecipue in grave praejudicium Imperii'.

[89] Ibid. II. ix (84): 'non longe foret ab haeresi pertinaciter negare temporalem Caesaris jurisdictionem a summo Pontifice derivare'.

[90] Ibid. I. ii (10): 'Ipse autem Jesus Christus vicarium suum constituit Petrum & successores . . . a quo Imperialis auctoritas, & deinceps ab Imperiali caetera regna, ducatus, principatus, & dominia mundi subalterna quadem emanatione defluxerunt'.

an important part of fifteenth-century thinking about monarchy. There is a counterpoint between this theme and the conciliarism which is the main focus of the next chapter, and indeed some consideration of conciliarist ideas has already been unavoidable here. So far as the papalist side of the argument is concerned, this was of course strongly developed by Roselli in the 1430s, even though his papalism is in a sense complicated by that rigorous dualism which has just been recalled. It may be that a clearer, if less elaborately developed, statement of the papalist position was being made at much the same time by Piero da Monte, in whose work there is certainly an emphatic and unequivocal rejection of the alternative conciliarist ecclesiology. In Rodrigo Sánchez de Arévalo, whose temporal political thought was considered in the previous chapter, there is a strong and even strident defence of the papal monarchy.[91] St Antoninus of Florence, in his influential mid-century *Summa theologica*, expounds more fully the view we have seen in Peter von Andlau, deriving all authority, in church and state alike, from the pope as vicar of Christ.[92] There can, however, be no question as to the identity of the most important exponent of a papalist ecclesiology at this time: Juan de Torquemada in his *Summa de ecclesia* (1449–53).[93]

It is important to observe that Torquemada, though most celebrated for his systematic exposition of papalist doctrine, was no stranger to the world of polemic and propaganda in which writers like Roselli, da Monte, and Piccolomini so largely worked. He was repeatedly involved on the papal side in the confrontation with the council of Basle: many columns in Mansi's *Amplissima Collectio* are filled with his swingeing attacks on the 'blasphemy and sacrilege' of the conciliarists. Much of the material that was thus deployed in the controversies of the 1430s and 1440s was to be incorporated in the more elaborate argumentation of the *Summa*. Torquemada's doctrinal position is as Thomist as one might expect of a Spanish Dominican; but Antony Black has argued persuasively

[91] On papalism in Monte and Arévalo, see Black, *Monarchy and Community*, *passim*; and cf. Becker, *Die Appellation vom Papst*, 332–3 (on Monte) and 352–3 (on Arévalo, whom Becker describes as 'entschiedener Befürworter einer absoluter Monarchie des Papstes').

[92] See J. H. Burns, 'Scholasticism: Survival and Revival', in Burns and Goldie (eds.), *Cambridge History of Political Thought 1450–1700*, 140–2.

[93] There is, somewhat surprisingly, no modern edn. of the text. Some useful extracts are printed by Black, *Monarchy and Community*, 162–72.

that it is the neoplatonic element in Thomism (perhaps more generally in the realist *via antiqua*) that accounts for what may be regarded as the most characteristic elements in Torquemada's ecclesiology.[94] He drew on what Black describes as 'an inexhaustible reservoir of analogies between cosmos and polity'. These analogies are pervaded by the notion of hierarchical dependence. The hierarchy is governed by the supreme power at its summit— by God in the cosmos as a whole, by the supreme ruler in the case of the polity. In such a theory there is really no place for any form of government other than monarchy. Aristotle is repeatedly cited in support of the monarchical principle, but it would be hard to guess from Torquemada's citations that Aristotle had recognized other constitutional forms as legitimate. All authority, all jurisdiction derives by way of 'effluence' from the head. No other element in the political system is granted any independent status.[95]

Faced with the argument that a council—*the* council in the case of the Church—may be regarded as representing reason in the body politic, while the ruler—pope, emperor, or king—supplies the element of will, Torquemada responded in a complex but quite unequivocal fashion. In the first place, he rejects the analogy: St John Chrysostom (he tells us) teaches that 'the intellect is high priest and king in man'; and so the sovereign pontiff provides the intellectual, the rational element in the mystical body of the Church. Even, however, if the analogy were allowed, the argument would fail; for without the imperative force of will the operations of reason are ineffectual.[96]

From the immense range of other points that could be extracted from Torquemada's remarkable work, one argument may be selected for consideration here, both because of its intrinsic interest and because it affords some indication of the stage of development reached by the middle of the fifteenth century in the theory of absolute monarchy. Citing no fewer than four passages from Aquinas in support, Torquemada (arguing originally against the conciliarists of Basle at the council of Florence in 1439) states a

---

[94] On this, see Black, *Monarchy and Community*, esp. 58–80.

[95] *Summa de Ecclesia*, II. 55 (Salamanca, 1560), 259; and cf. Black, *Monarchy and Community*, 167.

[96] Cf. *Solemnis Tractatus fratris Johannis de Turrecremata . . . contra decreta . . . concilii Constantiensis . . . & contra gesta concilii Basiliensis*, in Mansi, *Amplissima Collectio*, vol. xxx, cols. 571, 582–3.

theological postulate: namely, that even the whole creation, every created being, taken together with the creator himself, contains no more goodness than is to be found, independently of any creature, in God alone. The same is true in what we may term the political cosmos. All magistrates, officers, and judges, taken together with the king, do not dispose of any greater jurisdictional authority than does the king—or the emperor, or (of course) the pope—in himself. It follows that we cannot say, as the conciliarists said, that the pope is included in the council which represents or embodies the whole Church: we should perhaps say rather that the power of the council is, like every other jurisdictional authority in the Church, contained in the pope.[97] This was the kind of claim that had to be met and refuted by thinkers in the conciliarist tradition which is the central subject of the next chapter.

[97] *Oratio Synodalis de Primatu*, ed. E. Candal (Rome, 1954), 86. There is a translation of this address by T. M. Izbicki, entitled *A Disputation on the Authority of Pope and Council* (Oxford, Blackfriars, 1988): the passage referred to is on p. 68.

6

THE CONCILIARIST TRADITION
AND BEYOND

ONE of the points made in the opening chapter was that the historical and ecclesiological scholarship of recent decades has both broadened and deepened our understanding of the nature and significance of conciliarism as it developed from the late fourteenth to the early sixteenth century.[1] The conciliarist contribution to the theory of monarchy will be examined in this chapter mainly, though not exclusively, with reference to arguments deployed and developed from the mid-fifteenth century onwards—if only because the period down to the final closure of the council of Basle–Lausanne in 1449 has been studied so intensively as to leave little if anything that can be added within the compass of one chapter in a relatively short book. This chapter, however, also looks 'beyond' the conciliarist tradition in at least two ways. In the first place, some attention will be given to thinkers—notably Gabriel Biel—for whom the ecclesiological issue between conciliarism and papalism was not a major concern, but who none the less worked to a considerable extent in an intellectual milieu where conciliarist ideas are frequently found. (In any case, Biel in particular may be regarded as a major figure in late fifteenth-century thought whose 'political ideas' as such have received less attention than they merit.) The second way in which the discussion here moves outside the conciliarist tradition is in examining some relatively neglected aspects of the papalist response to the conciliarist challenge in the early sixteenth century, with particular reference to the work of Tommaso de Vio (Cajetan).

To start with, however, and despite what was said a moment ago about the intensive cultivation of the field of ecclesiological debate during the first half of the fifteenth century, it is worth while to

[1] Cf. Chap. 1, text at nn.13–17.

pause for a little in the period of the council of Basle, at least in order to establish a preliminary point of some importance. That point may be illustrated by considering the case of Juan González, bishop of Cadiz from 1426 until his death in 1440.[2] Between 1432 and 1434 González was active at the council of Basle; and it is not surprising to find a canonist who had served in the papal curia in the early years of Martin V's pontificate vigorously asserting the claims of the papacy. He argues in favour of the pope's maintaining *statum magnificum et gloriosum et potentem,* remarking that 'power, wisdom, and the worship of God are necessary in a true monarchy'.[3] In a particularly noteworthy passage González makes the point that to take 'executive power' *(potentiam executivam)* from the pope and give it to lesser prelates would mean subordinating the Church 'to kings and princes, under whose dominion and power those prelates are'.[4] Yet when, at the time of the fifth council of the Lateran, Domenico Giacobazzi compiled his massive *Tractatus de Concilio* (published posthumously in 1538), he appears to have regarded González as one who was prepared to follow Gerson's lead in upholding the prerogatives of the council against the pope.[5] When the evidence is systematically surveyed, as it has been by Erich Meuthen,[6] what seems to emerge is the picture of a man genuinely concerned to find and take the middle ground between the extreme positions that were being so strenuously asserted in the 1430s. Both those positions, González argued, were vitiated by a failure to observe the maxim *suum cuique*—the basic principle of distributive justice. Both pope and council had legitimate claims, and Christendom could only be harmed by denying what was due to either.[7]

---

[2] See E. Meuthen, 'Juan González, Bischof von Cadiz, auf dem Basler Konzil', *Annuarium Historiae Conciliorum,* 8 (1976), 250–93.

[3] Cf. ibid. 274.

[4] Ibid. 275.

[5] Giacobazzi, *Tractatus de Concilio* (Rome, 1538), 705 B, after referring to the view that full power, including coercive power in regard to the pope, belongs to the council representing the whole Church, adds: 'Istam etiam opinionem tenet quidam hispanus qui fuit episcopus gaddicen. qui colligit dicta gersonis & illa approbat.' There are frequent references to González in Giacobazzi's massive work.

[6] Meuthen's is the only comprehensive treatment of the subject: he himself refers to the discussion by V. Beltrán de Heredia, *Cartulario de la Universidad de Salamanca,* i (Salamanca, 1970), 159ʳ–190ᵛ.

[7] Cf. Meuthen, 'Juan González', 285, quoting from the bishop's 'Positio': 'Aliqua intendo allegare . . . in iusticiam reddendo unicuique quod suum est, videlicet pape, quod suum est, et concilio sacro, quod suum est; nam in hoc consistit vera iusticia.'

What this instance illustrates—and no doubt many others could be cited—is that, convenient as it no doubt is to make use of labels like 'papalist' and 'conciliarist' for analytical purposes in tracing the history of ideas, such labelling has its dangers. Individuals and groups are less securely categorized than the positions they may at one time or another choose to adopt. And with that in mind it will be useful to return briefly to Antonio de' Roselli and consider his views on the place of the council in the government of the Church. Roselli may well be regarded as a strong papalist: his activity on behalf of Eugenius and against Basle, especially his drafting of the pseudo-bull *Deus novit*, would support this view, as would the elaborate and detailed assertion of papal prerogatives in his *Monarchia*.[8] Yet elements of 'conciliarism' can also be detected in his thinking: he did, after all, extract from *Monarchia* material to be developed in a treatise on councils at a time when a conciliar solution to the problems of ecclesiastical allegiance in the 1440s was being considered.[9] And, as we have seen, there was a genuinely 'conciliar' element in Roselli's conception of monarchy.[10]

It is of course true to say that there could be opportunism as well as principle in what might then be seen essentially as 'trimming'. Roselli's situation and circumstances, for example, undoubtedly changed between the mid-1430s and the mid-1440s: his views may have altered somewhat accordingly. And there are celebrated, even notorious, cases of changing sides in the controversy: Nicholas of Cusa and Aeneas Sylvius may both be seen as exemplifying this. The more important point here, however, is that there was a perfectly genuine sense in which either extreme not only might but must be seen as mistaken. No one, in the end, could, without incurring a charge of heresy, take a stand exclusively for either pope or council. The strongest papalist—Juan de Torquemada, for instance—had to allow an essential and important place for the general council which represented or embodied the Church as a whole. It even had to be acknowledged that, in the case of a heretical pope (and schism might or might not be regarded as entailing heresy), the council had at least a declaratory function to perform in establishing that 'the throne was thereby become

---

[8] This is to be found above all in what became part IV of Goldast's edn. of Roselli's *Monarchia*.

[9] Cf. Chap. 5, text at nn. 21–2.

[10] Cf. Chap. 5, text at n. 18.

vacant'.[11] On the other side, not even the most vehement conciliarist could deny the place of the papacy in the supreme government of the Church. It is true that some were attracted by the classical mixed constitution as a model for the ecclesiastical polity, with the papacy supplying the monarchical element in the balanced tripartite system, the cardinals the aristocratic element, and the council the element (somewhat loosely construed) of democracy. Most conciliarists, however, would surely have agreed with John Mair, convinced defender of conciliar claims though he was, in arguing that the *politia mixta* was incompatible with the belief that Christ—'the best of legislators'—must have established in his Church the best of all forms of governments. And that was monarchy.[12]

This is indeed what makes the entire controversy between papalist and conciliarist views of the Church so crucial for our theme here. The argument reached—and no doubt passed—its peak in the period here under scrutiny; and it was at its heart—at least in so far as it is of concern to the historian of political thought—an argument about monarchy. What it was *not*, however, was an argument for and against monarchy as such: it was a debate, among thinkers who fully endorsed the monarchical principle, about what that principle properly implied. The central issue was the nature of monarchy and the basis of its claim to be regarded as, indeed, the best of all constitutions.

That argument was to be renewed vigorously in the early years of the sixteenth century. In the second half of the fifteenth, it is true, controversy was less sustained and somewhat muted. Yet it is a mistake to suppose that the controversy died away completely with the papal victory over the conciliar movement which had grown out of the crisis of the Great Schism. More than once, when conflicts of interest developed in the Church, and when a papal decision was resisted or rejected, the possibility of appealing to a council was raised. Pius II (that one-time conciliarist Aeneas Sylvius Piccolomini) expressly prohibited appeals from papal decisions to a

---

[11] See generally Thomson, *Popes and Princes*, 11, 13–14; also id., 'Papalism and Conciliarism in Antonio Roselli's *Monarchia*', 457–8. On Torquemada's position, see further Becker, *Die Appellation vom Papst*, 334–7; and cf. 337–8 on Antoninus of Florence, to whom Becker ascribes '[d]ie extremste Formulierung des päpstlichen Jurisdiktionsprimates'. Torquemada's views are also discussed by H. Smolinsky, *Domenico de' Domenichi und seine Schrift 'De potestate Pape et termino eius'* (Münster, 1976), 393–5.

[12] Mair, *In Mattheum ad literam expositio . . .* (Paris, 1518), fo. 69ᵛ.

future council by the bull *Execrabilis* (1460).[13] This, however, did not by any means put an end to the argument.[14] Yet it is true that such prospects as there were of reviving the conciliarist hopes of the two previous generations never materialized sufficiently to precipitate a sharp and extensive division along 'party lines'. If, as has been argued here, an essentially partisan interpretation can be misleading even at the height of the earlier controversy, such an approach must be still less appropriate in the 1450s and later.

A good illustration of this point may be found in the work of Denis Rijkel, commonly known as Denis the Carthusian.[15] Before exploring briefly some aspects of his thought, however, it is important to recall an essential factor in the situation of Western Christendom in the 1450s. With the fall of Constantinople in 1453 and the final extinction of the Byzantine empire, Europe faced a new onslaught from Islam, now spearheaded by the Ottoman Turks. The continuing disunity of Christendom in the face of this threat, the evident unwillingness of Christian princes to give that problem priority over their narrower interests and ambitions, led some churchmen to see a new council of the Church as the best, perhaps the only way of rallying Christian ranks and mobilizing the forces for a new crusade.[16] It was this, seemingly, that led Denis Rijkel—otherwise above all a mystical theologian (who became known as *doctor ecstaticus*)—to consider the role of the council and to urge the duty of the pope to summon one. To call him a 'conciliarist' may be to stretch the term too far: at best, his conciliarism was distinctly Laodicean. Yet, inspired by visions of the disasters that menaced Christendom, he does indeed see the

---

[13] See Thomson, *Popes and Princes*, 14–17: he observes (pp. 14–15) that *Execrabilis* 'was, in one sense, the most notable assertion of extreme claims by the fifteenth-century papacy, but at the same time, its text does not appear to have been widely circulated throughout Christendom, nor did the papacy employ it often in later controversies'.

[14] See Becker, *Die Appellation vom Papst*, esp. 162–202.

[15] On whom, see Black, *Monarchy and Community*, 42 n., 57, 61 n.; id., *Council and Commune*, 24, 153; Stieber, *Pope Eugenius IV*, 100–1, where the context is a more general discussion of Carthusian attitudes to issues in ecclesiastical politics in the Empire (see also pp. 338–9). Rijkel's voluminous works were published as *Opera Omnia* (Tournai, 1908); but it is also important here to note that many of his writings, including those most relevant in the present context, had been printed at Cologne in 1532.

[16] See Thomson, *Popes and Princes*, 115–19; and cf. Stieber, *Pope Eugenius IV*, 338–42.

convoking of a council as an essential means of averting them. His thinking on the matter has clear Thomist affinities; but yet again we have here Thomism with a strong neoplatonist tinge. Such ideas could be used—as they were used by Torquemada, for instance—in the service of papal absolutism. Denis the Carthusian used them to support a cautious and moderate conciliarism.[17]

The point just made is a valuable reminder of the fact that there is, in this period, no simple correlation between philosophical and theological positions and political or ecclesiological conclusions. Denis Rijkel had no doubt absorbed an Albertist realism as a student at Cologne; and that university was by no means the least important seminary of conciliarist ideas. On the other hand, it is well known that Parisian conciliarism was closely associated with the nominalism which frequently, if not always, prevailed in university teaching there. Rijkel, it may be worth noting, was perfectly prepared to follow where Gerson and d'Ailly had led in matters of ecclesiology. Perhaps the closest he came to resolving the potential contradictions in his compromise position was when he endorsed Pierre d'Ailly's suggestion that the best form of government for the Church would be that, under the pope as monarch, a number of persons were elected by and from every province. The cardinals should fulfil this role and should rule with the pope and under his authority.[18] It is important to notice here the phrase *cum Papa et sub eo*; if there is to be, in a sense, 'mixed government', it is still emphatically mixed *monarchy*. Rijkel makes it quite clear that he accepts the superiority of monarchy; and his fundamental position is one in which authority descends, ultimately, from God, who is the only true Lord.[19]

---

[17] Black (*Council and Commune*, 24) refers to 'such moderate quasi-conciliarists as Rickel', and describes him (p. 153) as 'a moderate conciliarist in the mould of the late d'Ailly'. At the same time it is worth bearing in mind that Rijkel's religious order had, in 1440, 'declared their full support of the Council of Basel and specifically recognized Felix V as pope' (Stieber, *Pope Eugenius IV*, 100). On the neoplatonic element in Rijkel's thought, see Black, *Monarchy and Community*, 57, and cf. 61 n. 2.

[18] Rijkel, *Opera Omnia*, xxxvi. 625. The chapter heading (p. 624) is *De triplici regimine et triplici politia Ecclesiae*.

[19] Cf. ibid xxvi. 24: 'secundum Philosophum . . . regimen monarchicum in quo unus tantum principatur, est optimum . . . et tale est regimen militantis Ecclesiae.' On dependence on divine *dominium*, cf. ibid. vi. 383: 'solus Deus est universalis Dominus et generalis rex. Creaturae vero sortiuntur ab eo aliquod particulare dominium specialeque regnum.'

Another point made by Denis the Carthusian may, in the perspective of later arguments, be at least as important as those already mentioned. At the very end of his most substantial work on these topics, he declares that the pope's rule over 'the Christian people' is not, whatever analogies there may be between the two, the same as the government of 'a civil society or political community'. The Christian community is 'formed by the faith and law of Christ': it is Christ's 'sheepfold and flock'. This means that it is a 'mystical body' in a sense that goes beyond what had become the accepted juristic usage of that term. It is over the body of Christ in its terrestrial life that the pope presides as 'ruler, head and judge'; and therefore to say that the Church is ruled by the pope as any other civil or political community is ruled runs counter to the very *raison d'être* of the Church and of the papal office.[20] We shall see later something of the significance of this recapture of the term *corpus mysticum* for the theological province where it had its origin.

There was of course nothing new in mystical theology and metaphysical philosophy having their share in what was said on these matters. Leaving aside the major work of Nicholas of Cusa,[21] we may note the case of Denis Rijkel's fellow-Netherlander Heimerich van de Velde (1396–1460). The work of Antony Black in particular has drawn attention to this remarkable figure, who developed (on the basis of what Black calls 'organic realism') an ecclesiology which was to prove compatible both with involvement in the council of Basle and subsequent support for Eugenius IV.[22] It may be hard to ascribe much direct influence to van de Velde's ideas: it is a striking fact that not a single work of his seems to have found its way into print—in sharp contrast with the thirteen volumes of Denis the Carthusian's writings published in the 1530s. Yet a discussion of ideas of monarchy in this period cannot simply pass by on the other side without taking note of a view of what may well be termed the economy of the Church as the household of the faith. In this view, Christ is the *paterfamilias*, the Church

---

[20] Cf. ibid. xxxvi. 673.

[21] On whom, see esp. P. E. Sigmund, *Nicholas of Cusa and Medieval Political Thought* (Cambridge, Mass., 1963).

[22] See Black, *Council and Commune*, 58–84. On van de Velde's influence on Cusa, whom he taught in the university of Cologne, see Sigmund, *Nicholas of Cusa*, 25–6.

herself is the *materfamilias*, while the pope's function is no more than that of the steward or *dispensator*.[23]

It was not only at such more or less visionary levels, however, that the issue of authority in the Church continued to be disputable. Other, more down-to-earth factors were at work in the era of the restored and reunited papacy. Pius II's decree against attempting to appeal from papal decisions has been noted already. In Germany especially, opposition to such assertions of papal power remained vigorous; and one instance of that opposition is relevant here because of the polemical interchanges it provoked and the particip-ants in them. The specific dispute in this instance arose from an election to the archbishopric of Mainz.[24] In February 1461 Diether von Issenburg, having been deposed by Pius II from the see to which he had been duly elected, appealed, in direct defiance of *Execrabilis*, to a council. To state his case he enlisted the services of a vigorous controversialist, Gregor Heimburg, already under sen-tence of excommunication for the part he had played in an earlier dispute.[25] On the papal side, Gabriel Biel—later to emerge as the leading theologian of the day—was briefed for what he himself called, in the title of the tract he wrote for the purpose, *The Defence of Apostolic Obedience* (1462).[26] This was a firm recapitulation of the papalist case, using at times what we may regard as the characteristic language of monarchical absolutism. Biel argues, for instance, that no positive law can bind the pope; 'and so', he goes on, 'should the sovereign pontiff, *ex certa scientia*, define, com-mand, or act otherwise than, or contrary to, what the positive law prescribes, such definitions and commands are to be obeyed with all reverence.'[27]

A quarter of a century later, writing towards the end of his life and in a much less polemical situation and context, in his *Exposition of the Canon of the Mass*, Biel is (no doubt predictably) more reserved. He is still emphatic as to the pope's position as head of the Church, though this is true only in a secondary sense: the

---

[23] See Black, *Council and Commune*, 75 ff.

[24] See on this dispute Becker, *Die Appellation vom Papst*, 346–52.

[25] See ibid. 167–201, 341–7; and for earlier phases in Heimburg's somewhat stormy career, Stieber, *Pope Eugenius IV*, esp. 235–6, 285–7.

[26] *Defensorium Obedientiae Apostolicae, et alia documenta*, ed. H. A. Oberman, D. E. Zerfoss, and W. J. Courtenay (Cambridge, Mass., 1968). The text was printed in several editions during the first two decades of the 16th cent.

[27] Ibid. 142.

primary headship can belong to no one but Christ himself.[28] Biel is clear too that the pope's headship is such that all subordinate authority 'flows' from the head to the members.[29] At the same time he is at pains to emphasize that the pope's authority over benefices, for example, is at most *dominium regitivum*, a lordship limited to some degree of regulatory control. Perhaps indeed, he adds, it is 'stewardship rather than lordship' (*dispensatio verius est quam dominium*).[30] Nor does Biel question the principle that councils have an essential part to play in the life of the Church. A general council is representative of the whole *congregatio fidelium*. As such, Biel argues, it is the 'supreme earthly tribunal' of the Church; and that supremacy prevails, in the last resort, even over the pope. On this point Biel cites the decree *Frequens* of the council of Constance.[31]

Neither a papalist nor a conciliarist in any simple partisan sense, Gabriel Biel was no doubt typical or many more churchmen than belonged to either party extreme. In a broader sense too he reflects a characteristic tendency in theological thinking, and therefore in ecclesiology, at this time. No doubt he may properly be regarded, as Heiko Oberman has presented him, as the essentially nominalist reaper of 'the harvest of medieval theology'.[32] Yet he wears his Ockhamism with a difference, with an eclecticism that takes him frequently from Ockham to Duns Scotus and, for that matter, to Thomas Aquinas, finding there views he is ready to respect and often to endorse. Biel's general theory of society, government, and law—never fully or systematically developed and still insufficiently studied—lies beyond the limits of the present discussion.[33] What is relevant for present purposes is to note that Biel's eclecticism illustrates the fact that the late fifteenth century was a period of fruitful cross-fertilization between schools of thought, if hardly between the parties in ecclesiastical politics.

Before turning, in the latter part of this chapter, to the early

---

[28] *Canonis Missae Expositio*, Oberman and Courtenay edn. i. 219–20.

[29] Ibid. 219: 'Dicitur [papa] etiam . . . caput propter virtutem influxivam, dependet siquidem ab eo omnis ordo ecclesiasticus . . . et ab ipso fluit mediate vel immediate omnis potestas spiritualis'.

[30] Ibid. 287.

[31] Ibid. 199.

[32] Oberman, *Harvest of Medieval Theology*.

[33] See further Burns, 'Scholasticism', in Burns and Goldie (eds.), *Cambridge History of Political Thought 1450–1700*, 137–9, 142–5.

sixteenth century and the circumstances in which such parties were again embroiled in vehement controversy, it is useful to pause and consider a late fifteenth-century figure who stands somewhat apart from the main line that is being examined here. John Wessel Gansfort may indeed be regarded as having developed a more radical attack on the monarchical principle than most others in the period.[34] This is not to say that he was a political 'radical' or that he advocated a constitutional alternative to monarchy. He did, it is true, express a preference for those political systems in which the authority of the ruler was institutionally circumscribed.[35] Such questions, however, were not in any sense the main focus of his concern. That lay rather in the spiritual life of the individual Christian believer. Gansfort gave his mind above all to the ways in which that spiritual life might be affected—might even be endangered—by a misconceived view of papal authority. Disputing on the subject of indulgences with his fellow-Netherlander Jacobus Hoeck, Gansfort took his stand firmly upon the nominalist foundations he had laid in Paris (having originally gone there with the aim of converting the nominalist teachers of the university to his own Thomist realism).[36] Nominalist theology led him inexorably to the conclusion that the reason and conscience of the individual, working upon the scriptures, afforded an authority that must, in the final analysis, prevail over that of the pope. As with Ockham before him, so with Gansfort now: the evident 'individualism' is less straightforward than it might seem. There is, for one thing, no question of attributing equal weight to all individuals. Gansfort is prepared to allow that an assembly of the weightier believers (the *valentior pars*, he might have said, though he did not) should be presumed not to err in its doctrinal definitions.[37] There is, so to speak, a latent conciliarism here; but it is some considerable way from the fully

---

[34] See generally E. W. Miller and J. W. Scudder, *Wessel Gansfort: Life and Writings* (2 vols.; New York and London, 1917), with extensive textual material in translation in vol. ii; M. van Rhijn, *Studiën over Wessel Gansfort* (Utrecht, 1933). On Gansfort's political ideas, see Ullman, *Law and Politics in the Middle Ages*, 305–6; F. Oakley 'Disobedience, Consent, Political Obligation: The Witness of Wessel Gansfort (*c.* 1419–1489)', *History of Political Thought*, 9 (1988), 211–21.

[35] *De dignitate et potestate ecclesiastica*, in *Opera quae inveniri potuerunt omnia* (Groningen, 1614; facsimile repr. Nieuwkoop, 1966), 765–6.

[36] See Miller and Scudder, *Wessel Gansfort*, i. 285; and cf. van Rhijn, *Studiën*, 30–2. See also Oakley, 'Disobedience, Consent, Political Obligation', 211–14.

[37] *Opera . . . omnia*, 781.

developed conciliarism in which a general council of the Church enjoyed a corporate authority directly bestowed upon it by Christ and exercised an infallible *magisterium* superior to that of the pope.

Conciliarism of that thoroughgoing kind was still the received wisdom in more than one centre of theological learning as the fifteenth century gave way to the sixteenth. This was true, above all, of the university of Paris. Yet, like received wisdom in all periods and in many different contexts, it might well be seen as having become a somewhat inert force at that stage in its history. As ever, it needed a political issue, something in the nature of a crisis, to restore to conciliarist thinking the momentum it had had in the great days of Constance and Basle. The crisis or crises then had of course had a secular or temporal aspect; but the Conciliar Movement of the period, when it is defensible to refer to it by that name, was above all the product of a great scandal within the Church itself, the scandal of schism compounded by the challenge of heresy. It is true that when the argument between conciliarists and papalists was renewed a hundred years later, a far greater heretical challenge than that of the Hussites and a split in Catholic Christendom deeper and more permanent than the Great Schism lay just below the horizon. Nor should we underestimate the seriousness with which the issue of reform in the Church was being raised before the period of what we call the Reformation. The council of Pisa and Milan around which, in 1511 and 1512, the old controversies were revived and extended, was, at least initially and in part, the result of that reforming concern. And the fifth council of the Lateran, summoned to overshadow what from a papal point of view was no more than the *conciliabulum* in northern Italy, certainly had reform prominently on its agenda, however little action came of it. Yet, when all is said and done, it is hard to believe that the controversy we are about to examine would have developed as it did had not Francis I of France seen in the assembly at Pisa a weapon to be used in his political conflict with Julius II. Certainly that specifically political element in the situation added to the polemical vitality of the debate. Yet the debate itself, drawing as it did on doctrinal resources built up and developed over a century and more (and grounded, for that matter, in much earlier thinking), had a momentum that carried it beyond the moment of political convenience. It is noteworthy that neither the concordat between

Francis I and Leo X in 1516 nor the king's concomitant order that the debate on authority in the Church should cease brought about a complete closure. The theologians of Paris—John Mair prominent among them—were far from acquiescing in the defeat of their traditional arguments. And if the conciliar attempt, at Trent, to deal with the problems brought to a head by the Protestant challenge had little to do with conciliar*ism*, that view of the polity of the Church was not quite extinct even then.[38]

However that may be, the conciliarist view was still very much alive in 1511. Indeed, even before the crisis precipitated in that year by the dissident cardinals who summoned the council at Pisa, there were indications that the papalist view did not monopolize opinion in the curia itself.[39] This is not simply a matter of the pope's being urged as a matter of prudent policy to summon a reform council, though it is certainly not without interest to observe that this is, for instance, the case of Giovanni Francesco Poggio, whose systematic refutation of conciliarism will be considered in a moment.[40] In the case of Poggio's colleague in the curia, Giovanni Gozzadini, however, we are dealing with 'a conciliarist at the court of Julius II'. The 'conciliarism' in Gozzadini's *De electione Romani Pontificis* may be far from extreme. Yet he does maintain that conciliar decisions have 'greater authority, strength and power than the pope's statutes'; he does assert vigorously that the right to appeal from the pope to a council cannot be abrogated by any papal decree.[41] That is striking language from a curial jurist writing half a century after Pius II's *Execrabilis*.

---

[38] See O. de La Brosse, *Le Pape et le Concile: La Comparaison de leurs pouvoirs à la veille de la Réforme* (Paris, 1965), esp. part 1, chap. 2; A. Renaudet, *Le Concile Gallican de Pise-Milan: Documents florentins (1510–1512)* (Paris, 1922); P. Imbart de la Tour, *Les Origines de la Réforme*, ii. *L'Église Catholique: La Crise de la Renaissance* (Paris, 1909; 2nd edn. rev. Melun, 1946), esp. i. ii–iii and ii. i–11; W. Ullmann, 'Julius II and the Schismatic Cardinals', in *Studies in Church History*, ix. *Schism, Heresy and Religious Protest* (Cambridge, 1972), 177–93.

[39] See on this esp. Ullman, 'Julius II and the Schismatic Cardinals', Becker, *Die Appellation vom Papst*, 231–5, 356–65.

[40] Cf. G. F. Poggio, *De officio principis* (Rome, 1504), addressed to Julius II, sig. [a 6]ᵛ.

[41] See H. Jedin, 'Giovanni Gozzadini, ein Konziliarist am Hofe Julius II', in id., *Kirche des Glaubens, Kirche der Geschichte: Ausgewälte Aufsätze und Vorträge*, ii. *Konzil und Kirchenreform* (2 vols., Freiburg, 1966), 17–74, where 23 'conclusions' from the *De electione* are printed on pp. 27–30. The point about conciliar and papal decisions and decrees is in the tenth conclusion (p. 28); and cf., for the right of appeal, the extract from the same text printed by Becker, *Die Appellation vom Papst*, 442–7.

Yet possibly the most interesting point in Gozzadini's *De electione* is one which was about to be used powerfully on the other side of the argument and against the conciliarist view. Gozzadini insists that the inerrancy of the whole Church as represented in the council inheres in it as 'a mystical body, but not a body politic'. He argues that a body politic might err and might mislead, might even 'come to an end'—and all these are inconceivable in the Church which is the mystical body of Christ himself.[42] Now it was an established part of the conciliarist argument that crucial questions about authority in the Church were answerable on the basis of the parallel that could be drawn between the ecclesial community and political communities in general: it was assumed and asserted that the Church *was* a political community, was indeed the most perfect of all such communities. We shall find this view being vigorously attacked and defended in that phase of the controversy over the council of Pisa which was carried on by theological writers—in particular, by Cajetan, Almain, and Mair. There is, however, a less familiar but interesting discussion of the matter by canonists who viewed the matter from the papal curia and who did not follow the conciliarist lead given by Gozzadini. One instance of this kind of thinking merits some attention here.

This is the work of G. F. Poggio, who was mentioned above in connection with his having urged Julius II to summon a council at the outset of his pontificate. When, probably during the short and troubled duration of the council of Pisa–Milan, Poggio wrote his *De potestate papae et concilii*, his purpose was to review and to refute all the major arguments on the conciliarist side.[43] In doing so, he develops with some care the argument that the Church is not ruled by any kind of *regimen politicum*. It is a monarchy established by Christ. The monarchy Poggio has in mind, moreover, is royal monarchy, or kingship. In developing the analogy between royal and papal power, Poggio interprets both in what may be termed a patriarchal sense. Thus the pope, as vicar of Christ, is *paterfamilias ipsius domus*, the paternal ruler of the household of the faith. This

---

[42] *De electione*, conclusion VII, in Jedin, 'Giovanni Gozzadini', 28.

[43] Giovanni Francesco Poggio (1442–1522), one of the five legitimate sons of Poggio Bracciolini, became secretary to Leo X. His *De potestate papae et concilii* was published in Rome, without date, but probably in or about 1512. For the mostly brief references to him in the secondary literature, see Becker, *Die Appellation vom Papst*, 356 n. 4.

is, obviously, to be compared and contrasted with the views of such earlier writers as Heimerich van de Velde and Gabriel Biel, where the pope emerged as essentially a steward acting on behalf of the true *paterfamilias*, Christ himself. This leads Poggio to argue that, while the papal headship of the Church is in certain respects distinct from that of Christ, the distinction cannot be absolute: in the end, there is and can be only one headship; and Poggio certainly believed that, so far as jurisdiction was concerned, all the Church's power (*vis*) subsisted in Peter and each of his papal successors 'as in the head and foundation'.[44] The distinction between the Church as embodying a necessary hierarchy of authority and the Church as the Bride of Christ dispensing the means to salvation is of course crucial. In that connection Poggio makes use of terminology we encountered in an earlier chapter. The sacramental Church, so to call it, dispenses *gratia gratum faciens*; the Church as a jurisdictional entity exercises authority which rests upon *gratia gratis data*. It follows that the pope's monarchical authority is not abrogated by sin: he may be less virtuous than many—or any—of those who are subject to him without for this reason losing any part of his absolute authority over them.[45]

At least as important for our investigation into ideas of monarchy is the vehemence with which Poggio insists that royal and papal power is to be sharply differentiated from anything that, in his sense of the term, may properly be called 'political'. The reasons for this bring out some of the most significant points in his discussion. Insisting on the crucial difference between *regimen politicum* and the government of the Church, which 'is monarchical, not political', he argues that the essential feature of monarchy is that, under it, the fullness of power lies with the monarch, not with the community. In a 'polity' the opposite is true; and conciliarism would make a polity of the Church. To admit such a view is to open the way for even worse errors, in particular that which Poggio attributes to the Hussites—the view that any individual subject may rise and punish an oppressive ruler. It is still the case that a pope who behaves so as to bring scandal and detriment upon the Church may be resisted; but there can be no

---

[44] *De potestate*, sigs. E2ᵛ, F1ᵛ.
[45] Ibid. sigs. H[4]ᵛ–I1ʳ. On the terminology of grace used here, cf. Chap 2, text at nn. 42–4.

question of punishment in the case, and deposition is explicitly ruled out.[46]

As already noted, Poggio's argument along these lines refers to the kind of monarchical authority that belongs to a king or pope. He does not deny that there can be rule by one man under a 'political' system. Such a ruler (*princeps*) derives his authority from the community and, accordingly, he may be deprived of it by the community. None of this applies to the pope, who exercises authority directly conferred upon him by Christ. An 'earthly society' (*civitas terrena*) may be suitable for 'political' rule—which is not to say that all such societies either are or should be so governed. The essential point for Poggio is that the Christian community—the Church—is simply incapable of such a regime.[47]

The same line of argument was followed by other canonists in defence of the papal position against the pretensions of the conciliarists.[48] The most direct polemical interchange, however, was the work of theologians rather than jurists. It began in the autumn of 1511 with a swingeing attack on the assembly at Pisa by Tommaso de Vio, OP, later and better known, from his birthplace (Gaeta), as Cajetan. Apart from his celebrated controversy with Luther, Cajetan became the leading Thomist theologian of the first half of the sixteenth century.[49] As master-general of the Dominicans he was to play a major part in the fifth council of the Lateran; and from his point of view Pisa was no more than a schismatic *conciliabulum*. Its claims nevertheless called for refutation, and Cajetan sought to provide this in his *Auctoritas Pape & Concilii siue Ecclesie comparata*, completed before mid-October and printed by 19 November 1511.[50]

---

[46] Ibid. sigs. [13]$^{r-v}$, [F4]^v.

[47] Ibid. sig. [H4]^v: 'ciuitas terrena est capax huiusmodi politiae, Fidelium uero uniuersitas huiusmodi potestatis prorsus est incapax'. (Some manifest misprints have been silently corrected: the quality of the printing may indicate that the book was somewhat hurriedly brought out in view of the controversial need it was intended to meet.)

[48] Notably by Domenico Giacobazzi in his *De concilio*, already referred to (n. 5 above): cf. 1538 edn. 389. Giacobazzi (1443–1527) was a contemporary and curial colleague of Poggio, made cardinal by Leo X in 1517.

[49] On Cajetan (1468–1534), see esp. La Brosse, *Le Pape et le Concile*; G. Hennig, *Cajetan und Luther: Ein historischer Beitrag zur Begegnung von Thomismus und Reformation* (Stuttgart, 1966); and cf. Becker, *Die Appellation vom Papst*, 356–8.

[50] References here are to the critical edn. in Cajetan's *Scripta Theologica*, i, ed. V. M. J. Pollet (no more published; Rome, 1936).

At an early stage in his argument Cajetan invokes a distinction drawn from Aquinas (though perhaps not used in quite the way St Thomas intended). This is between *potestas executiva*, which has to do with government (*gubernatio*), and *potestas praeceptiva* which has to do with *imperium* (with sovereignty, we might say). In the Church, Cajetan argues, the former, executive power, having been entrusted to all the apostles, is shared by their successors in the episcopate. But the supreme 'preceptive' power, or *auctoritas regiminis*, was conferred only upon Peter and thus belongs exclusively to his successors.[51] The Church is, essentially, a monarchical system. True, the pope is *dispensator* not *dominus*—a steward not a lord over the Church's goods. True again, he is *princeps* only as 'servant and vicar of that natural prince who is the highest good'.[52] Yet it remains fundamentally true that monarchy is the sovereign element in the Church. The conciliarist position 'perverts the constitutional order' of the Church and would make it 'a democratic or popular regime, in which all authority would reside, not in any one person, but in the whole community'. On this view, moreover, the Church is a *libera communitas*, having the same corporate power over the pope as a 'free community' has over its king. In fact, Cajetan maintains, Christ gave the fullness of power to one man, and not to the community.[53] Arguing in a way we have encountered in Torquemada (whose authority Cajetan repeatedly invokes), he insists that all powers of ecclesiastical jurisdiction are inherent in the papacy, so that no additional weight is carried by decisions in which 'the whole Church', represented in a council, is associated with the pope.[54]

Faced with this outright rejection of the traditional conciliarist view which had just been reasserted by a council enjoying the political backing of the French crown, the university of Paris resolved, in the early months of 1512, upon an immediate reply. The task of writing this was entrusted to one of the youngest members of the faculty of theology, Jacques Almain.[55] His *Libellus*

---

[51] *Auctoritas comparata*, chap. 3 (Pollet edn. 29–30).
[52] Ibid. chap. 5 (Pollet edn. 39) and chap. 9 (69).
[53] Ibid. chap. 6 (Pollet edn. 47). [54] Ibid. chap. 6 (Pollet edn. 45).
[55] Almain, perhaps the most brilliant of the Parisian pupils of John Mair, died prematurely, aged about 35, in 1515. On his ecclesiology and the circumstances of his involvement in the controversy with Cajetan, see esp. La Brosse, *Le Pape et le Concile*; and cf. the references given by Becker, *Die Appellation vom Papst*, 357 n. 31.

de auctoritate Ecclesie, completed (it seems) in May 1512, was a direct reply to Cajetan's attack. The 'political ideas' deployed in it and developed in Almain's other writings have been extensively studied and analysed.[56] All that is necessary here is to draw attention to points lying near the heart of the ecclesiological debate.

In doing so, however, it is proper to emphasize that Almain's thought brings out with particular clarity the extent to which that debate had become a matter of political theory as well as of theology and scriptural exegesis. At the very beginning of the *Libellus*, he takes up, not the immediate issue of authority in the Church, but the question of the relationship between a community and its individual members. His concern here, as elsewhere in his work, is with the various kinds of *dominium*.[57] There is, for Almain, a natural, divinely constituted order, in terms of which the individual has an inalienable right to preserve and defend himself and what is his. However, an equally natural right, also divinely constituted, belongs to the community: this right, to promote and uphold the common good, while parallel to the rights of individuals, is not derived from them.[58] It is from the community as a whole that those who exercise political power derive their authority to do so; and they may be legitimately deprived of it if they abuse their power.[59]

This general theory of society and government applies as much to monarchy, to kingship, as to any other constitutional system. It

---

[56] See F. Oakley, 'Almain and Major: Conciliar Theory on the Eve of the Reformation', *American Historical Review*, 70 (1964–5), 673–90; id., 'Conciliarism in the Sixteenth Century: Jacques Almain again', *Archiv für Reformationsgeschichte*, 68 (1977), 111–32; Q. R. D. Skinner, *The Foundations of Modern Political Thought*, ii. *The Age of Reformation* (2 vols., Cambridge, 1978), 43, 119–20 (and cf. J. H. Burns, '*Jus gladii* and *jurisdictio*: Jacques Almain and John Locke', *Historical Journal*, 26 (1983), 369–74); Burns and Goldie (eds.), *Cambridge History of Political Thought 1450–1700*, 147–51.

[57] References here are to the original (Paris, 1512) edn. of the *Libellus de Auctoritate Ecclesie . . . editus a magistro Iacobo Almain . . . contra Thomam de Vio . . .* The text was included in Almain's *Aurea . . . opuscula* (Paris, 1518) and in later edns., the bibliography of which is complex. It was also included in the edns. of Gerson's *Opera* published in Paris in 1606 and (the most generally accessible text) 1706. There are useful extracts from the *Libellus* and from Almain's other writings in Carlyle, *Medieval Political Theroy*, vi. 241–6, citing the 1606 Gerson edn. (where the titles do not correspond to those in the original edns.). For the individual/community relationship, see *Libellus*, chap. 1, sig. Ai^r–aii^r.

[58] See on this esp. Almain's *Questio in vesperiis habita*, in *Aurea opuscula*, fos. 62 f.; and cf. the discussion in Burns, '*Jus gladii* and *jurisdictio*'.

[59] *Libellus*, chap. 1, sig. Ai^r.

is here that Almain comes to grips with Cajetan's argument. In his view, to attribute ultimate sovereign power to the community as a whole, to assert a corporate right (exercised, as it must be in practice, through representatives) to call to account and if need be to depose a ruler guilty of misgovernment, are positions wholly compatible with monarchical, with royal government. Indeed, he would argue (as John Mair, his teacher, was also to do) that the virtue of kingship, the claim that *politia regalis* is the best of polities, is actually inseparable from the recognition of the community's ultimate right to self-protection against misrule. To be rooted in the community in such a way as to preserve the community's last-resort superiority to the king is a defining characteristic of kingship properly understood.[60]

All this, according to Almain, is applicable to the monarchy established by Christ in the Church. There too, the community, represented by the council, has the ultimate power of deposing a pope who has abused his power so as to imperil the well-being—in this case the eternal salvation—of his subjects. There was, however, a problem in this simple interchange of arguments between the civil and the ecclesiastical context. In the former case the *libera communitas* could exercise its freedom by varying the constitutional order under which political authority was exercised. This, manifestly, was not the case in the Church, where the monarchical system established by Christ himself was not subject to alteration by any merely human authority, however exalted.[61] This unavoidable admission was eagerly seized upon by Cajetan when he resumed the controversy in his *Apologia . . . De Comparata Auctoritate Papae et Concilii*, completed in late November 1512.[62]

Cajetan, for his part, concedes that a *libera communitas* does indeed have all the powers that Almain and others ascribed to it, including the power to change the location of political power. He goes further. He says that it may well be the case that, in the temporal order, political authority *always* derives in some sense (under God, of course, as was acknowledged on both sides of the debate) from the community. What he resolutely denies is that this is true of the Church. There, unquestionably, we are confronted by

---

[60] Ibid. sigs. Ai^v–Aii^r.
[61] Ibid. chap. 7, sigs. Biv^r–Ci^v; chap. 8, sigs. Civ^r–Di^r; chap. 12, sigs. Ei^v–Eiv^r.
[62] References here are to the critical edn. in *Scripta Theologica* (above, n. 50).

a form of government directly and unalterably ordained by God in the person of Christ.[63]

Cajetan also takes up once again his earlier insistence that there can be no compromise as to the essential character of a political system. The determining factor, he argues, is the location of the *summum regimen*, or as he also significantly calls it, 'the supreme tribunal' (*summum tribunal*). If issues are to be finally resolved by the people (or by whatever body is held to represent the community as a whole), then the system is, quite simply, democratic or 'popular'. This fundamental point is not affected or modified in any way by the various arrangements that may be made for what Cajetan calls the *regimen medium*, by which is meant the ordinary process of government.[64] This clearly echoes the distinction made in Cajetan's earlier tract between 'executive' and 'preceptive' power, though it is important to note that the echo or parallel is not exact. Even the Petrine or papal *potestas praeceptiva*, after all, does not extend to what we might term 'constituent' authority, such as belongs, in a *libera communitas*, to the people, and, in the Church, to Christ alone.

What seems to emerge, then, is a contrast between a conciliarist view in which there is a marked and perhaps increasing tendency to push the parallel between civil and ecclesiastical authority as far as possible, and a papalist view which rejects that parallel completely in favour of what we might call a rigorous and exclusive 'divine right' view of the papal monarchy. In Cajetan's case the latter view is presented with notable sophistication and with implications of considerable historical importance. He was not prepared to rest content with the alternative parallelism which had satisfied earlier papalists. In that view, what was claimed for the pope was, *mutatis mutandis*, also claimed for others who were kings in the true sense, and not merely supreme magistrates under some kind of non-royal sovereign power. Cajetan's willingness to grant, in principle, the 'communitarian' basis of all temporal authority, however royal or kingly it might be, was carefully calculated in ideological terms. Its effect was to establish the unique character and status of the papal monarchy, which belonged to a supernatural order utterly different

---

[63] *Apologia*, chap. 1 (Pollet edn. 204–5).
[64] Ibid. chap. [8] (Pollet edn. 236–7). The enumeration of chapters in the early edns. is defective and has been corrected and supplied by Pollet.

from that natural order in which temporal authority operated.[65] What this foreshadowed was a renewal of the papal claim to supremacy over temporal rulers, although it was now to be represented as an 'indirect power'. The revived and revised Thomism of the later sixteenth and early seventeenth centuries took its cue, in this context, from Cajetan's suggestion that temporal authority, subject to temporal sanctions because it was based ultimately on community consent, and operating in a purely natural order, must acknowledge its subordination to the supreme and supernatural power of the pope as the vicar of Christ. Absolute monarchs in the early modern period would find it hard to see as an ally the monarch who claimed, as it were, to be more absolute still.

The immediate controversy died away with the collapse of the council of Pisa–Milan and the negotiation of the 1516 Concordat. Yet despite this, and despite Francis I's decree against continuing the debate, when John Mair wrote his commentary on St Matthew's gospel (published in 1518), he decided to take up at length, as he had not done in his voluminous earlier writings, the issue of conciliar and papal power. There is no doubt that he did so with Cajetan's polemic very much in mind.[66] Some elements in Mair's theory will be considered towards the end of the next chapter; but there is at least one point worth emphasizing here because it brings out something not especially evident in the statement of the conciliarist case by Almain. Indeed, even in Mair's case it is necessary to look beyond the 1518 commentary where his conciliarism is most fully expressed if we are to appreciate properly the view he takes of monarchy—the *politia regalis et optima* of which he finds instances in his native Scotland, in France, and above all in the Church. What becomes clear in this broader perspective is that kingship for Mair is far from being a narrowly restricted or inhibited form of political power. The king he has in mind does indeed depend for this authority upon the consent of the community; and that consent may be withdrawn if he abuses that authority.

[65] Cf. e.g. ibid. chap. [9] (Pollet edn. 245–6).
[66] At the very outset of his discussion (*In Mattheum*, fo. 68ᵛ) Mair remarks that the Thomists generally took the papalist view and that in Rome no one (it was said) was allowed to give public support to the conciliarist position. There are several later hostile references to the Thomist attitude to ecclesiastical authority: cf. fos. 69ᵛ, 72ʳ.

Again, his *dominium* never extends to such absolute control over the realm as a private individual enjoys over his possessions.[67] Yet while he remains king he rules with real power and far-reaching competence. In particular, it is the king who, in Mair's view, has the legislative power, saving only the right of the community through its representatives (the three estates of the realm, the council in the Church) to lay down fundamental norms regulating such matters as the succession and the conservation of the public domain.[68] On this score and on other counts too, Mair was consistently of the opinion that monarchy was clearly superior to all other constitutions. And the monarchy he had in mind was a system in which, while the king was of course obliged to take counsel, the decision as to what was to be done was his alone.[69] It may be recalled that Mair went out of his way to dissociate himself from the view that a mixed constitution afforded the ideal model for the government of the Church.[70] There could be no clearer reminder of the fact that conciliarism remained, for the most part at least, a theory of monarchy. And that is not the least important point to be made about the significance of conciliarist thought for the history of political ideas.

The evidence surveyed in this chapter perhaps indicates a notable shift in the theory and ideology of monarchy between the middle decades of the fifteenth century and the first quarter of the sixteenth. In the earlier period, papalism and what we may perhaps

---

[67] *In Mattheum*, chap. 16, fo. 63ᵛ '[rex] non habet ita pingue ius in regno suo sicut ego in caputio meo'; and cf. *In quartum sententiarum* (Paris, 1516), fo. 76ʳ: 'rex non habet ita liberum dominium in regno sicut ego in biblia mea.'

[68] For the king's legislative power, cf. e.g. *In secundum sententiarum* (Paris, 1510), fo. 100ʳ: '[rex] auctoritatiue condit leges positiuas in quibus dispensat'. The power of the representative body to impose laws on the ruler is most fully dealt with in Mair's *Historia Majoris Britanniae*; but the essential point is succinctly made in the *In Mattheum*, chap. 18, fo. 70ᵛ: 'sicut populus virtualiter est super regem, & in casu, ut in rebus arduis in quibus conuocantur tres status regni, qui regem in casibus ancipitibus habent dirigere; sic in casibus arduis concilium vniuersale rite congregatum habet legem obligatoriam pontifici imponere'.

[69] *Quartus sententiarum* (Paris, 1509), fo. 87ʳ: 'prestat habere unum supremum monarchamn in regno a cuius nutu omnia diriguntur dummodo is utatur consilio sapientum et postea eis consentientibus vel dissentientibus concludat a parte que sibi placet.' Mair's preference for monarchy, and specifically for hereditary monarchy, is expressed again at the very end of his active career: cf. *Ethica Aristotelis cum commentariis* . . . (Paris, 1530), VII. x, fos. 134ᵛ–135ʳ.

[70] *In Mattheum*, fo. 71ʳ: 'aliqui dicunt policiam ecclesiasticam esse mixtam; sed non sic dico.'

call royalism (looking towards royal absolutism) had been able, at least to a considerable extent, to make common cause against forces and doctrines that seemed to threaten the monarchical principle. Thus Antonio de' Roselli could sustain a dualism in which pope and emperor alike disposed of absolute power within their respective areas of competence. A staunch papalist like Rodrigo Sánchez de Arévalo had no difficulty in upholding at the same time the absolute claims of his temporal sovereign in Castile. In the generation of Cajetan, Almain, and Mair, a somewhat different picture seems to emerge. The conciliarism which, in the days of the council of Basle, might have seemed to be associated with radical (even, in a loose sense, 'democratic') ideas had moved (though perhaps 'reverted' would be a more appropriate verb) to an alliance with royal power against papal pretensions. Certainly the papalist strategy adopted by Cajetan, claiming for the papacy a kind of 'divine right' to be enjoyed by no other ruler, might seem to imply a 'triumphalism' unlikely to find much favour in the eyes of temporal monarchs. That suggests part—perhaps a rather ironic part—of the background to the final chapter in this investigation.

7

THE TRIUMPH OF MONARCHY?

IT may be that the only secure element in the title of this chapter is the mark of interrogation at the end. The notion of a 'triumph of monarchy' achieved by the early sixteenth century, whether in ideological or in institutional terms, may well seem puzzling and problematic. 'Triumph over what?' would be one obvious question. It may seem clear, even obvious, that no viable alternative to monarchy was available in late medieval and early modern Europe. And the position of monarchy might appear to be equally unchallenged—and therefore in no need of any 'triumph'—in the realm of theory. There were, it is true, republican ideas that commanded a good deal of intellectual attention—more and more attention, indeed, as humanism took a firmer and firmer hold on the minds of educated men. The familiar point can be illustrated from what may be a less familiar source, in Thomas More's epigram *Quis optimus reipublicae status?* The title, of course, recalls that of More's *Utopia*; and his answer to his own question is decidedly in favour of the 'republican' alternative—in favour of government by a number of men rather than by a single ruler—

inque bonis multis plus reor esse boni.[1]

A case might even be made for claiming that, in the sphere of ideas, it was republicanism that triumphed, not monarchy. That case becomes progessively stronger, no doubt, if one looks forward from the sixteenth to the seventeenth and indeed the eighteenth century. Much recent scholarship has emphasized and elucidated the historical importance for the political culture of the Atlantic world of the classical republicanism that stems from the Renaissance.[2]

Yet the harvest from the seed sown by the humanists was long in

---

[1] *Thomae Mori . . . Lucubrationes . . .* (Basle, 1563), 242.
[2] See esp. Pocock, *The Machiavellian Moment*.

its ripening and late in its gathering. Nearly two centuries after the period in which the present enquiry draws to a close, monarchical systems preponderated even more than they had done in the fifteenth century. Of the experiments in extending republican institutions and principles from their origins in the city-states to the territorial states of early modern Europe, the one in mid-seventeenth-century England had been short-lived, while the United Provinces in the Netherlands constituted at best an ambiguous and peculiar testimony to the vitality of the republican idea. As the seventeenth century gave way to the eighteenth, it would surely be safe to claim that the royalist doctrines of a Bossuet commanded more support and were of greater practical significance than the republican visions of a Harrington or a Milton.

This is not of course to say that, within the period under scrutiny here, the monarchical principle was unquestioned and entirely unchallenged. It has been pointed out above that monarchist ideology in the 1430s and 1440s was based on the hypothesis that there was indeed a subversive threat which monarchs must unite to repel. Two decades or so later, it seems that Pope Paul II saw sufficient menace in the republican ideas of Pomponius Laetus to warrant the humanist's detention in Castel Sant' Angelo (with, as it happens, Rodrigo Sánchez de Arévalo as his gaoler).[3] One may allow oneself some scepticism as to how much genuine uneasiness the pope experienced in this instance; but the episode is, in its odd way, some indication of the fact that republican ideas could be regarded as having more than academic interest in the middle decades of the fifteenth century. And of course republican government itself was no mere Roman myth or scholar's daydream. It was very much in being, with the city-republics of northern Italy still embodying it in no inconsiderable majesty and prosperity. Nor could anyone schooled in Aristotelian political analysis question the validity of such regimes; no one conscious of the contemporary facts could deny them a degree of viability. How viable, how stable, how durable they might be was another matter. John Mair was, for a scholastic theologian, no mean observer of the facts of political life—'kings', he once said, 'keep peace treaties when it suits them.'[4] Contemplating Florence and Venice from his Parisian lecture-room

---

[3] See on this episode Trame, *Sánchez de Arévalo*, 172–82.
[4] *Historia Majoris Britanniae*, fo. 45^r: 'Reges pacem servant quando volunt.'

in 1509 or thereabouts, Mair remarked that *communitates*—republican regimes—'have rarely lasted long'.[5] Developments in Florence at least within his own long lifetime (from the late 1460s to the midpoint of the sixteenth century) might well have led him to claim a degree of prophetic insight in that judgement. Whatever the grand duchy of Tuscany may have been, it was not what Mair meant by a *communitas*, nor what we mean by a republic.

There was indeed, in this period, no real possibility that the states—at all events the major states—of Christendom would, in any foreseeable future, develop any form of government that was not in some substantive sense monarchical. This does not, however, mean that what I have called 'the triumph of monarchy' was the kind of triumph that is achieved by pushing at an open door or advancing to the next round in a contest because an opponent has failed to appear or field a team. Two ways at least can be suggested in which the notion of a 'triumph of monarchy' can be sustained. One of these belongs primarily to the history of institutions or to political history; and this will receive only brief consideration here. The other, appertaining more directly to the history of ideas, calls for fuller discussion.

Where institutions are concerned, one might perhaps put a 'counterfactual' question: what would have happened to political life in Western Europe if monarchy had failed to 'triumph', in the sense here envisaged, over the threats it faced during the fifteenth and early sixteenth centuries? These threats did not, to reiterate, manifest themselves as revolutionary alternatives to monarchical government as such. Though sometimes represented by those who opposed them as 'democratic', they were not republican. And if they were often, in a reasonably meaningful sense, oligarchic (or, more favourably construed, aristocratic), this does not mean that they looked to constitutions of those Aristotelian types as replacements for the established monarchies. What movements of the kind in question might have entailed had *they* triumphed over the monarchies they challenged, may be tentatively illustrated from two instances which, in respect of ideas or doctrines, have been considered above.

In the Spanish kingdoms the outcome of such a development would presumably have been the preservation and intensification

---

[5] *Quartus sententiarum*, fo. 87ʳ.

of deep-rooted movements favouring corporate privilege, particularism, and the fragmentation of authority. As it was, for all the achievements of Ferdinand and Isabella from 1474 onwards, it would be misleading to think of those achievements as involving 'the end of medieval Spain' and the establishment of a 'modern state' free of all trace of such immemorial obstacles to royal absolutism.[6] Yet if we accept the view that the reign of the Catholic Monarchs saw firmly established 'the hegemony of Castile'—of a realm, that is to say, where the principles and practices of absolute monarchy had already made significant advances, the notion of a triumph of monarchy may well appear to have considerable substance.[7]

The second illustrative instance is the papal monarchy. Here indeed the Conciliar Movement had failed decisively to bring about the changes in the constitutional structure of the Church which some at least of its supporters had hoped for. That, however, did not rule out less radical possibilities which might have qualified substantially the papalist victory of the mid-fifteenth century. One such possibility would have been to enhance and to entrench the authority of the college of cardinals. There had always been a 'cardinalist' element of this kind within conciliarism; and a movement in that direction was still very much alive in the 1460s. It may indeed well have been a more serious source of anxiety to the popes of that period than the academic republicanism of the humanists.[8] It was, for that matter, still a movement to be taken with some seriousness half a century later, at the time of the councils of Pisa–Milan and Lateran V.[9] Against such stubbornly persistent tendencies, the papacy of the Counter-Reformation surely embod-

---

[6] See on this theme Hillgarth, *Spanish Kingdoms*, ii. 604–28.

[7] Hillgarth, *Spanish Kingdoms*, uses the phrase 'Castilian hegemony' as the subtitle of his second volume, though he points out (pp. 626–7) that the hegemony established between 1250 and 1516 was challenged and eroded by later developments—a process from which it 'was not to recover'. On the 15th cent. establishment of absolutism, cf. MacKay, *Spain in the Middle Ages*, 141: 'The Catholic kings, Ferdinand and Isabella, who have so often been credited with founding the early modern state in Spain, were to receive the power of absolutism intact. They did not have to struggle to gain an acceptance of the theory since these powers were not in dispute. The key political problem consisted in determining who was to enjoy the benefits of wielding the royal powers.'

[8] See on this Thomson, *Popes and Princes*, ch. 3, 37–77.

[9] Cf. Ullman, 'Julius II and the Schismatic Cardinals'; Becker, *Die Appellation vom Papst*, 203–43.

ied a considerable triumph, as did the Spanish monarchy of the
Golden Age, over the forces that might have hindered the consolidation of royal absolutism.

Consolidation seems indeed to be the appropriate word for the
developments which, in the area of practical politics, might be
regarded as constituting 'the triumph of monarchy'. That triumph
was above all a matter of ensuring that the diverse bodies and
authorities within the realm answered to its head in the knowledge
that the headship was secure and, if not beyond challenge, at least
unlikely to be challenged with lasting success. In such processes of
consolidation, ideas and doctrines had their part to play alongside
institutional development and political manœuvre. To that 'ideological' aspect of the matter the remainder of this chapter will be
addressed.

The problem here is, obviously, to elucidate the notion of a
'triumph of monarchy' in the realm of ideas. A first step in that
direction may be taken by suggesting that, if there was no significant or sustained confrontation, in this period, between monarchism
and republicanism as such, it is none the less true that the term
respublica is crucially important in this context. This is a point
which can perhaps be clarified by moving, not for the first time,
outside the specific period under investigation here. Whereas,
however, in the discussion of *dominium* it was necessary to look at
evidence from before 1400, the present case is one where we can
usefully move forward—though not very far forward—from 1525.

In June 1564 the problems of Christian obedience and political
authority were debated at some length in the general assembly of
the Scottish Church. Towards the end of that debate, an opinion
was sought from John Craig, who was then John Knox's colleague
in the ministry of the High Kirk of Edinburgh. Craig was a former
Dominican, having indeed been prior of the Order of Preachers in
Bologna. There, ten years previously, he had 'heard reasoned,
determined, and concluded' the principle he now wished to uphold. The proposition stated was that because 'the band betuix the
Prince and the people is reciprocal', princes who violate their oath
may be 'reformed or deposed by those by whom they are elected'.
To this it was objected by one whom Knox (who reported the
debate in his *History of the Reformation*) contemptuously called 'a
claw-back [back-scratcher, toady] of that corrupt Court' that
Craig's point was irrelevant, because 'we [in Scotland] are a

kingdom, and they [in Bologna] are but a commonwealth'. It is Craig's rejoinder to this objection that is important here: 'my judgment is, that every kingdom is, or at least should be a commonwealth, albeit that every commonwealth is not a kingdom.'[10] Now there was, of course, nothing novel or unusual in associating *respublica* with *regnum*. Indeed, to use the term 'republican' as it has been used here would be wholly misleading and anachronistic if it were to conceal the ordinary medieval assumption that a kingdom exists, and ought to function, for the common good, for the common weal, for the *respublica*. The two terms are closely associated by Jean de Terrevermeille, to cite only one instance; and the association could be traced far back into the earlier history of medieval political discourse. Nor, again, was there anything out of the way in the 'contractual' thesis Craig had heard debated in Bologna and repeated in the Edinburgh assembly. That is not to say that the thesis was uncontroversial: we have indeed seen how vigorously it was contexted in the political literature of fifteenth-century monarchism. Yet the context in which the argument was used in 1564 has perhaps its own distinctive character. The heckler in the assembly—'claw-back' or not—was assuming that there was a political system or regime to which the term *respublica* or 'commonwealth' applied in a particular way, *par excellence*; and such a regime embodied principles that did *not* apply to a kingdom or *regnum*. Craig, however, insisted that all legitimate polities are, fundamentally, commonwealths or *respublicae*, even though some—most indeed in his day—were ruled as kingdoms. All, that is to say, should be governed by principles shared in common with what we would call republics. This may, from one point of view, strike one as an interesting anticipation of something Rousseau was to say two centuries later.[11] More interesting historically, however, may be the point that Craig's position stands on common ground with an argument we have encountered

---

[10] *John Knox's History of the Reformation in Scotland*, ed. W. C. Dickinson (2 vols.; London, 1949), ii. 133; and cf. Knox, *Works*, ed. D. Laing (6 vols.; Edinburgh, 1846–64), ii. 458.

[11] *Du contrat social*, II. vi: in *The Political Writings of Jean Jacques Rousseau*, ed. C. E. Vaughan (2 vols.; Cambridge, 1915; repr. Oxford, 1962), ii. 50: 'Tout Gouvernement légitime est républicain.' Rousseau adds in a footnote: 'Pour être légitime, il ne faut pas que le Gouvernement se confonde avec le souverain, mais qu'il en soit le ministre: alors la Monarchie elle même est République.' Obviously the 'anticipation' suggested above must not be pressed too far.

in a more celebrated member of his former religious order: Cajetan, after all, had been prepared to acknowledge that in all temporal polities the authority of rulers was derived from the consent of the community.[12]

The themes here, the underlying issues in the view Craig presented to the 1564 assembly are familiar. The notion of a mutual agreement or pact between ruler and people, under which, *inter alia*, the law should be upheld and no new law made without the subjects' consent—themes like these have occurred here in various contexts and in different forms. They make part, for example, of Fortescue's *dominium politicum et regale*; and they figure in various expressions and elaborations of the conciliarist view of the polity of the Church. By the time Craig took up this kind of argument, the same points could have been illustrated from, for instance, the interpretation of English government advanced by John Ponet in 1556.[13] In Spain, to the extent that vestiges of Aragonese and Catalan *pactismo* survived, in France on at least some current views of the constitutional structure of the realm, it might still be possible to see the kingdom as, in a measure at least, a commonwealth in Craig's sense.[14] And it may not be too extravagant to suggest that there was in this view a certain latent or implicit 'republicanism'. It was all still a very long way indeed from the kind of constitutional monarchy H. G. Wells was to call 'a crowned republic'. Yet already in the sixteenth century the argument implied by Craig's 'clawback' adversary was to be given serious expression. One of the arguments used against George Buchanan's *De jure regni apud Scotos*—written only two or three years after the 1564 debate—was precisely that he reduced the royal office to something comparable, at best, with the chief magistracy in such regimes as that of Venice.[15]

---

[12] Cf. Chap. 6, text at n. 63.

[13] For Ponet's *Shorte Treatise of Politike Power*, see the facsimile repr. in W. S. Hudson, *John Ponet (1516?–1556): Advocate of Limited Monarchy* (Chicago, 1842); and cf. esp. sig. [Dvii]r: 'men ought to haue more respecte to their countrey. than to their prince: to the common wealthe, than to any onepersone/ For the countrey and common wealthe is a degree aboue the king.'

[14] See Hillgarth, *Spanish Kingdoms*, ii. 515–16, 627; and cf. for ideological trends in the 16th cent., Giesey, *If Not, Not*.

[15] Cf. e.g. Adam Blackwood, *Adversus Georgii Buchanani Dialogum ... pro Regibus Apologia* (Poitiers, 1581), 54: 'aristocratica Venetorum respublica, cuius princeps non regis sed ducis nomine, viuit iis fere legibus, quibus caeteri ciues: neque statuere quidquam potest, nisi vel sex minimum, vel decem viris in consilium adhibitis'.

The 'triumph of monarchy' consisted, it may now be suggested, in the extent to which that 'anti-monarchomach' view prevailed, and did so by developing the 'absolutist' themes we have found in the political discourse of the fifteenth and early sixteenth centuries.

Attention has already been drawn to a certain parallelism between the position taken by John Craig and one element in the political doctrine of Cajetan. That doctrine had been developed in defence of the papal monarchy against the conciliarist challenge; and it is of some interest to note that the Bologna debate to which Craig referred had involved the authority of the pope, or at least of those who claimed to act on the pope's behalf. The matters at issue, however, arose from the pope's position as temporal ruler in the States of the Church, not as the spiritual ruler of Christendom.[16] In the latter capacity, Cajetan had maintained, the monarchical authority of the pope was unique. The only monarchy with which it could even be compared was the kingship directly instituted by God over the people of Israel. In all other monarchies, Cajetan had been ready to grant, there must always be an ultimate sovereignty vested in the community, from which all ordinary political jurisdiction was derived.

Arguments of this latter kind might be deployed by conciliarists, or by advocates of the right of subjects to resist their rulers; they might be manipulated by papalists, or—in the later context James VI and I knew so well—by papists. And it was against such arguments that what James called 'the true law of free monarchy' had to be asserted. The foundations of that assertion had, it is suggested, been firmly laid in the period we have been exploring.

The king—or the emperor (and after all every king was increasingly seen as 'emperor in his own kingdom')— was God's vicar. It is tempting to elaborate that point by adopting Anglican terminol-

---

[16] Cf. the report of Craig's speech in Knox, *History of the Reformation*, ii. 132. 'The occasion of this disputation and conclusion, was a certain disorder and tyranny that was attempted by the Pope's governors, who began to make innovations in the country against the laws that were before established, alleging themselves not to be subject to such laws, by reason that they were not instituted by the people, but by the Pope, who was King of that country.' The 'conclusion' maintained by Vincentius de Placentia, OP, was as follows: 'Principes omnes, tam supremi, quam inferiores, possunt et debent reformari, vel deponi per eos, per quos eliguntur, confirmantur, vel admittuntur ad officium, quoties a fide praestita subditis per juramentum deficiunt: Quoniam relatio juramenti subditorum et principum mutua est, et utriusque aequo jure servanda et reformanda, juxta legem et conditionem juramenti ab utraque parte fact' (ibid.; and cf. Knox, *Works*, ii. 458).

ogy: the king was indeed no mere curate, taking services on behalf of *the* vicar, the pope. The king himself—always, of course, within his temporal sphere—had, so to speak, parson's freehold, of which no power on earth could deprive him. He held his authority—an authority entrusted to him by God—for the good of his people, it is true: there was a sense in which his essential function was to serve them. The pope, after all—who, on this view of the matter, held a precisely similar monarchical power in the spiritual realm— was 'the servant of the servants of God'. The ministry exercised by the king or the pope, however, was emphatically a ministry of ruling. Kings, emperors, popes were all indeed *ministri Dei*; but they were, by the same token, *rectores*, rulers. That terminology, reaching back at least as far as Gregory the Great in the sixth century, points to a complex set of terms in which the verb *regere* and the noun *regnum* are perhaps the most important.[17]

Within that terminological complex we also find the adjective *rectus* and its derivatives, reminding us that kingship, lordship, and empire have to do with what is right and fitting. The ruler is to direct, to guide; and government in this sense (*gubernatio*, the handling of the tiller or helm, the *gubernaculum*) is absolutely necessary for human well-being. This would always have been true, even if the consequences of sin had not brought the element of coercive control into the matter. Here and elsewhere the ruler represents—presents the image of—the God who 'leads men in the paths of righteousness'. It is worth recalling that the psalm in which these words occur, which we know as 'The Lord is my shepherd', begins, in the Latin Vulgate text, with the words *Dominus regit me*. To be *pastor*, the shepherd of his people, the king must also be *rector* and *dominus*.

The paths of righteousness are the paths of justice; and it is of course the king's business to do justice and to uphold equity. This latter responsibility authorizes and indeed requires him to sub- ordinate the letter of the law to its spirit and purpose. It is, however, the spirit and purpose of the *law* that are to guide even the most flexible equitable procedures. Law is inseparable from

---

[17] On Gregory the Great, see R. A. Markus, 'The Latin Fathers', in Burns (ed.), *Cambridge History of Medieval Political Thought*, 116–22; and cf. Carlyle, *Medieval Political Theory*, esp. i. 152–60. The Carlyles regarded Gregory as having made the first full statement of the 'theory of Divine Right' and as being the main source for that view in later medieval thinking: cf. i. 218–19; iii. 116.

kingship, and law is a meaningless concept if we separate it from justice. It thus becomes crucially important to determine the source of law, the location of legislative authority. Among the authors discussed in earlier chapters it is perhaps Fortescue who manifests the clearest awareness of this point, basing his differentiation of different regimes precisely on this criterion. What is in some ways more striking, however, is the readiness of thinkers in this period, even if they differ on other elements in the concept of monarchy, to accept—almost to take for granted—the king's position as lawgiver. John Mair provides a notable illustration of this. As we have seen, while he insists that, both in the Church and in the temporal realm, it is for the representative assembly to prescribe rules governing such matters as the succession and the public domain, he is equally clear that in other respects legislative power is best placed in the hands of the monarch. The rule of a good man, the *bonus legislator*, is preferable to the impersonal rule of law because it brings to bear on the common affairs and interests of the community a special kind of skill or wisdom. This *prudentia legis civilis* is more likely to be found in one man than in any group. These views appear to have been held consistently through the period of more than twenty years during which Mair developed his ideas.[18]

The ruler Mair has in mind, the king who 'lays down the laws authoritatively and dispenses from them', would seem, then, to be *legibus solutus*; and this suggests the conclusion that his power is absolute. To state such a conclusion naturally prompts the question whether 'the triumph of monarchy' means in effect the triumph of absolutism. In one sense that question must be answered in the affirmative. What we know as 'absolute monarchy' certainly became the prevailing political system in Europe from the sixteenth century to the end of the eighteenth; and the predominant ideology in that long period was inevitably an ideology of absolutism. Yet the fact that what may well seem to be essential principles of monarchical absolutism have just been illustrated here from the works of a writer generally regarded as an important proponent of the opposite, 'constitutionalist' conception of monarchy (and sometimes, more debatably, as a radical advocate of limited

---

[18] Cf. Chap. 6, n. 69.

monarchy[19]) hints at a paradox. That paradox in turn may serve to alert us to problematic elements in the notion of absolutism itself.[20]

David Hume, in his *History of Great Britain*, remarks, apropos of the reign of James I, 'I have not met with any English writer of that age, who speaks of England as a limited monarchy, but as an absolute one.' He cites in this connection Sir Walter Raleigh's distinction between monarchies that are 'entire' and those that are 'limited or restrained', and his insistence that 'the English kingdom' belongs to the former category: the reason is that 'the prince hath the power to make laws, league and war; to create magistracies; to pardon life; of appeal, &c.'[21] Jean Bodin, again, had found no difficulty in including England (along with Scotland, France, Spain, and a formidable list of other realms) among countries where the prince was 'an absolute sovereign', where 'the kings themselves have the sovereignty without all doubt or question'.[22] Yet Bodin had distinguished the absolutism (which is, of course, our word, not his) of 'royal monarchy' as he understood it from despotic or seigneurial rule as well as from mere and sheer tyranny. Raleigh for his part drew a firm line between the absolute monarchy he saw in England and, on the other hand, the regime Philip II sought to impose on the Netherlands, intending 'Turk-like to tread under his feet all their natural and fundamental laws, privileges, and ancient rights'.[23]

[19] This is the view, particularly, of Quentin Skinner, who repeatedly uses the term 'radical' in regard to the political and ecclesiological views of Mair (together with Almain and others in the same Parisian tradition): cf. e.g. *Foundations of Modern Political Thought*, ii. 323, 340, 342.

[20] See on these J. H. Burns, *Absolutism: The History of an Idea* (The Creighton Trust Lecture 1986; London, 1987); id., 'The Idea of Absolutism', in J. Miller (ed.), *Absolutism in Seventeenth-Century Europe* (London, 1990), 21–42; J. P. Sommerville, 'Absolutism and Royalism', in Burns and Goldie (eds.), *Cambridge History of Political Thought 1450–1700*, 347–73.

[21] Cf. Hume, *The History of Great Britain: The Reigns of James I and Charles I*, ed. D. Forbes (Harmondsworth, 1970), 80 n. 1; 222 n. 4.

[22] Cf. Bodin, *Les Six Livres de la République* (1576), II v; *Six Books of the Commonwealth*, trans. and ed. M. J. Tooley (Oxford, n.d. [1955]) 67; *The Six Bookes of a Commonweale*, trans. Richard Knolles and ed. K. D. McRae (Cambridge, Mass., 1962), 222. The list of absolute monarchies in the original French text—'France, Spain, England, Scotland, Ethiopia, Turkey, Persia, and Muscovy'— was later expanded: in Richard Knolles's English version of 1606, based on a conflation of the French text with the Latin *De republica libri sex* first published in 1586, it includes France, Spain, England, Scotland, Turkey, Muscovy, Tartary, Persia, Ethiopia, India, 'and. almost all the kingdomes of Affricke, and Asia'.

[23] For Bodin's account of the different types of monarchy, see *République*, II. ii–v. Raleigh's distinction between English and Spanish kingship is cited by Hume, *History of Great Britain*, 80 n. 1.

What this seems to suggest is that, in the late sixteenth and the early seventeenth century, there was, firmly established (and to that extent at least 'triumphant'), a concept of absolute monarchy which was not only compatible with but in fact inseparable from a framework of fundamental laws. The last word has been put in the plural because it seems clear that the framework for absolute monarchy in this understanding of it is constituted by different kinds of fundamental law. One of these was, of course, the law of God. John Knox, in the remarkable sermon he preached in Edinburgh on 19 August 1565, insisted that, just because 'the royal throne of kings' was established by 'the onely and perfect ordinance of God, who willeth his power, terror, and Majestie in a parte, to shine in the thrones of Kings', those kings 'have not an absolute power in their regiment, what pleaseth them, but their power is limitted by God's word'.[24] None of the advocates of what they would still have called absolute monarchy would have disagreed, however much they might have sympathized with Mary Queen of Scots in her rejection of Knox's interpretation of 'God's word'.[25]

Nor would any of the varied interpreters of the monarchical principle whom we have encountered in these pages have hesitated in asserting or accepting the proposition that royal power was limited by the moral principles of the law of nature. To claim, for instance, as Rodrigo Sánchez de Arévalo did, that hereditary kings ruled 'by natural right' was to presuppose the validity of the natural law which vindicated that right. Different positions, whether philosophical or theological, could be and were taken as to the precise basis of that law and its relationship to divine law; but both its reality and its efficacy were universally acknowledged.

There is, however, a third element in the framework referred to above; and this third element is problematic in a sense that does not apply to the laws of God and of nature (problematic as they no doubt were in their own fashion and as they certainly are for many people today). It is in this third context that the specific term 'fundamental law' is itself most commonly used. What is at issue here is a form of law that is neither God-given nor simply accessible to natural reason. It is neither cosmic nor transcendent: it is

---

[24] Knox, *Works*, vi. 236, 238.
[25] Knox records his discussion with Mary in *History of the Reformation*, ii. 15–17; cf. id., *Works*, ii. 279–83.

terrestrial, sublunar, human. Though it must be consonant with divine and natural law (else it would be invalid), it is essentially distinct from those categories and capable of variations to which they are not subject. A diversity of terms came to be applied to it. Sir James Whitelock, in the English Parliament of 1610, called it *jus publicum regni*.[26] The Scots controversialist Ninian Winzet, in his 1582 attack on the political ideas of George Buchanan, had used a term with a long history ahead of it—*leges politicae*.[27] John Mair among others employed a term susceptible of various meanings but plainly indicative in this context of fundamental norms of the political system or regime—the term *leges regni*.[28]

A problem arises here because the concept of law—whether the Latin word used for it be *lex* or *jus*—is applied, on the one hand, to the product of a legislative process, and, on the other hand, to the organizational principles which determine how and by whom that process—and all other political processes—shall be carried on. That ambiguity is conveniently avoided by a term we encountered at an early stage in this enquiry, in the work of Jean de Terrevermeille. The term in question is *status*, whether in its application to the Church (*status ecclesiae*) or to the realm (*status publicus regni*) or to political systems generally (*status reipublicae*). None of the theories of monarchy that have been considered here would (it seems safe to say) leave the *status* in this sense at the arbitrary disposal of the monarch. It is obviously tempting to add that the equivalent of *status* in later political discourse is 'constitution'. If we make that translation, however, it would seem to follow that all the forms of monarchy regarded as legitimate in this period are to be classified as 'constitutional'.

Now this is not, as it may at first sight appear to be, a conclusion to be dismissed out of hand by way of a firm Euclidean *which is*

---

[26] Cited by McIlwain, *Constitutionalism Ancient and Modern*, 13–14: cf. n. 16 (p. 152) for the attribution to Whitelocke.

[27] Winzet, *Velitatio in Georgium Buchananum* . . . (Ingolstadt, 1582; published, and continuously paginated, with the author's *Flagellum Sectariorum*), 273–4: 'scis . . . Regem . . . legibus bifariam inseruire debere: primum vt se suamque vitam legibus maxime diuinis moderetur, deinde vt se & subditum sibi populum secundum leges politicas gubernet'.

[28] Cf. e.g. Mair, *In secundum sententiarum* (1510), fo. 101ᵛ: 'rex non debet imponere aliquid in humeris populi ultra leges regni . . . Rex . . . deuincitur tenere leges consuetudinales regni'. In his *Historia* (1521), IV. v, fo. 58ᵛ, Mair argues that the Scottish estates should enact a *legem regni* forbidding the king to alienate any part of the domain without parliamentary consent.

absurd. It is in fact, so far as it goes, an entirely valid and meaningful conclusion, and one which says something of considerable importance about the way in which monarchy was understood in late medieval and early modern thinking on the subject. It does leave us, however, with a further question. If we cannot use the acceptance of the *status regni* as something beyond the reach of royal authority as a sufficient criterion for distinguishing 'constitutionalism' from 'absolutism', and if we are not prepared to abandon that distinction altogether in our attempts to reach a historical understanding of political ideas in this period—which would perhaps be a prematurely desperate expedient—where are we to find a better touchstone?

All that will be offered here by way of an answer to that question is a provisional hypothesis. To formulate that hypothesis it will be necessary to return to points that emerged in sources examined in earlier chapters. Sánchex de Arévalo, for example, insists at one point that the estates of the realm have no authority to alter either the *regimen regni* or the *status regni*.[29] By the first of these terms he seems to mean the location of royal power in the hands of one person rather than another. By denying the estates power in regard to the second term, he surely means to debar them from undertaking what we might call fundamental constitutional change. Half a century later, the Parisian conciliarists John Mair and Jacques Almain were equally insistent that a *libera communitas*, a free community, *did* have the power to choose between different constitutional forms.[30] They acknowledged that not all communities were free in this sense; but we saw that their adversary Cajetan was ready, for his own polemical purposes, to come close to saying that *all* temporal societies, unlike the Church with its divinely ordained constitution, had this power over their own basic organization. Such constituent authority (for that would seem to be the appropriate modern term for it) is, on this view of the matter, the most fundamental of all the powers vested in and reserved to the community: other powers—to enact laws specifically limiting royal authority, for instance, or to control rulers by the ultimate sanction of deposition—are all in the end derivations from it.

[29] Arévalo. *De origine* (1521), fo. 73ᵛ.
[30] Cf. e.g. Mair, *In Mattheum* (1518), fo. 70ᵛ: 'Populus autem liber pro raionabili causa potest policiam mutare.'

This would suggest that the concept of constitutionalism, in regard to late medieval and early modern monarchy, rests on the assertion that the *status publicus regni* is ultimately determined by the community. There may be—in some sense, indeed, there must be—a place within the constitutional system so conceived for absolute power. No one, in the end, would have disagreed with Fortescue (for instance) in his insistence that *dominium regale* (even if it is also *politicum*) necessarily includes an element of *potestas absoluta*. To acknowledge this, however, did not entail an acceptance of 'absolute monarchy' as that system came to be so widely recognized by the end of the sixteenth century. Essential to that form of absolute monarchy was the notion that royal power was not absolute only in the sense of being (as all political power necessarily was in some circumstances) *legibus solutus*. It was absolute also in the sense of being—to borrow a phrase from John Donne and at the same time to recall a point made by his older contemporary Raleigh—'entire of itself'. The power of an absolute monarch, that is to say, was independent of any other power, save only that of God, 'by whom kings reign'.

In the final stage of this enquiry, an attempt will be made to explore a little further this notion of a power that is independent. For this purpose it is helpful to turn yet again, paradoxically perhaps, to a theory commonly regarded as belonging to the constitutionalist side of the argument. In the theory expounded by such conciliarists as Almain and Mair there is a crucial distinction (looking back to Ockham among others) between power that is exercised *regulariter* and power that comes into operation only *casualiter*—that is, in certain cases or eventualities. The latter is the power Mair and Almain regard as being lodged inalienably with the community; and to it the 'regular' power of the ruler is in the end subordinate. The power of the king or the pope, then, is ultimately dependent upon the power of the community. Of these two powers, Mair says, one—the power of the community—is, therefore, *superior et illimitatior*. He does *not* say that it is an *un*limited power; only that it is 'more unlimited' than the 'regular' power of the ruler. Nor does he say that the community's power is independent; only that the ruler's power is dependent upon it. In the Church, however—which, for thinkers like Mair and Almain, is the most important of all communities—there *is* a genuinely independent power, a power not merely superior but supreme. This power is also, in the phrase used here a moment ago, 'entire of itself': it includes both 'regular' and 'casual' authority. It is summed up by Mair in the comprehensive phrase *suprema potestas casualis et regularis independens*. Such a power, however, belongs to no human authority: it belongs only to Christ, who is not only the *legislator optimus* but, as the second person of the Trinity, is capable of doing anything that does not involve contradiction.[31]

Could such a concept of monarchy be brought, as it were, down to earth? Could any terrestrial ruler be conceived to possess a power so comprehensive in its competence, so absolute in its independence? Papalist writers, certainly—and by no means only those who wrote within the period examined here—had gone very close to claiming for the pope as Christ's vicar the kind of authority Mair reserved for Christ alone. Yet even the most extreme papal apologist had to concede that there were restraints on papal authority other than those that were imposed even on the power of God by the principle of contradiction. The pope, to take one crucial example, could not institute a sacrament as Christ had done. Papalist and conciliarist ideologies alike met at certain points the impenetrable, unshakable bedrock of the theological principles both sides necessarily acknowledged.

Such theological truths were of course as valid and as authoritative for exponents of temporal authority as they were for those concerned with ecclesiastical government. Yet their bearing on political issues in the temporal realm was naturally rather different. After all, the denial of freedom to do something one has never conceived of the possibility of doing is no very severe restraint; and no late medieval or early modern king (or pope, for that matter) was likely to fret greatly over the fact that he could not add an eighth sacrament to the existing seven. It is worth bearing in mind too the tendency for royal power in ecclesiastical matters to grow—and sometimes to be dramatically increased—as medieval Christendom gave way to the Europe of the Reformation and Counter-Reformation. Most rulers, it is true, had to stop short of the claim by Henry VIII in England to be supreme head of the Church within the realm; but few, on the other hand, were likely to experience the degree of frustration to which papal jurisdiction had sometimes subjected their medieval predecessors.

[31] Cf. ibid. fos. 70^v–71^r.

What mattered more, we may suppose, to the absolute or would-be-absolute king in the sixteenth century and later was the principle that his authority was supreme in the one sense in which, for John Mair, that adjective can properly be applied only to the community and *not* to its ruler. The striking phrase Mair uses in this context is *suprema fontalis potestas inabrogabilis;*[32] and the greatest of these terms is surely *fontalis*. To be the source, the one supreme source of all other forms of jurisdictional authority—this was what mattered above all in the developing theory of monarchy, from which the modern theory of sovereignty was emerging in this period. That divine law, natural law, and fundamental constitutional law all imposed limits more rigorous than were acceptable in the fully developed juridical theory of sovereignty as it was to be expounded by an Austin or a Dicey is both true and important. Yet none of these factors struck at the heart of the matter—the *suprema potestas fontalis*. The future—and there were of course to be several different futures—lay with the authority which commanded that power and was recognized as possessing it.

---

[32] Ibid. fo. 71ᵛ: 'in regno et in toto populo libero est suprema fontalis potestas inabrogabilis'.

BIBLIOGRAPHY

PRIMARY SOURCES

ALMAIN, JACQUES, *Libellus de auctoritate Ecclesie* . . . (Paris, 1512).
—— *Aurea . . . opuscula* . . . (Paris, 1518).
ANDLAU, PETER VON, *De Imperio Romano-Germanico libri duo*, in *Repraesentatio Reipub. Germanicae sive Tractatus varii de Sacri Romani-Germanici Imperii regimine* (Nuremberg, 1657; first published Strasburg, 1612), 1–115.
AQUINAS, ST THOMAS, *Summa Theologiae*, ed. T. Gilby *et al.* (61 vols.; Blackfriars: London, 1964–80).
ARÉVALO, RODRIGO SÁNCHEZ DE, *De origine ac differentia principatus imperialis et regalis* . . . (Rome, 1521).
—— *Suma de la política*, in M. Penna (ed.), *Prosistas castellanos del siglo XV*, i (Biblioteca de Autores Españoles; Madrid, 1959), 247–341.
BIEL, GABRIEL, *Canonis Missae Expositio*, ed. H. A. Oberman and W. J. Courtenay (5 vols.; Wiesbaden, 1963–7).
—— *Defensorium Obedientiae Apostolicae*, ed. H. A. Oberman, D. E. Zerfoss, and W. J. Courtenay (Cambridge, Mass., 1968).
BLACKWOOD, ADAM, *Adversus Georgii Buchanani Dialogum . . . pro Regibus Apologia* (Poitiers, 1581).
BODIN, JEAN, *Six Books of the Commonwealth*, trans. and ed. M. J. Tooley (Oxford, n.d. [1955]).
—— *The Six Bookes of a Commonweale*, trans. Richard Knolles, ed. K. D. McRae (Cambridge, Mass., 1962).
BURKE, EDMUND, *Reflections on the Revolution in France*, in *The Works of the Right Honourable Edmund Burke* (8 vols.; London, 1801), v. 75–488.
CAJETAN, TOMMASO DE VIO, *Auctoritas Pape & Concilii siue Ecclesie comparata* (Rome, 1511).
—— *Opuscula omnia* (3 vols.; Turin, 1582).
—— *Scripta Theologica*, i (no more published), ed. V. M. J. Pollet (Rome, 1936).
Deutsche Reichstagsakten, xv, ed. H. Herre (Gotha, 1912, 1914; repr. Göttingen, 1957).
EIXIMENIS, FRANCESC, *La Societat catalan al siglo XIV*, ed. J. Webster (Barcelona, 1967).

FITZRALPH, RICHARD, *Summa . . . in Questionibus Armeniorum* (Paris, 1512).

—— *De pauperie Salvatoris*, in *Johannis Wycliffe De Dominio Divino Libri Tres*, ed. R. L. Poole (London, 1890).

FORTESCUE, Sir JOHN, *Works*, ed. Thomas [Fortescue], Lord Clermont, and Chichester Fortescue [later Lord Carlingford] (2 vols.; London, 1869).

—— *The Governance of England*, ed. C. Plummer (Oxford, 1885).

—— *De laudibus legum Anglie*, ed. S. B. Chrimes (Cambridge, 1949; first published 1942).

GANSFORT, JOHN WESSEL, *Opera quae inveniri potuerunt omnia* (Groningen, 1614; facsimile repr. Nieuwkoop, 1966).

—— *Life and Writings*, ed. E. W. Miller and J. W. Scudder (2 vols.; New York, 1917).

GERSON, JEAN, *Œuvres complètes*, ed. P. Glorieux, iii. *L'œuvre magistrale*, (Paris, 1962); vi. *L'œuvre ecclésiologique* (Paris, 1965).

GIACOBAZZI, DOMENICO, *Tractatus de Concilio* (Rome, 1538).

GILES OF ROME, *De regimine principum* (Venice, 1502).

—— *Liber de renunciatione papae*, in J. T. de Rocaberti (ed.), *Bibliotheca Maxima Pontificia*, ii (Rome, 1698).

—— *De ecclesiastica potestate*, ed R. Scholz (Weimar, 1929; repr. Aalen, 1961).

HOBBES, THOMAS, *Leviathan*, ed. R. Tuck (Cambridge Texts in the History of Political Thought; Cambridge, 1991).

HUGH OF ST VICTOR, *De sacramentis*, in Migne, *Patrologia Latina*, clxxvi.

KNOX, JOHN, *Works*, ed. D. Laing (6 vols.; Edinburgh, 1846–64).

—— *History of the Reformation in Scotland*, ed. W. Croft Dickinson (2 vols.; London, 1949).

KRÄMER, HEINRICH, *Opusculum in errores Monarchie* (Venice, 1499).

MAIR, JOHN, *Quartus sententiarum* (Paris, 1509).

—— *In secundum sententiarum* (Paris, 1510).

—— *In quartum sententiarum* (Paris, 1516).

—— *In Mattheum ad literam expositio* (Paris, 1518).

—— *Historia Majoris Britanniae, tam Angliae q. Scotiae* (Paris, 1521).

—— *In tertium sententiarum* (Paris, 1528).

—— *Ethica Aristotelis cum commentariis* (Paris, 1530).

MONTE, PIERO DA, *Repertorium Juris* (Nuremberg, 1476).

—— *De potestate Romani Pontificis et Generalis Concilii* (Rome, 1476 or 1477).

—— *Monarchia* (Lyons, 1512).

MORE, THOMAS, *Lucubrationes* (Basle, 1563).

PICCOLOMINI, AENEAS SYLVIUS, *De ortu & auctoritate Sacri Romani Imperii lib. I* (Mainz, 1535).

—— *De ortu et auctoritate Imperii Romani*, in G. Kallen, *Aeneas Silvius Piccolomini*, as under secondary sources below.

POGGIO, GIOVANNI FRANCESCO, *De officio principis* (Rome, 1504).

—— *De potestate Papae et Concilii* (Rome?, 1512?).

PONET, JOHN, *A Shorte Treatise of Politike Power*, in W. S. Hudson, *John Ponet (1516?–1556): Advocate of Limited Monarchy* (Chicago, 1942).

RIJKEL, DENIS (the Carthusian), *Opera omnia* (38 vols.; Tournai, 1894–1908).

ROGADEO, E. (ed.), *Diplomatico Aragonese, Re Alfonso V (1435–58)* (Codice diplomatico barese 11; Bari, 1931).

ROSELLI, ANTONIO DE', *Monarchia*, in M. Goldast (ed.), *Monarchia S. Romani Imperii*, i (Hanover, 1611; repr. Graz, 1960), 252–556.

ROUSSEAU, JEAN JACQUES, *Political Writings*, ed. C. E. Vaughan (2 vols.; Cambridge, 1915; repr. Oxford, 1962).

Somnium Viridarii, in M. Goldast (ed.), *Monarchia S. Romani Imperii*, i (Hanover, 1611), i. 58–229.

TERREVERMEILLE, JEAN DE, *Contra rebelles suorum regum* (Lyons, 1526).

—— *Tractatus de iure legitimi successoris in hereditate regni Galliae* [= *Tractatus I–II* of the *Contra rebelles*], in F. Hotman, *Disputatio de controversia successionis regiae . . .* (Frankfurt, 1585).

TORQUEMADA, JUAN DE, *Summa de Ecclesia* (Salamanca, 1560).

—— *Solemnis Tractatus . . . contra decreta concilii Constantiensis . . . & contra gesta in concilio Basilensi . . .*, in Mansi, *Sacrorum Conciliorum nova et amplissima collectio*, xxx (Venice, 1798), cols. 550–90.

—— *Oratio Synodalis de Primatu*, ed. E. Candal (Rome, 1954).

WINZET, NINIAN, *Velitatio in Georgium Buchananum . . .* (Ingolstadt, 1582).

SECONDARY SOURCES

ACTON, Lord, *The History of Freedom and Other Essays*, ed. J. N. Figgis and R. V. Laurence (London, 1907).

—— *Lectures on the French Revolution*, ed. J. N. Figgis and R. V. Laurence (London, 1910).

—— *Essays on Church and State*, ed. D. Woodruff (London, 1952).

BARBEY, J., *La Fonction royale: Essence et légitimité d'après les TRACTA-TUS de Jean de Terrevermeille* (Paris, 1983).

BÄUMER, R., *Nachwirkungen des konziliaren Gedankens in der Theologie und Kanonistik des frühen 16. Jahrhunderts* (Münster, 1971).

BECKER, H.-J., *Die Appellation vom Papst an ein allgemeines Konzil:*

Historische Entwicklung und kanonistische Diskussion im späten Mittelalter und in der frühen Neuzeit (Cologne, 1988).

BELLONI, A., *Professori giuristi a Padova nel secolo XV* (Frankfurt-am-Main, 1986).

BELTRÁN DE HEREDIA, V., *Cartulario de la Universidad de Salamanca*, i (Salamanca, 1970).

BLACK, A. J., *Monarchy and Community: Political Ideas in the Later Conciliar Controversy 1430–1450* (Cambridge Studies in Medieval Life and Thought, 3rd Series, 2; Cambridge, 1970).

—— *Council and Commune: The Conciliar Movement and the Council of Basle* (London, 1979).

—— 'The Conciliar Movement', in J. H. Burns (ed.), *The Cambridge History of Medieval Political Thought c.350–c.1450* (Cambridge, 1988), 573–87.

—— 'The Individual and Society', ibid., 588–606.

BROADIE, A., *George Lokert: Late Scholastic Logician* (Edinburgh, 1983).

—— *The Circle of John Mair* (Oxford, 1985).

BUCKLAND, W. W., *A Text-Book of Roman Law from Augustus to Justinian*, ed. P. Stein, 3rd edn. (Cambridge, 1975).

BURNS, J. H., *'Politia regalis et optima*: The Political Ideas of John Mair', *History of Political Thought*, 2 (1981), 31–61.

—— *'Jus gladii* and *jurisdictio*: Jacques Almain and John Locke', *Historical Journal*, 26 (1983), 369–74.

—— 'Fortescue and the Political Theory of *Dominium*', *Historical Journal*, 28 (1985), 777–97.

—— *Absolutism: The History of an Idea* (The Creighton Trust Lecture, 1986; London, 1987).

—— 'The Idea of Absolutism', in J. Miller (ed.), *Absolutism in Seventeenth-Century Europe* (London, 1990), 21–42.

—— 'Scholasticism: Survival and Revival', in J. H. Burns and M. Goldie (eds.), *The Cambridge History of Political Thought 1450–1700* (Cambridge, 1991), 132–55.

—— 'The "Monarchia" of Antonio de' Roselli (1380–1466): Text, Context and Controversy', in *Proceedings of the Eighth International Congress of Medieval Canon Law San Diego, 1988* (Vatican City 1991).

CANNING, J. P., 'Introduction [to Part V, c.1150–c.1450]: Politics, Institutions and Ideas', in Burns (ed.), *Cambridge History of Medieval Political Thought*, 341–66.

—— 'Law, Sovereignty and Corporation Theory, 1300–1450', ibid., 454–76.

CARLYLE, Sir R. W., and CARLYLE, A. J., *A History of Mediaeval Political Theory in the West* (6 vols.; Edinburgh, 1903–36).

CHRIMES, S. B., *English Constitutional Ideas in the Fifteenth Century* (Cambridge, 1936).

COLEMAN, J., '*Dominium* in Thirteenth- and Fourteenth-Century Political Thought and its Seventeenth-Century Heirs: John of Paris and Locke', *Political Studies*, 33 (1985), 73–100.

—— 'Property and Poverty', in Burns (ed.), *Cambridge History of Medieval Political Thought*, 607–48.

DOE, N., 'Fifteenth-Century Concepts of Law: Fortescue and Pecock', *History of Political Thought*, 10 (1989), 257–80.

DUNBABIN, J., 'Government', in Burns (ed.), *Cambridge History of Medieval Political Thought*, 477–519.

ECKERMANN, K., *Studien zur Geschichte des monarchischen Gedankens im 15. Jahrhundert* (Berlin, 1933).

ERCOLE, F., 'Impero e papato nella tradizione giuridica bolognese e nel diritto pubblico italiano del rinascimento', *Atti e memorie della R. Diputazione di Storia Patria per le provincie di Romagna* (IV. ser., 1; Bologna, 1911), 1–223.

FERGUSON, A. B., 'Fortescue and the Renaissance: A Study of Transition', *Studies in the Renaissance*, 6 (1959), 175–94.

—— *The Articulate Citizen and the English Renaissance* (Durham, NC, 1965).

FIGGIS, J. N., *Political Thought from Gerson to Grotius 1414–1625: Seven Studies* (New York, 1960; first published Cambridge, 1907).

FRANKLIN, J. II., 'Sovereignty and the Mixed Constitution: Bodin and his Critics', in Burns and Goldie (eds.), *Cambridge History of Political Thought 1450–1700*, 298–328.

GIBBON, E., *The History of the Decline and Fall of the Roman Empire*, ed. W. Smith (8 vols.; London, 1854–5).

GIESEY, R. E., *If Not, Not: The Oath of the Aragonese and the Legendary Laws of Sobrarbe* (Princeton, NJ, 1968).

GILL, P. E., 'Politics and Propaganda in Fifteenth-Century England: The Polemical Writings of Sir John Fortescue', *Speculum*, 46 (1971), 333–47.

GILL, R. H., 'Political Theory at the Court of Charles V of France, 1364–80', Ph.D. thesis (London, 1988).

GILLESPIE, J. L., 'Sir John Fortescue's Concept of Royal Will', *Birmingham Medieval Studies*, 23 (1979), 47–65.

GUENÉE, B., *States and Rulers in Later Medieval Europe*, trans. J. Vale (Oxford, 1985).

HALLER, J., *Piero da Monte: Ein Gelehrter und päpstlicher Beamter des 15. Jahrhunderts: Seine Briefsammlung* (Rome, 1941).

HAY, D., *The Church in Italy in the Fifteenth Century* (Cambridge, 1977; repr. 1979).

HAZELTINE, H. D., 'General Preface', in S. B. Chrimes (ed.), *Sir John Fortescue: De laudibus legum Anglie* (Cambridge, 1949; 1st edn. 1942).

HENNIG, G., *Cajetan und Luther: Ein historischer Beitrag zur Begegnung von Thomismus und Reformation* (Stuttgart, 1966).

HILLGARTH, J. N., *The Spanish Kingdoms 1250–1516* (2 vols.; Oxford, 1976, 1978).

HOLMES, G., *Europe: Hierarchy and Revolt 1320–1450* (Fontana History of Europe; London, 1975).

HUME, D., *The History of Great Britain: The Reigns of James I and Charles I*, ed. D. Forbes (Harmondsworth, 1970).

JEDIN, H., 'Sanchez de Arevalo und die Konzilsfrage unter Paul II', *Historisches Jahrbuch*, 73 (1954), 95–119.

—— 'Giovanni Gozzadini, ein Konziliarist am Hofe Julius' II', in id., *Kirche des Glaubens, Kirche der Geschichte* (2 vols.; Freiburg, 1966), ii. 17–74.

KALLEN, G., *Aeneas Silvius Piccolomini als Publizist in der 'Epistola de ortu et auctoritate Imperii Romani'* (Cologne, 1939).

KANTOROWICZ, E. H., *The King's Two Bodies: A Study in Medieval Political Theology* (Princeton, NJ, 1957).

KRETZMANN, N., KENNY, A., and PINBORG, J. (eds.), *The Cambridge History of Later Medieval Philosophy from the Rediscovery of Aristotle to the Disintegration of Scholasticism 1100–1600* (Cambridge, 1982).

LA BROSSE, O. DE, *Le Pape et le Concile: La Comparaison de leurs pouvoirs à la veille de la Réforme* (Paris, 1965).

LÓPEZ AMO Y MARIN, A., 'El pensamiento político de Eximeniç en su tratado de "Regiment de Princeps"', *Anuario de Historia del Derecho Español*, 17 (1946), 5–139.

McGRADE, A. S., *The Political Thought of William of Ockham: Personal and Institutional Principles* (Cambridge, 1974).

McILWAIN, C. H., *Constitutionalism Ancient and Modern*, 2nd edn. rev. (Ithaca, NY, 1947; first published 1940).

MacKAY, A., *Spain in the Middle Ages: From Frontier to Empire, 1000–1500* (London, 1977).

—— 'Ritual and Propaganda in Fifteenth-Century Castile', *Past and Present*, 107 (May 1985), 3–43.

MAFFEI, D., *La donazione di Costantino nei giuristi medievali* (Milan, 1969).

MARKUS, R. A., *Saeculum: History and Society in the Theology of St Augustine* (Cambridge, 1988; first publ. 1970).

—— 'The Latin Fathers', in Burns (ed.), *Cambridge History of Medieval Political Thought*, 92–122.

MERRIMAN, R. B., *The Rise of the Spanish Empire in the Old World and the New* (2 vols.; New York, 1918).

MEUTHEN, E., 'Juan González, Bischof von Cadiz, auf dem Basler Konzil', *Annuarium Historiae Conciliorum*, 8 (1976), 250–93.

—— 'Antonio Rosellis Gutachten für Heinrich Schlick im Freisinger Bistumsstreit (1444)', in H. Mordek (ed.), *Aus Kirche und Reich: Studien zu Theologie, Politik und Recht im Mittelalter (Festschrift für Friedrich Kempf . . .*) (Sigmaringen, 1983), 461–72.

MEYNIAL, E., 'Notes sur la formation du domaine divisé du XIIe au XIVe siècle dans les romanistes', *Mélanges Fitting*, ii (Montpellier, 1908), 409–61.

MORRALL, J. B., *Gerson and the Great Schism* (Manchester, 1960).

NADER, H. B., *The Mendoza Family and the Spanish Renaissance 1350 to 1550* (New Brunswick, NJ, 1979).

NARDI, B., 'Fortuna della "Monarchia" nei sec. XIV e XV', in id., *Nel mondo di Dante* (Rome, 1944), 161–205.

OAKLEY, F., *The Political Thought of Pierre d'Ailly: The Voluntarist Tradition* (New Haven, Conn., 1964).

—— 'Almain and Major: Conciliar Theory on the Eve of the Reformation', *American Historical Review*, 70 (1964–5), 673–90.

—— 'Conciliarism in the Sixteenth Century: Jacques Almain again', *Archiv für Reformationsgeschichte*, 68 (1977), 111–32.

—— *The Western Church in the Later Middle Ages* (Ithaca, NY, 1979).

—— *Omnipotence, Covenant, and Order: An Excursion in the History of Ideas from Abelard to Leibniz* (Ithaca, NY, 1984).

—— 'Disobedience, Consent, Political Obligation: The Witness of Wessel Gansfort (c.1419–1489)', *History of Political Thought*, 9 (1988), 211–21.

OBERMAN, H. A., *The Harvest of Medieval Theology: Gabriel Biel and Late Medieval Nominalism*, 2nd edn. rev. (Grand Rapids, Mich., 1967; first published 1963).

OURLIAC, P., 'La Sociologie du Concile de Bâle', *Revue d'Histoire Ecclésiastique*, 56 (1961), 2–32.

PASCOE, L. B., *Jean Gerson: Principles of Church Reform* (Leiden, 1973).

POCOCK, J. G. A., *The Machiavellian Moment: Florentine Political Thought and the Atlantic Republican Tradition* (Princeton, NJ, 1975).

QUILLET, J., *La Philosophie politique de Marsile de Padoue* (Paris, 1970).

—— *La Philosophie politique du Songe du Vergier (1378): Sources doctrinales* (Paris, 1977).

—— 'Community, Counsel and Representation', in Burns (ed.), *Cambridge History of Medieval Political Thought*, 520–72.

RENAUDET, A., *Préréforme et humanisme à Paris pendant les premières guerres d'Italie (1494–1517)*, 2nd edn. (Paris, 1953; first published 1916).

—— (ed.), *Le Concile Gallican de Pise–Milan: Documents florentins (1510–1512)* (Paris, 1922).

ROUND, N., *The Greatest Man Uncrowned: A Study of the Fall of Don Alvaro de Luna* (London, 1986).

RYDER, A., 'The Evolution of Imperial Government in Naples under Alfonso V', in J. R. Hale, R. Highfield, and B. Smalley (eds.), *Europe in the Late Middle Ages* (London, 1965), 332–57.

—— *The Kingdom of Naples under Alfonso the Magnanimous: The Making of a Modern State* (Oxford, 1976).

SIGMUND, P. E., *Nicholas of Cusa and Medieval Political Thought* (Cambridge, Mass., 1963).

SKINNER, Q. R. D., *The Foundations of Modern Political Thought* (2 vols.; Cambridge, 1978).

SMOLINSKY, H., *Domenico de' Domenichi und seine Schrift 'De potestate Pape et termino eius'* (Münster, 1976).

STARKEY, D., 'Which Age of Reform?', in D. Starkey and C. H. D. Coleman (eds.), *Revolution Reassessed: Revisions in the History of Tudor Government and Administration* (Oxford, 1986), 13–27.

STIEBER, J. W., *Pope Eugenius IV, the Council of Basel and the Secular and Ecclesiastical Authorities in the Empire: The Conflict over Supreme Authority and Power in the Church* (Leiden, 1978).

SUÁREZ FERNÁNDEZ, L., *Nobleza y Monarquía: Puntos de vista sobre la historia castellana del siglo XV* (Valladolid, 1959).

TATE, R. B., *Joan Margarit i Pau* (Manchester, 1955).

—— *Joan Margarit i Pau, Cardenal i Bisbe de Girona, la seva vida i les seves obres* (Barcelona, 1976).

THOMSON, J. A. F., 'Papalism and Conciliarism in Antonio Roselli's *Monarchia*', *Medieval Studies*, 37 (1975), 445–58.

—— *Popes and Princes 1417–1517: Politics and Polity in the Late Medieval Church* (London, 1980).

TIERNEY, B., *Foundations of the Conciliar Theory: The Contribution of the Medieval Canonists from Gratian to the Great Schism* (Cambridge, 1955).

—— *Origins of Papal Infallibility 1150–1350: A Study on the Concepts of Infallibility, Sovereignty and Tradition in the Middle Ages* (Leiden, 1972).

—— *Religion, Law, and the Growth of Constitutional Thought 1150–1650* (Cambridge, 1982).

—— 'Tuck on Rights: Some Medieval Problems', *History of Political Thought*, 4 (1983), 429–41.

—— 'Origins of Natural Rights Language: Texts and Contexts, 1150–1250', *History of Political Thought*, 10 (1989), 615–46.

TOEWS, J. B., 'The View of Empire in Aeneas Sylvius Piccolomini (Pope Pius II)', *Traditio*, 24 (1968), 471–87.

TRAME, R. H., *Rodrigo Sánchez de Arévalo 1404–1470: Spanish Diplomat and Champion of the Papacy* (Washington, DC, 1958).

TUCK, R., *Natural Rights Theories: Their Origin and Development* (Cambridge, 1979).

ULLMANN, W., *Principles of Government and Politics in the Middle Ages* (London, 1961).

—— *A History of Political Thought: The Middle Ages* (Harmondsworth, 1965).

—— 'Julius II and the Schismatic Cardinals', *Studies in Church History*, ix. *Schism, Heresy and Religious Protest* (Cambridge, 1972), 177–93.

—— *Law and Politics in the Middle Ages: An Introduction to the Sources of Medieval Political Ideas* (London/Cambridge, 1975).

—— '"This Realm of England is an Empire"', *Journal of Ecclesiastical History*, 30 (1979), 175–203.

VAN CAENEGEM, R. C., 'Government, Law and Society', in Burns (ed.), *Cambridge History of Medieval Political Thought*, 174–210.

VAN RHIJN, M., *Studiën over Wessel Gansfort* (Utrecht, 1933).

WALSH, K., *A Fourteenth-Century Scholar and Primate: Richard FitzRalph in Oxford, Avignon and Armagh* (Oxford, 1981).

WATT, J. A., 'Spiritual and Temporal Powers', in Burns (ed.), *Cambridge History of Medieval Political Thought*, 367–423.

WORMALD, J., *Court, Kirk, and Community: Scotland 1470–1625* (The New History of Scotland, 4; London, 1981).

Index